The Impact of Political Economy

Piet Naudé | Michael Welker | John Witte, Jr. (Eds.)

The Impact of Political Economy

on Character Formation, Ethical Education,
and the Communication of Values
in Late Modern Pluralistic Societies

WIPF & STOCK · Eugene, Oregon

Wipf and Stock Publishers
199 W 8th Ave, Suite 3
Eugene, OR 97401

The Impact of Political Economy
on Character Formation, Ethical Education, and the Communication
of Values in Late Modern Pluralistic Societies
By Naude, Piet and Welker, Michael
Copyright © 2023 Evangelische Verlagsanstalt GmbH All rights reserved.
Softcover ISBN-13: 978-1-6667-8061-1
Hardcover ISBN-13: 978-1-6667-8062-8
Publication date 5/22/2023
Previously published by Evangelische Verlagsanstalt GmbH, 2023

Table of Contents

Acknowledgments 7

Preface to the Series 9

Piet J. Naudé
Introduction 13

PART ONE: RETHINKING ETHICS

Amanda Gouws
Neoliberal Political Economy and Value Transmission: What We Can
Learn from Feminist Care Ethics 31

Andreas Glaeser
Ethics' Political Imperative: Moving Toward Better Institutions 45

Roshan Allpress
Philanthropic Formation at the Intersection of Mercantile and Religious
Networks: The Thornton Family in Their Eighteenth-Century Contexts   67

PART TWO: INTEGRATING SOCIAL SYSTEMS

Nicholas Aroney
Economics, Law, Education, and Religion—Contributions to the
Composition of a Good Society 81

Sergio Belardinelli
Social Systems, Moral Individualism, and Education 101

Paul Oslington
Why Is the Conversation between Theologians and Economists So
Difficult? 115

Part Three: Evaluating Liberal Capitalism

Rüdiger Bittner
Our Political Economy's Moral Teaching 137

David McIlroy
The Devaluing of Virtue: The Global Financial Crisis of 2007–10 as a Test Case of the Effect of Moral Formation 151

Jonathan Cole
Twitter: A Case-Study in the Character-Malformation Potential of Twenty-First-Century Digital Technology 169

Part Four: Navigating State Power

John Witte Jr.
Resisting Political Authority to Protect Faith and Morality: Enduring Lessons from the Lutheran Reformation 189

Nathan S. Chapman
Constitutional Rules and the Political Economy of Character Formation: Conditions on Government Aid to Religious Schools as a Case Study ... 209

Contributors 231

Acknowledgments

A consultation leading to this volume took place at the Forschungszentrum Internationale und Interdisziplinäre Theologie (FIIT) at the University of Heidelberg in 2021. We are grateful to the McDonald Agape Foundation for the generous support of the consultation and this publication.

Piet J. Naudé, Michael Welker, John Witte Jr.

Preface to the Series

Five hundred years ago, Protestant reformer Martin Luther argued that "three estates" (*drei Stände*) lie at the foundation of a just and orderly society—marital families, religious communities, and political authorities. Parents in the home; pastors in the church; magistrates in the state—these, said Luther, are the three authorities whom God appointed to represent divine justice and mercy in the world, to protect peace and liberty in earthly life. Household, church, and state—these are the three institutional pillars on which to build social systems of education and schooling, charity and social welfare, economy and architecture, art and publication. Family, faith, and freedom—these are the three things that people will die for.

In the half millennium since Luther, historians have uncovered various classical and Christian antecedents to these early Protestant views. Numerous later theorists have propounded all manner of variations and applications of this three-estates theory, many increasingly abstracted from Luther's overtly Christian worldview. Early modern covenant theologians, both Christian and Jewish, described the marital, confessional, and political covenants that God calls human beings to form, each directed to interrelated personal and public ends. Social-contract theorists differentiated the three contracts that humans enter as they move from the state of nature to an organized society protective of their natural rights—the marital contract of husband and wife; the government contract of rulers and citizens; and, for some, the religious contracts of preachers and parishioners. Early anthropologists posited three stages of development of civilization—from family-based tribes and clans, to priest-run theocracies, to fully organized states that embraced all three institutions. Sociologists distinguished three main forms of authority in an organized community: "traditional" authority that begins in the home, "charismatic" authority that is exemplified by the church, and "legal" authority that is rooted in the state. Legal historians outlined three stages of development of legal norms—from the habits and rules of the family, to the customs and canons of religion, to the statutes and codes of the state.

Already a century ago, however, scholars in different fields began to flatten out this hierarchical theory of social institutions and to emphasize the foundational role of other social institutions alongside the family, church, and state in shaping private and public life and character. Sociologists like Max Weber and Talcott Parsons emphasized the shaping powers of "technical rationality" exemplified especially in new industry, scientific education, and market economies. Legal scholars like Otto von Gierke and F. W. Maitland emphasized the critical roles of nonstate legal associations (*Genossenschaften*) in maintaining a just social, political, and legal order historically and today. Catholic subsidiarity theories of Popes Leo XIII and Pius XI emphasized the essential task of mediating social units between the individual and the state to cater to the full range of needs, interests, rights, and duties of individuals. Protestant theories of sphere sovereignty, inspired by Abraham Kuyper, argued that not only churches, states, and families but also the social spheres of art, labor, education, economics, agriculture, recreation, and more should enjoy a level of independence from others, especially an overreaching church or state. Various theories of social or structural pluralism, civil society, voluntary associations, the independent sector, multiculturalism, multinormativity, and other such labels have now come to the fore in the ensuing decades—both liberal and conservative, religious and secular, and featuring all manner of methods and logics.

Pluralism of all sorts is now a commonplace of late modern societies. At minimum, this means a multitude of free and equal individuals and a multitude of groups and institutions, each with very different political, moral, religious, and professional interests and orientations. It includes the sundry associations, interest groups, parties, lobbies, and social movements that often rapidly flourish and fade around a common cause, especially when aided by modern technology and various social media. Some see in this texture of plurality an enormous potential for colorful and creative development and a robust expression of human and cultural freedom. Others see a chaotic individualism and radical relativism, which endangers normative education, moral character formation, and effective cultivation of enduring values or virtues.

Pluralism viewed as vague plurality, however, focuses on only one aspect of late modern societies—the equality of individuals, and their almost unlimited freedom to participate peaceably at any time as a respected voice in the moral reasoning and civil interactions of a society. But this view does not adequately recognize that, beneath the shifting cacophony of social forms and norms that constitute modernity, pluralistic societies have heavy normative codes that shape their individual and collective values and morals, preferences and prejudices.

The sources of much of this normative coding and moral education in late modern pluralistic societies are the deep and powerful social systems that are the pillars of every advanced culture. The most powerful and pervasive of these are the social systems of law, religion, politics, science/academy, market, media, family, education, medicine, and national defense. The actual empirical forms of each of these powerful social systems can and do vary greatly, even in the relatively homogeneous societies of the late modern West. But these deeper social systems in one form or another are structurally essential and often normatively decisive in individual and communal lives.

Every advanced society has a comprehensive legal system of justice and order, religious systems of ritual and doctrine, a family system of procreation and love, an economic system of trade and value, a media system of communication and dissemination of news and information, and an educational system of creation, preservation, and application of knowledge and scientific advance. Many advanced societies also have massive systems of science, technology, health care, and national defense with vast influence over and through all of these other social systems. These pervasive social systems lie at the foundation of modern advanced societies, and they anchor the vast pluralities of associations and social interactions that might happen to exist at any given time.

Each of these social systems has internal value systems, institutionalized rationalities, and normative expectations that together help to shape each individual's morality and character. Each of these social spheres, moreover, has its own professionals and experts who shape and implement its internal structures and processes. The normative network created by these social spheres is often harder to grasp today, since late modern pluralistic societies usually do not bring these different value systems to light under the dominance of just one organization, institution, and power. And this normative network has also become more shifting and fragile, especially since traditional social systems, such as religion and the family, have eroded in their durability and power, and other social systems, such as science, the market, healthcare, defense, and the media, have become more powerful.

The aim of this project on "Character Formation and Ethical Education in Late Modern Pluralistic Societies" is to identify the realities and potentials of these core social systems to provide moral orientation and character formation in our day. What can and should these social spheres, separately and together, do in shaping the moral character of late modern individuals who, by nature, culture, and constitutional norms, are free and equal in dignity and rights? What are and should be the core educational functions and moral responsibilities of each of these social spheres? How can we better understand and better influence the complex interactions among individualism, the normative binding powers of these social systems, and the creativity of civil groups and institutions? How can we map and measure the different hierarchies of values that govern each of these social systems, and that are also interwoven and interconnected in various ways in shaping late modern understandings of the common good? How do we negotiate the boundaries and conflicts between and among these social systems when one encroaches on the other, or imposes its values and rationalities on individuals at the cost of the other social spheres or of the common good? What and where are the intrinsic strengths of each social sphere that should be made more overt in character formation, public education, and the shaping of minds and mentalities?

These are some of the guiding questions at work in this project and in this volume. Our project aims to provide a systematic account of the role of these powerful normative codes operating in the social spheres of law, religion, the family, the market, the media, science and technology, the academy, health care, and defense in the late modern liberal West. Our focus is on selected examples and case studies drawn from Western Europe, North America, South Africa, and Australia, which together provide just enough diversity to test out broader theories of character formation and moral education. Our scholars are drawn from across the academy, with representative voices from the humanities, social sciences, and natural sciences as well as the professions of theology, law, business, medicine, and more. While most of our scholars come from the Protestant and Catholic worlds, our endeavor is to offer comparative insights that will help scholars from any profession or confession. While our laboratory is principally Western liberal societies, the modern forces of globalization will soon make these issues of moral character formation a concern for every culture and region of the world—given the power of global social media, entertainment, and sports; the pervasiveness of global finance, business, trade, and law; and the perennial global worries over food, health care, environmental degradation, and natural disasters.

In this volume, we focus in on the role of the political economy in shaping character development, ethical education, and the communication of values in late modern pluralistic societies.

Michael Welker, University of Heidelberg
John Witte Jr., Emory University
Piet J. Naudé, University of Stellenbosch

Introduction

Piet J. Naudé

In the preface to this book series, the editors state that the aim of this project on "Character Formation and Ethical Education in Late Modern Pluralistic Societies" is to identify the realities and potentials of core social systems to provide moral orientation and character formation in our day. The volumes already published in the series addressed various key social systems, and in this volume—one of the last in the series—the focus is on political economy.

We were fortunate to gather potential authors in the postpandemic time in Heidelberg, Germany, during May 2021. As in the previous projects, the editors did not provide contributors with a standard definition of the social system under discussion (for example, "What is political economy?") accompanied by suggested topics associated with this guiding definition. Nor did we attempt to tell the complex story of how political economy developed as a distinct field of inquiry and use that as a basis to design academic contributions to the field. In the context of the social systems focus of the bigger project, we expected that economics, public policy, ethics, sociology, and politics would all be associated with a rather wide understanding of "political economy" as a fundamentally interdisciplinary endeavor studying the economic aspects of government.

The weakness of this approach is obviously that it may lead to a lack of coherence and no clear boundaries of inquiry. The advantage is the possibility of novel approaches, allowing each author to bring her or his strengths to the table, culminating in a richer diversity. We believe the risk of the second approach was worth taking, and present this volume for readers to enjoy and comment on.

The values project focuses on late modern (mostly) Western societies. This choice naturally limits diversity. Contributors do represent a fair mix of geographies, which include Australia, Germany, South Africa, the United Kingdom, and the United States, and provide in some chapters highly informative contextual considerations related to the political economy with implications much wider than Western societies.

The contributions to this volume are presented in four sections. These sections are somewhat artificial, as chapters cross boundaries, and one could have used different designations. But they hopefully provide some order and allow a quick overview of the book's content.

Part One, "Rethinking Ethics," includes the chapters on a feminist ethics of care (Gouws), the ethics of institutions (Glaeser), and an example of a biographical account of moral formation (Allpress). These chapters are grouped together and deliberately put at the beginning because they provide theoretical proposals of how to frame character formation and moral communication from different perspectives.

Part Two, "Integrating Social Systems," includes chapters on how social systems indeed operate separately but could still be held as complementary, despite difficulties in this regard. The contributions by Aroney, Belardinelli, and Oslington refer in different ways to economics, education, law, and religion.

Part Three, "Evaluating Liberal Capitalism," includes the view that there is no specific ethos and moral formation associated with liberal capitalism (Bittner), followed by two case studies on the global financial crisis (McIlroy) and the design of Twitter (Cole), both highly critical of how moral deformation occurs in the market.

Part Four, "Navigating State Power," includes a chapter on the conditions and grounds for resistance to state power (Witte) and one on how state power could be negotiated via constitutional deliberation (Chapman).

To give a preview and overview of the contributions, I present each chapter here in a few paragraphs in the order of appearance. Readers are advised to read the full chapters, because much of the detail and nuances are lost in these summaries.

Part One: Rethinking Ethics

"Neoliberal Political Economy and Value Transmission: What We Can Learn from Feminist Care Ethics," by Amanda Gouws, describes late modern Western societies as multicultural and subject to the dominance of a neoliberal political economy. The social fabric of pluralistic societies is assured by values such as social inclusion, more inclusive resource distribution, and acceptance of differing value options. These values are transmitted by a variety of socialization agents. However, since neoliberal policies came to dominate our political economy, these values are compromised: "Neoliberal competitiveness and a focus on independence, combined with the commoditization of care, undermine care ethics that embodies interdependence as an important value in multicultural societies." The privileging of the individual, the economization of subjectivity, and an encompassing self-referential consumer culture create a narcissistic value system, namely, "that of manipulating relationships and the lack of deep interpersonal connections." Reinforced by social media, there is a slow corrosion of interrelational values like attentiveness and care.

The outcome of this shift in values is the reinforcement of asymmetrical power relations between those who cannot successfully participate in the market and those who are economically empowered. The fringes of society are mostly occupied by women and people of color, constituting neoliberalism as both a raced and gendered process. In a patriarchal society, care and the value of care are usually associated with (often unpaid) women's work, creating not only a binary gender distinction, but also a divide between a productive economy and a reproductive economy, the latter associated with feminization of poverty.

Gouws then introduces the concept of "precarity": "Precarity is caused and fueled by neoliberalism and the way it assigns value to human interactions, with large numbers of people now living outside a safety net that would ensure their survival. It is now widely acknowledged that we have a care crisis," partially attributed to the privatization of care and the scaling back of the welfare state. To address this crisis, she turns in the second part of her chapter to highlight the importance of care ethics in late modern societies. Care ethics is incompatible with neoliberal values of individualization and a competition imperative, as care ethics promotes principles of interdependence, relationality, and acknowledging the "affective turn" where emotions supporting solidarity are nurtured. Care ethics builds on a notion of an ontologically constituted relational moral subject dependent on a collective community and a focus on distributive justice that seeks to overcome precarity. The argument for a *feminist* ethics of care is based on the gendered nature of the "robust masculine market" in general, but more specifically in relation to the task of caring. "A feminist care ethic socializes values such as attentiveness (to the care recipient), responsiveness, responsibility, and relationality," and it applies such values on a personal, interpersonal, and planetary scale. What is needed are different types of socialization agents "that [focus] on relationality, community, and care."

Gouws concludes her discussion with the question why care is not in the forefront of late modern societies if there is indeed a care crisis? The answer lies in the fact that care is taken for granted; "care is something without which humans cannot exist," and we live by the assumption that we all know how to care, including honoring the emotional and affective dimensions of care. Yet care is devalued because it is embedded in the value dominance of the neoliberal market, where care is relegated, undervalued, and feminized. There are thus no proper socialization options for care that relate from the individual to the state and to the global community. "We ignore a care ethics at our own peril," is her concluding remark.

"Ethics' Political Imperative: Moving Toward Better Institutions" is the title of Andreas Glaeser's chapter. The discussion about character formation and moral communication in late modern societies is directed away from the merely personal toward the ethical importance of institutions. From a sociological perspective, institutions encompass all forms of regularized human behavior and "exist in the enchainment of self-similar action-reaction effect flows involving at least two, but often very many, spatially and temporally distributed persons."

Human beings, living their lives in and through institutional arrangements, not only are formed by those institutions, but their acts in turn impact the formation of institutions. This impact is designated as "political," because it remakes "the world in and through which a larger community acts and as such they are part of the *res publica*." And the consequences of reforming institutions "could become subject to political effort if actors would be made aware of them."

If ethics is, inter alia, concerned with the consequences of one's actions, and if most consequences of human action are mediated by institutions, then the goodness of those institutions should be the subject of ethical reflection. It is thus not merely the moral quality of individual actions but rather the goodness of "institutional fabrics" that is at stake. The Kantian question of "what ought I to do?" is not wide enough in scope and should much rather be framed as "what assemblage of institutions ought we to form, such that we are all more likely to act ethically in the sense stipulated by us together?" The task of building good and better institutions is the political imperative of ethics.

Glaeser proceeds to propose three "general evaluative criteria" or "metaethical principles" against which the goodness of institutions could be ethically judged.

Transparency, without which accountability is impossible, refers to the open and ethically relevant knowledge of consequences that an institution generates in its interaction with concrete others and the environment. Alterability or malleability refers to the degree in which people through various means (personal effort, social movements, or state policy) are able "to intervene positively in reshaping the institutional fabric through which they live"—in other words, making institutional changes for the better. The third principle is called public goal and value conformity, by which institutions are assessed regarding their embodiment of a comprehensive vision in which a good life and a good society are closely intertwined. Glaeser argues for open fora in which all people can deliberate and participate equally in answering the question of a good life and a good society.

Late modern societies are "morally unhinged" because "the privilege of ignorance has made possible the creation of an institutional world in which people not only do not know, but they are kept from knowing what they are doing." What Glaeser calls "a new civic ethos" will become possible only if the ethics of institutions enables us to know, assess, and change the consequences of our institutionally mediated actions.

"Philanthropic Formation at the Intersection of Mercantile and Religious Networks: The Thornton Family in Their Eighteenth-Century Contexts" is the contribution by Roshan Allpress. Instead of discussing the formative role of different social systems in general, Allpress uses salient bibliographical and biographical information about Henry Thorton, an eighteenth-century English merchant, to describe how moral formation actually occured in different social settings. His intention is to identify—via historical analysis—"potentials for the formation of character and vocation in the late modern context."

Allpress tells the story of how two institutional contexts provide definitive formative experiences. He focuses on the particular mercantile context of the Russia Company, where—unlike in other companies—collective decision-making, voluntary work, and building networks of interpersonal trust were strengthened by a culture of associational honor and formation in commercial *habitus.* The rise of the evangelical movement from 1730 onward also created an overlaying institutional context marked by personal commitment and "the cultivation of the inner life," character formation, creation of new charitable organizations, and engaging in philanthropic activism.

Thornton's most influential intellectual contribution was his *Enquiry into the Paper Credit of Great Britain* (1802). His original insight "was to recognize that the speed of circulation of paper credit reflected not the wealth of the nation, but the net trust of the commercial community. . . . Thornton argued that moral duty and, therefore, moral formation require the cultivation of trust and trustworthiness—and that the basis of the good society and wealthy economy was the cultural accumulation and maintenance of reciprocal trust."

Allpress then infers that the formative experiences on a personal level, in the intergenerational Thornton family context, as well as mercantile and religious neworks all provided multilayered experiences which formed habits and perspectives that resulted in both financial innovation and philanthropy for the common good. The interactions between these layers are often constructed in contemporay societies as oppositional or reactive, but this biography—though from a different time and context—provides clues to the potential synergies of moral formation that are "constructive of new identities."

Part Two: Integrating Social Systems

"Economics, Law, Education, and Religion—Contributions to the Composition of a Good Society," by Nicholas Aroney, acknowledges that late modern liberal societies rely on economics, law, and education to imagine and build a "good society." He demonstrates that each of these social systems may be understood in a positivist (value-neutral) way or as being informed by values with a distinct effect on the common good. Economics is often defined in positive, "value-free" terms, but is also conceived of as directed at moral ends. Law may be defined in positive terms "by reference to the will and power of the lawmaker," while one may also focus on the ethical content and purpose of the law. In the same way, education is sometimes understood as the simple transfer of knowledge and development of appropriate skills, while for some it is about character development, aiming for wisdom and virtue.

Aroney regards these three systems as crucial for the building of a good society, especially if the normative definition of each is upheld and there is respect for the sphere-specific role of each: economics sustains human welfare; law ensures justice and order; education provides skills and knowledge and builds character.

He then proceeds to argue for the inclusion of religion into the social imagination of building of a good society. Religion can also be defined in a purely secular, sociological, or phenomenological way (positivist), or in terms of *religio*, "conceived not as a system of beliefs and practices but as a personal virtue or quality of character." Drawing on classical sources, he refers to the importance of overcoming human pride, "for it infects us even at our very best moments when we appear to be doing good. But because the desire for glory and honor only motivates us to appear to be good, it doesn't motivate us to do what is right when no one is looking, when no one sees, or when we can get away with it. And herein lies the seed of all our problems."

His conclusion is that religion provides for a missing dimension in the other three social systems, because it addresses the goodness of the will. "Education without religion can only inform the mind and train the hand; it cannot convert the soul. Law without religion can only require outward conformity and punish when there is disobedience; it cannot redirect the heart. Economics without religion provides the necessities of life but does not give us the good life. Law, education, and economics therefore need to leave room for religion, so that religion can do what it alone is capable of: softening the heart and redirecting the will."

Where the normative quality of these four social systems is affirmed and brought into synergy, the possibility for the formation of a good society is increased. A purely secular society will not achieve this because "religion, properly understood, is what motivates and empowers people to acts that are not only prudentially wise and minimally right, but also heroic and supererogatory."

In the first part of "Social Systems, Moral Individualism, and Education," Sergio Belardinelli discusses the perennial sociological question regarding the relation between individuals and social systems. Over against a notion of self-referential social systems, he proposes that we should recover the human dimension both within each system and in the broader society. We should accept that "the individual and society are distinct, but also constantly permeating each other," thus avoiding both the individualistic and the collectivist view.

Belardinelli then asserts the intrinsic normative dimension of this individual-societal continuum with human dignity and freedom as criteria for both human action and institutions. This makes it possible to "maintain the firm distinction between what is right and what is not, between what promotes human freedom and dignity and what instead it inhibits them," and allows us to apply normative terms like "justice" and "good" to the constellation of political- economic institutions in liberal democracies: "Does what I do promote or inhibit the dignity and freedom of others? Does this institution promote or inhibit the dignity and freedom of citizens? These are the questions we should ask ourselves if we are interested in the human quality, the good, of our individual and social life."

The second part of the chapter explains that to build a good and just society is, however, subject to the limits of our rationality to understand complexity and uncertainty, specifically the unintended and unforeseen consequences of free human actions. Despite the rise and importance of a techno-shaped society, the reality is that "(t)here are no algorithms for predicting the future."

The implication is that we need to understand and deal with the risks and uncertainty which are given with the human condition. Due to the growing control that we have gradually acquired over reality, our desire for security also has increased. This yearning for security leads to overloaded expectations from social systems which in some cases abuse the power conferred on them in this regard. A good example is the overloaded security expectations from the state and those holding political power. They are "happy to take on these tasks, as they greatly increase its power and its claim to be able to control every area of our social and individual life," thus limiting freedom in the name of control and predictability.

The third and last part of the chapter turns to the importance of education to espouse the liberal democratic values of late modern Western societies. Belardinelli argues against both the perceived or claimed value neutrality and functionalization that mark contemporary Western education. Despite the aspirations for ethically neutral education, he claims that "an educational process is always a relationship in which someone (the teacher) takes on the responsibility of teaching another (the student) something that is considered good." There are virtues intrinsic to every educational practice: "knowledge, honesty, discipline, respect, freedom, solidarity—in short, a certain moral ideal, let's say a certain ideal of humanity."

He acknowledges that practice-oriented education for the world of work is important for the economy but argues that even this type of education should enable "a passion for truth, freedom, beauty, the comparison of ideas, respect for all, and human solidarity." For him "the only real purpose of every educational practice" is to assist a new generation to find its way in a complex, uncertain world, guided by the values that confirm human freedom in tandem with duties and responsibilities we hold in our foundational relationships

"Why Is the Conversation between Theologians and Economists So Difficult?," by Paul Oslington, must be read from the perspective that constructive and fruitful interdisciplinary conversation is desirable among disciplines that represent the different social systems of late modern societies. A wide conception of "political economy" brings into play education, law, religion, politics, sociology, and economics. In his contribution, Oslington investigates why the conversation between theologians and economists are fraught with difficulties.

He first provides a brief survey of the current state of the conversation between theologians and economists by looking at the problem from theologians' side. After a critical rendering of well-known theologians who write about economics, Oslington finds a few shared factors: a strong prejudicial approach, relying on secondary texts without proper contextualization, and a collapsing of the critique of capitalism into a critique of economics. The perspective from economists' side is even bleaker. There is at least a strong growth in theological literature on economics, but there is little interest among contemporary economists to engage with theologians. Stemming from a kind of disciplinary superiority complex, "the dominant view among contemporary mainstream economists is that engaging with theologians is a waste of time."

Oslington then lists and discusses several reasons for this difficult conversation that range from contrasting disciplinary cultures, difficulty of access to sufficiently master the other discipline, reciprocal ideological perceptions, and even jealously from theologians who realize that economics has become the dominant frame for public discourse. While these factors all play a part, Oslington resorts to economics itself to provide an alternative explanation. "I suggest that the conversation suffers from a similar incentive problem that the economics Nobel Laureate Geoff Akerlof identified with the used car market. In a situation where buyers cannot easily judge quality of the product, there is an incentive for sellers to flood the market with poor quality products (known as lemons), so that the good products are not offered for sale and the market collapses." For Oslington, it seems that readers and writers of interdisciplinary research on economics and theology face an analogous situation, with theological literature mostly contributing to the poor quality, but both sides—especially economists—not finding the incentives to engage attractive enough.

Oslington is nevertheless hopeful that the relatively new "interdisciplinary field of economics and theology" can overcome past barriers and result in conversations that are mutually beneficial, especially where cooperation between economists and theologians addresses public issues that involve both disciplines. He ends his chapter with a list of recommendations to bring this interdisciplinary academic conversation to fruition, which may benefit a broad understanding of political economy.

Part Three: Evaluating Liberal Capitalism

Rüdiger Bittner begins his chapter, "Our Political Economy's Moral Teaching," by asserting that the contemporary political economy of the West is that of liberal capitalism. "Capitalism" refers to an economic system of exchange via markets, and "liberal" means that these markets are regulated and function under the rule of law to ensure civil liberties like freedom of expression, movement, and association. In terms of the theme of this book series, the question arises whether liberal capitalism is "fertile ground for particular moral conceptions or, indeed, misconceptions?"

Bittner then notes that one of the innovations brought about by the rise of capitalism is that of widespread educational institutions to develop and transfer knowledge. These institutions indeed contribute to character formation and the transmission of values both at individual and societal levels. But the issue is whether "liberal capitalism all by itself, with or without schools, is already a moral teacher." And Bittner denies this moral formative aspect of the market because "markets do not teach any morality, whether right or wrong. Neither does capitalism when it allocates goods by means of this mechanism."

He argues that the widely held belief that the market economy undermines morality is based on three false assumptions. First, the fact that people choose what to buy and sell and lead their life-path based on independent choice "makes them more resistant to guidance by representatives of a traditional morality, which gives the appearance, especially to these representatives, of their having put aside moral concerns altogether." Second, markets are assumed to be hostile to morality based on the false conviction that rational agents are bound to be selfish, which in turn is fed by the myth of the sinfulness of each human person. Third, there is—since Plato—an intellectual class prejudice against those who work with material things that they sell and buy on the market.

The conclusion then is clear, namely, that "there is no such thing as an ethos of liberal capitalism. Our political economy does not teach us any morals, either good or bad. It does invite us to cast off the merely given ones of old, but which to adopt it does not say." Bittner then addresses the critique about material losses (human and ecological) attributed to liberal capitalism. His response rests—as elsewhere in the chapter—on the notion that liberal capitalism has been and is still abused by people. "People suffer ... but their suffering is not owed to liberal capitalism. It is owed to what is currently done within liberal capitalism and done in preference to other things that could as well be done within liberal capitalism." Terribly wrong choices and abuse of the system of distribution should not be laid at the door of liberal capitalism itself. In fact, liberal capitalism—because it is an open-choice system—allows us the freedom to correct past judgments and "to leave behind the errors and habits that caused our going wrong before."

Does this mean that liberal capitalism is beyond criticism? No, but such criticism should be aimed at the proper target, which is the political use of the system rather than system itself. In terms of the theme of this book series, Bittner would respond that "it is not through our political economy that characters are formed and values transmitted. Liberal capitalism is morally neutral, for as long as it is liberal it presents to people a whole range of courses to take. What makes them think of good and bad the way they do is not liberal capitalism, but the particular experience they go through within liberal capitalism."

"The Devaluing of Virtue: The Global Financial Crisis of 2007-10 as a Test Case of the Effect of Moral Formation," by David McIlroy, describes the global financial crisis of 2007-10 as fundamentally a crisis of the banking system. From a technical perspective, the crisis was caused by the significant proportion of debt that banks took on to finance their trading in financial instruments while transferring liabilities to other actors in the financial markets. But McIlroy is interested in the ethical perspective on this crisis. The crisis was not caused by a few errant individuals, but by the dominant "antisocial" culture in the banking sector as a whole, described in the title of his contribution as a "devaluing of virtue."

As to the source of this culture, McIlroy points to the cumulative negative moral effect of a line of economic thinking that he attributes to the Chicago School of Economics. This school operates based on four (contested) assumptions: 1. Economics is by nature equivalent to the natural sciences, and its account of human behavior is nonnormative and purely empirical-descriptive. (The school denies any social and normative nature of economic inquiry). 2. Maximizing shareholder return is the sole measure of success. (The returns and costs for broader stakeholder groups and society at large are ignored). 3. Markets are amoral and should be trusted to self-regulate. (Financial reporting, reputational incentives, and competition will be sufficient to ensure good aggregate outcomes regardless of personal and corporate motivations). 4. Ethics and setting moral standards are the tasks of industry regulators and—ultimately—governments. (Banks and specifically top management absolve themselves from accountability for personal and corporate ethics).

How can this view "that regarded markets as intrinsically amoral and affirmed no value other than money" be countered? In terms of the topic addressed in this book, how can the dominant paradigm of the political economy be challenged and changed? In McIlroy's terms, how can virtue be revalued?

For him, the "antidote lies in four E's: Education, Empathy, Example, and Enforcement." On the firm assumption that virtues can indeed be taught, *education* counters "the normalization of selfishness" by expressly aiming at the inculcation of virtue and building of character. Where *empathy* informs and guides our self-interest, greed and selfishness are controlled. As to the banking industry, instead of viewing a bank purely as a financial business, it should be understood as part of a service industry. This will change the purpose of banking from a focus on short term profits "to serving the common good indirectly by serving customers directly." We learn by following *examples* as our self-interest includes aiming to be held in esteem by those whose judgment we trust. Business needs to produce new, alternative heroes to the Gordon Gekko stereotype, enabling social confirmation and approbation of ethical leaders. Last, the amoral culture will not change unless *enforcement* is seen to be implemented with negative sanctions for ethical lapses. Enforcement starts with a commitment to and examples of institutional ethics by business leaders themselves, complementing the standards set by regulators or the laws enacted by the state.

McIlroy concludes that the global financial crisis "shows the disastrous effects of taking ethics out of the financial markets." The culture that enabled actions at that time must change to ensure that financial markets in fact serve society at large.

Jonathan Cole contributes a critical assessment of technology markets in "Twitter: A Case-Study in the Character-Malformation Potential of Twenty-First-Century Digital Technology." Based on the hypothesis "that Twitter users are more likely to experience harassment and abuse, increased stress levels, and regret from using Twitter than is usual in social interactions in other contexts," the question arises as to what specific characteristics of Twitter causes this higher level of negative experiences? Cole identifies and explains five design features/consequences of Twitter that lift or remove norms that govern civil human interaction. These features are: (1) anonymity, or participation on the platform without personal identification after registration; (2) brevity, the limitation on characters which makes constructive conversation on controversial topics impossible; (3) interpolation, or the fact that "Twitter algorithms expose conversations to hostile voices in a way that is far less common in physical-analogue social systems"; (4) unmoderatability, the impossible task of moderating the number of tweets on accounts that have a large following; and (5) invisibility of mitigating circumstances—a design consequence—or the fact that context, crucial for adjusting communication appropriate to circumstances, is absent from Twitter. For Cole the conclusion is clear: "Rather than promoting 'healthy conversations,' the stated social goal of Twitter, the platform is contributing to the malformation of human character by subverting norms that exist to promote constructive human engagement in physical/analogue social systems."

Cole then points to the tension at the heart of Twitter as a public company. Its stated aim of facilitating healthy conversations is pure corporate rhetoric and is not the aim of the company at all. It is a byproduct of the real purpose, namely, increasing advertising revenue by selling user data. Twitter, Inc., is in fact a digital advertising company, says Cole, and uncivil or unhealthy conversations—because they usually attract more users—are in fact more profitable to host.

The design features coupled to the business model work together to undermine civility and constructive conversations. Cole then makes a few very insightful general comments on the "adverse ecological effects of purposeless, sovereign, and monetizable technologies like Twitter" because of their ability to distort "human culture, anthropological character, social systems, and even political economy." This case study provides food for thought about the too quick and too enthusiastic embrace of technology advances that might seem useful at first, but may later purposefully undermine civility in late modern democratic societies.

Part Four: Navigating State Power

In his chapter "Resisting Political Authority to Protect Faith and Morality: Enduring Lessons from the Lutheran Reformation," John Witte Jr. recognizes that the modern state—through various means like laws, policies, and procedures—plays a key role to shape and direct ethics, character, and moral habits. The question is what happens when the state betrays its responsibilities or even, in a tyrannical way, turns against the freedoms of its own citizens. "When, how, and on what grounds may citizens reject, resist, and even revolt against the state altogether?" asks Witte, in a question related to the political economy. Witte answers this question with a careful analysis of the Lutheran Reformation, which he views as a powerful resistance movement, "indeed a revolution." He starts with specific reference to Martin Luther himself and, subsequently, refers to the Magdeburg Confession of 1550.

Luther challenged canon law on the grounds that it gives the pope unbridled powers of legislation and adjudication; it was abusive and self-serving by elevating clergy with all sorts of special benefits above laity; it became "an instrument of greed and exploitation," and, according to Luther, it carried no legal authority. God bestowed that authority on the prince and civil magistrates, while the pope and clerics were delegated to preach the gospel and administer the sacraments. As a public act of defiance and resistance against an oppressive religious-political order, Luther (in December 1520) burned the books of the canon law.

In what one may call a separation of church and state—a radical idea at that time—Luther insisted that the nature of the church is a community of faith and not one of law and politics. Hence Luther commended and confirmed civil law and the political authority of the state as represented by (Christian) magistrates, called "vice-regents" of God and "loving fathers" of the communities they serve.

After Luther's death, the prosecution of Protestants continued, especially by Emperor Charles V, who attempted to impose by civil law the Catholic doctrines accepted by the Council of Trent. The leaders of Magdeburg drafted a confession in 1550 in which they explained their resistance to new imperial law. A key argument was that God ordained the three estates of church, state, and family to keep social order. The magistrates linked two conditions to the exercise of the respective authorities: no one estate should intrude on the mandate given to another (separation of authorities); and if any authority acts against the will of God, it loses its legitimacy. "Yes, the Confession argued, we must honor the authorities 'so that our days may be long.' But if our days are being cut short, then we should not honor those authorities who shorten them." Furthermore, the Confession insisted on the right to fair procedures in hearing their case. When these conditions are not met and these freedoms are not granted, the people have grounds for the duty to self-defense and resistance against tyrannical abuse of power. In the end, the people of Magdeburg prevailed, and the famous Peace of Augsburg was concluded in 1555 on the principle of *cuius regio, eius religio*.

Witte then brings the historical events into relation to questions of political authority in late modern societies. The distinction between "softer" and "harder" force provides some clues to the measures those affected by abusive power may take. In liberal democracies, "soft force" (filing of an injunction, public protests, publication in a free press) is the means to ensure public accountability of an overreaching state. But in some cases—as we have seen during the Nazi regime and in many contemporary examples around the globe—"harder force" might be required. "When the rule of law breaks, when oppression and tyranny break out, a whole community can resort to revolt and rebellion, even organized revolution and regicide."

The Lutheran Reformation was indeed a revolution in many respects and provides fruitful bases to deliberate on the grounds for resistance when the political-economic order of the day intrudes on what Witte calls "liberty, morality and conscience."

The chapter by Nathan S. Chapman, "Constitutional Rules and the Political Economy of Character Formation: Conditions on Government Aid to Religious Schools as a Case Study," addresses the constitutional rules that govern U.S. school education to demonstrate the political economy of character formation. As a test case, Chapman takes on the difficult constitutional questions involved in state funding for private schools. "The question is this: when the government provides funds to private religious schools, may it condition those funds on the school's acceptance of a policy of nondiscrimination against employees or students because of their sexual or gender status or identity?"

Chapman first outlines the current constitutional principles governing school education in the United States. These principles establish the state's primary authority over education; they also grant parents and teachers a fundamental right to private education; they expressly prohibit public schools to engage in religious instruction; and "the government may provide some indirect funding to religious schools, so long as it is religiously neutral and the product of the free, independent choice of parents and students."

According to Chapman, citing many constitutional court cases, these principles do not provide clarity on the difficult question whether the state may provide funding to private schools on the condition that those schools adopt an LGBT nondiscrimination policy, especially when the recipient school objects to such a policy on religious grounds. The outcome of this constitutional tension is difficult to predict, but Chapman argues for the likelihood that the U.S. Supreme Court will adopt one of three possible rules.

First, the no-conditions rule (in favor of private schools) "would hold that the government may not secure as a condition for receiving public funds a promise to forgo any constitutional right," which includes the right to free religious association. Second, the nondiscrimination rule (in favor of government) would allow the government to indeed impose a nondiscrimination condition (for example, regarding LGBT persons) for receipt of funding. He points to a possible third rule that may bridge the gap between the competing views: "In exchange for the same funding available to other private schools, the religious school agrees to not discriminate against staff or students on the basis of their status and conduct but may continue to discriminate against them on the basis of their religious beliefs."

Chapman's contribution confirms the key role that school education plays in character formation. In a liberal democracy like the United States, conflicts about the role of the state and private concerns in education end up being constitutional questions. This may reflect the political dimension of the struggle. In this specific case, there are serious financial implications for schools, whatever way the Court may decide. These implications reflect the economic dimension of the conflict—hence, the "political economy of character formation" in the title.

A key insight is that underlying this seemingly legal-political-economic court battle is the philosophical question of paradigm-dependent thinking. Chapman observes that "the Supreme Court's articulation of such rules is, of course, itself a product of a political economy that shaped the terms of the Constitution and the contours of the prior doctrine. No court is an island; the constitutional doctrines the Supreme Court announces are creatures of political economy as much as they affect it." With regard to the specific case of nondiscrimination and possible conditional funding, there is a clash of values typical of incommensurable paradigms which makes the resolution of political economic questions more difficult to answer.

He finally notes the aspirations of American constitutionalism to religious neutrality, but there is in this case "no entirely neutral viewpoint from which to adjudicate the dispute."

Tentative Conclusion

Summarizing the themes addressed in the collection of essays, one might suggest the following: character formation and moral communication in the political economy are best approached from integrating and seeing the connections in an ethical approach that includes global, institutional, and personal dimensions. There is consensus that liberal capitalism is the dominant description of political economy in late modern Western societies. If divorced from ethics, liberal capitalism yields negative and even catastrophic results. Again, it is best to view the formative impact of liberal capitalism in tandem with social systems like law, religion, and, specifically, education. Avenues to address the use and possible abuse of political or state power are resistance in the form of "soft" or—in extreme cases—"hard" power, and where the rule of law governs, contestation is possible and desirable via constitutional means.

Part One:
Rethinking Ethics

Neoliberal Political Economy and Value Transmission: What We Can Learn from Feminist Care Ethics

Amanda Gouws

Introduction

Multicultural plural societies are "imagined communities" formed out of indigenous populations, colonizing settlers, and people migrating across borders. Pluralism brings together people with diverse cultures, languages, ethnicities, and understandings of ways of being governed. The creation of multicultural societies into one body politic has been successful because of liberal constitutions and multicultural governance, in which the state had a role to play in providing a social safety net, through social welfare, for those who are socially excluded and marginalized. Some of the core values of multicultural societies are tolerance, recognition of identities, acceptance of differing value systems, social inclusion, and a more inclusive redistribution of resources. But undergirding the success of multicultural societies is an ethic of care that needs a more prominent place among the values and behavior of citizens in multicultural societies.

Multicultural societies need social engineering to prevent conflict and to create greater acceptance of difference. Values like tolerance, respect, and human dignity need to be socialized in order for citizens to live in harmony. Socialization agents, such as parents, peers, schools, and institutions like the state, play an important role in the transmission of these values. In the past two decades, with the rise of populism and rightwing nationalism, the marketplace of ideas has shrunk, and agents of socialization have to face the impact of neoliberal policies that focus on individualism, competitiveness, the profit motive, and the echo chambers of social media that have led to serious fractures and polarization in multicultural societies. Those on the receiving end of intolerance and violence are often women, migrants, and nonconforming bodies (LGBTIQ and transgender persons). With the ever-shrinking role of the state and neoliberal privatization of care, value transmission that will support the social fabric of multicultural societies becomes compromised.

In this chapter, I first analyze the effect of neoliberalism on societies in general, and more specifically on how it creates precariousness for citizens. Neoliberal competitiveness and a focus on independence, combined with the commoditization of care, undermine care ethics that embodies interdependence as an important value in multicultural societies. I then focus on what we can learn from a feminist ethics of care in late modernity.

The Effects of Neoliberalism Globally

The main characteristic of neoliberalism is the rolling back of the state with dwindling contributions toward the provision of social welfare, and the rolling out of financialization, marketization, globalization, privatization, deregulation, and austerity measures that contribute to greater human inequality and dissociability.[1] Neoliberalism changes the egalitarian distribution of a previous era to a market fundamentalism that radically changes the relationship between state and society. Vivien A. Schmidt and Mark Thatcher contend that neoliberalism has the following characteristics:[2]

1. A confidence in the market as an efficient mechanism for the allocation of scarce resources.
2. A belief in the desirability of a global trade regime for free trade and free capital mobility.
3. A belief in the desirability, all things being equal, of a limited and non-interventionist role of the state and of the state as a facilitator and custodian rather than a substitute for market mechanisms.
4. A rejection of Keynesian demand-management techniques in favour of monetarism, neo-monetarism, and supply-side economics.
5. A commitment to the removal of those welfare benefits that might be seen to act as disincentives to market participation—subordinating principles of social justice to those of perceived economic imperatives.
6. A defence of labour-market flexibility and the promotion and nurturing of cost competitiveness.

Under neoliberalism, markets should be as free as possible based on the idea that the state is inherently inefficient and that the private sector can do better

---

[1] Louise Morley, "Gender in the Neo-liberal Research Economy: An Enervating and Exclusionary Entanglement," in *Gender Studies and the New Academic Governance*, ed. Heike Kahlert (Wiesbaden: Springer, 2018), 16–17.

[2] Vivien A. Schmidt and Mark Thatcher, "Theorizing Ideational Continuity: The Resilience of Neo-Liberal Ideas in Europe," LSE Research Online, 2013, http://eprints.lse.ac.uk/84379/1/Thatcher_Theorizing%20ideational%20continuity_2017.pdf, at p. 5. Here they draw on Colin Hay, "The Normalization Role of Rationalist Assumptions in the Institutionalist Embedding of Neo-Liberalism," *Economy and Society* 33, no. 4 (2004): 500–27.

service delivery (of course, at a cost).³ What makes neoliberalism dangerous is its ability to adapt to new circumstances while maintaining certain key elements, therefore making it very difficult for a coherent set of criticisms to be successful. It is also dangerous because it depoliticizes processes through which social phenomena are maintained.⁴ Deregulation allows hypermobility of capital and the increased power of capital interests, leading to an overreliance on capital growth and investment, rather than providing for human well-being and the sustainability of resources.⁵ This resilience of neoliberalism leads to an exclusion of alternative frameworks of managing economies, the formation of subjectivities that embrace neoliberal principles, and the unequal redistribution of resources.

Neoliberalism has a serious impact on democracy because it undermines practices, cultures, and institutions of democracy as rule by the people, and instead privileges the individual over the collective of the polity.⁶ The focus of all transactions becomes the human being as an economic unit, rather than the distribution of resources among the collective that can lead to socially responsible and critical citizenship. Change therefore becomes the restructuring of individual agency rather than the restructuring of conditions that lead to inequality, discrimination, and precariousness.⁷ When neoliberalism becomes a pervasive ethos, it influences value transmission through which subjectivities are formed. The economization of subjectivity reinforces asymmetrical power relations that disproportionately affect those who cannot access the market successfully and those on the fringes of societies—often women and people of color—because neoliberal globalization is a raced and gendered process through which economically disempowered people often are exploited to the benefit of those who are economically empowered.

One outcome of neoliberalism on the subject formation of humans is a narcissistic value system—that of manipulating relationships and the lack of deep interpersonal connections. This value permeates social institutions, leading, for example, to children internalizing the values, beliefs, and practices of a consumer culture's individualized demands.⁸ This trend is enhanced and reproduced through the exposure to social media that drives consumer culture and self-representation, rather than deeper values of attentiveness and care that is interrela-

---

[3] Schmidt and Thatcher, "Theorizing Ideational Continuity," 17.
[4] Ibid., 15.
[5] V. Spike Peterson, "International/Global Political Economy," in *Gender Matters in Global Politics*, ed. Laura J. Shepherd (London: Routledge, 2015), 173–85.
[6] Morley, "Gender in the Neo-Liberal Research Economy," 20.
[7] Ibid., 26.
[8] Sami Timimi, "The McDonaldization of Childhood: Children's Mental Health in Neo-Liberal Market Cultures," *Transcultural Psychiatry* 47, no. 5 (2010): 686–706, at 686.

tional. The free market exercises social control in aggressive and punitive ways, through making those who are not successful feel like failures, not fitting in and not belonging.[9] Many children are now preoccupied with issues that show a lack of psychological well-being, such as anxiety, depression, and feelings of exclusion—feeling that they do not belong, manifesting as emotional insecurity. In what Sami Timimi calls the "McDonaldization" of children's mental health— where pharmaceutical interventions can be bought as fast as a takeaway hamburger—children are not made to feel secure and connected, but rather are pathologized because they do not fit in. Children need webs of care outside the education system that focus on respect, dignity, and interdependence.[10] As Michael Rustin argues,[11] the development of human potentialities and capabilities is dependent on the quality of the relationships in which they are nurtured, and this also to a large extent determines their future contributions to society.

Quentin Duroy maintains that certain mental constructs legitimize the dominance of neoliberal institutions and policies.[12] Drawing on the work of Thorstein Veblen,[13] he argues that habits of mind are the guides to an individual's interpretation of the world and actions that has an institutional, cultural, and individual dimension. Neoliberalism produces ideas and habits of mind (subjectivities) that foreground the individual's access to the market that has also influenced cultural expressions. On an institutional level, neoliberalism has delegitimized the ability of the state to assert its political sovereignty in the market, and culture has become instrumentalized for the purposes of making money. Culture and institutions therefore conspire to socialize values that support neoliberal capitalism. This includes objectifying relations and individuals through commodification in terms of their productivity, efficiency, and profit. A person's value is therefore contingent on his or her relations to profit.[14] Education itself has become instrumentalized to meet ends that suit the market, rather than valorized for the values it can transfer.

The consequences of neoliberalism are powerful and have culminated in a global project, through which space is reconfigured. Neoliberalism has become institutionalized through governmental programs, social formations, as well as

---

[9] Ibid., 696.

[10] Dympna Devine and Wendy Lutrell, "Children and Value—Education in Neo-Liberal Times," *Children and Society* 27, no. 4 (2013): 231–44.

[11] Michael Rustin, "A Relational Society," *Soundings* 54 (2013): 23–36.

[12] Quentin Duroy, "Thinking Like a Trader: The Impact of Neoliberal Doctrine on Habits of Thought," *Journal of Economic Issues* 50, no. 2 (2016): 603–10.

[13] Thorstein Veblen, *The Vested Interests and the State of the Industrial Arts* (New Brunswick, N.J.: Transaction Publishers, 1919).

[14] Ryan Willilams LaMothe, "The Colonizing Realities of Neoliberal Capitalism," *Pastoral Psychology* 65 (2016): 23–40, at 28.

political projects and global governmental bodies.¹⁵ Its institutionalization means that socialization agents, such as schools and tertiary institutions, also become embedded in neoliberal value systems. Institutions are crucial for how they shape values and ideas. Once certain values and ideas become institutionalized, they present powerful forces for continuity that rest on established path dependencies. When care and the bodies who care are not configured into these path dependencies, the contribution of women (carers) to sustaining human societies is erased.

The value of care in patriarchal societies is usually associated with women's work that is unpaid and happens in the privacy of the home. Neoliberal globalization as a gendered process devalorizes women's bodies and care work, especially where global care chains consist of mostly migrant women from developing countries. When this sex/gender system (which determines a gendered division of labor) is socialized to be "natural," the gender binary becomes internalized, and care is devalued. This system also reinforces the idea of the binary between the productive and reproductive economy—where the productive economy is viewed as male, paid for, and rewarded, while reproductive work is viewed as elastic and mostly unpaid, contributing to the feminization of poverty. Neoliberalism has contributed to a crisis in social reproduction because it depletes the emotional, cultural, and material resources necessary to sustain the well-being of human beings.¹⁶ Effective socialization of the sex/gender system matters structurally for masculinized economic relations that, on one hand, value men's work and, on the other hand, devalue women's work that maintains the emotional and physical health of people.¹⁷ The devaluing of women's work also contributes to the concentration of women in precarious work that has become characteristic of late modernity. This is work that is short term, low paid, and without benefits.

Neoliberalism's logic of commodification and capital accumulation has contributed to the dismantling of welfare states that offered a safety net to poor and vulnerable people, contributing to the greater precariousness of work, access to housing, and health. Precariousness is a consequence of the hegemony of the free market. The compact of labor, the state, and the private sector has shifted to erode workers' rights and bargaining power with a concomitant decrease in government's social expenditure through austerity measures. Precarity is both a social and a structural economic condition and is a consequence of the erosion of the state's welfare provisioning that has fueled migration from developing regions to developed countries. This migration enables a flexible labor market embedded in an international division of labor that is raced and gendered, with

---

¹⁵ Sylvia Walby, *Globalization and Inequalities* (London: Sage, 2009), 42–45.
¹⁶ Peterson, "International/Global Political Economy," 180–82.
¹⁷ Ibid., 181.

more women and people of color relegated to low-paying, precarious jobs, of which care work is one of the biggest sectors. This situation normalizes the devaluation of care work. When market crises occur, the costs are gendered because of the concentration of women in precarious forms of employment. Women often are the buffer for the impact of reduced household income, leading to a deterioration of their own health, taking girls out of school to work, increasing sex work, and escalating violence against women.[18] Precarity combined with the fast pace of change caused by ever-changing technology induces what David Theo Goldberg has called "dread."[19] For him, dread has become the driving force of the palpable anxieties of our time caused by wars, climate disasters, pandemics, and the inability to cope with the pace of technological change and to distinguish lies from truth. Dread is the outcome of precarity. The very stark difference between those whose situation is precarious and those whose is not creates an "us and them"—the ones with access to the market and the precarious ones, prompting Judith Butler to ask: what is a livable life? who counts as human? and what makes for a grievable life?[20]

Precarity has very serious implications for plural societies, where differences of race, class, religion, and culture have been incorporated into a single polity. Multicultural societies governed in ways that draw on the strengths of these divisions have retreated in the face of large-scale migration of people from conflict zones. Migrants and refugees may not want or be able to assimilate into existing societies, aggravating already existing schisms around race, religion, and culture. In the wake of 9/11 and the war on terror, we see greater and greater polarization of people around clashing value systems and the rise of a populist response globally that generally resists gender equality and adheres to a gender ideology that questions nonbinary gender identities and sexualities, therefore also challenging human-rights regimes. Human rights do not protect everyone equally, because they have been used to impose and legitimize Western political hegemony, neoliberal politics, and serious structural inequalities, so that rights have become essentialized as universal, as though they apply to everyone equally. In many ways they have begun to limit social, economic, and political possibilities for change, and to open doors for new forms of imperialism and antidemocratic politics.[21] Rights talk conceals the structural conditions that

---

[18] Ibid., 181; and Walby, *Globalization and Inequalities*.
[19] David Theo Goldberg, *Dread–Facing Futureless Futures* (Newark, N.J.: Polity Press, 2021).
[20] Judith Butler, *Precarious Life: The Powers of Mourning and Violence* (London: Verso, 2004).
[21] Vivienne Bozalek and Michalinos Zembylas, "A Critical Engagement with the Social and Political Consequences of Human Rights: The Contribution of the Affective Turn and Posthumanism," *Acta Academia* 46, no. 4 (2014): 29–47.

produce dependency, in which needs unfold for those who are poor or marginalized. Dependent people often cannot recognize the language of rights, because their needs are constructed outside entitlements to rights, thus making rights meaningless.[22]

The racial logic of power embedded in rights (of lives that are racially distinct, less than human, and subjected to exceptional violence—for example, migrants crossing the Mediterranean) is inherent in the global order that universalizes Western experience and human-rights regimes. Human-rights regimes are criticized by scholars such as Judith Butler, David Theo Goldberg, and Wendy Brown,[23] because such regimes focus on the "independent" individual, who ostensibly has no need for interdependence or life in communities, and also because rights talk does not acknowledge the raced, gendered, and classed nature of incorporation into citizenship and regimes of rule. Brown contests the view that liberal rights have the ability to address the causes of social grievance and suffering, because rights do not erode structures of exploitation and oppression in a way that leads to social justice. These critiques demand that we draw on alternatives for rights regimes, such as an ethic of care.

The Importance of Care Ethics in Late Modernity

Precarity is not a passing condition or an episode.[24] Precarity is caused and fueled by neoliberalism and the way it assigns value to human interactions, with large numbers of people now living outside a safety net that would ensure their survival. It is now widely acknowledged that we have a care crisis. This crisis is a consequence of the relational harm of neoliberalism, planetary neglect, and constant warfare.[25] As Wendy Brown puts it:

> It [neo-liberalism] has economised everything and everyone, it's rendered everything as a market and it's rendered everything we do as market action. When rights are adjudicated through that frame, human beings get figured as little capitals, and

---

[22] Amanda Gouws and Mikki van Zyl, "Feminist Ethics of Care through a Southern Lens," in *Care in Context–Transnational Gender Perspectives*, ed. Vasu Reddy et al. (Cape Town: HSRC Press, 2014), 99–124.

[23] Wendy Brown, *States of Injury: Power and Freedom in Late Modernity* (Princeton: Princeton University Press, 1995).

[24] Maurice Hamington and Michael A. Flower, *Care Ethics in an Age of Precarity* (Minneapolis: University of Minnesota Press, 2021), 1.

[25] Ibid., 15.

all of civic and political life gets rendered as market spheres. That means that rights increasingly get allocated not as civil rights, not as civil liberties, not as rights to empower the disempowered, but as capital rights.[26]

The harms of neoliberalism manifest themselves in the lack of care, in exclusions from life-sustaining conditions and services, and in environmental degradation in the name of profit, based on an unjust neoliberal global order that rests on raced and gendered geopolitics.[27] There is therefore also the need to counter the impact of neoliberalism on care ethics. Care ethics is incompatible with individualization and competition as an imperative. Care ethics itself has become precarious because of marketization, when the market undermines interdependence and shifts the responsibility of care work onto women. The market is "free" because women do the unpaid care work that sustains a free-market economy, in which care is viewed as a burden on the state and the market treats it as a commodity to be bought by self-reliant individuals.[28] The adoption of an ethics of care by women facilitates the smooth functioning of globalized neoliberalism.[29] Who cares is deeply gendered and related to the boundary maintenance of citizenship. Neoliberal regimes determine who is entitled to receive care and who is not, which bodies provide care and which bodies are exempt from providing care.[30]

Care involves principles, practices, and emotions that the market is not able to deliver, because care is embodied, relational, and multiscalar. The multiscalarity of care is linked to transnational and international care chains made up mostly of women.[31] Care involves fundamentally different normative and ontological assumptions about the nature of injustice and the moral subject,[32] and draws our attention to distributive justice, because of the relationality of care that involves every dimension of life, such as care for babies and children, for the elderly, for the disabled, reproductive care, and care to sustain households and the planet. The interpersonal nature of care is not recognized when women are perceived as workers and not caregivers for the purpose of legitimizing their

---

[26] Katie Cruz and Wendy Brown, "Feminism, Law, and Neoliberalism: An Interview and Discussion with Wendy Brown," *Feminist Legal Studies* 24, no. 1 (2016): 69–89, at 72.

[27] Fiona Robinson, "Global Care Ethics: Beyond Distribution, Beyond Justice," *Journal of Global Ethics* 9, no. 2 (2013): 131–43, at 133.

[28] Sabrina Schmitt, Gerd Mutz, and Brigit Erbe, "Care Economies—Feminist Contributions and Debates in Economic Theory," *Osterreich, Z. Soziol* 43 (2018): 7–18, at 11–15.

[29] Nira Yuval-Davis, "Nationalism, Belonging, Globalization and the 'Ethics of Care,'" *Kinder, Kon & Forskning* 2–3 (2007): 91–100, at 91.

[30] Ibid., 93.

[31] Robinson, "Global Care Ethics," 131.

[32] Ibid., 135.

labor migration.³³ In the face of a care deficit in neoliberal societies, the way migrant women's labor is used reproduces and reinforces the public/private dichotomy. When care is devalued, it is relegated to the private sphere of the home, done by migrant women whose lives are also devalued because they often lack citizenship. Such devaluation sets in motion a chain of injustices that are multiscalar, starting at the household level and rising to the state and the global order.³⁴ For example, the injustices extend to the migrant caregiver's family when her children have to forgo a mother's care. The public devaluing of care is related to a discourse of globalization that feminizes the state in relation to a robust masculine market.³⁵ The marketization of care puts care out of reach for a majority of the global population, while women in the care chain suffer from a care penalty because of the low pay relative to the time-intense nature of the work.³⁶

When the basic ontology of independence is altered to show that subjects are dependent, vulnerable, self-sacrificing, emotional, embodied, and partial toward each other, it negates the rationalist model of distributive justice.³⁷ As Robinson makes clear, it is not about an obligation to care, because we all care—often because we do not have a choice (and more often it is women who do not have a choice), but when the values of care are internalized, they become constitutive of our subjectivities and identities in an ontological and moral sense.

The consequences of the devaluation of care are enormous, because they extend way beyond the individual. Devaluation of care has planetary consequences with environmental disasters, irreversible climate change, and the possibility of nuclear catastrophes. What is needed is a different type of value socialization that focuses on relationality, community, and care. Whereas human-rights regimes favor the "independent" liberal subject, care values put the emphasis on relationality. Care stands in opposition to precarity. Care is what Joan C. Tronto defined long ago as "everything we do to maintain, continue and repair 'our world'. . . to interweave a complex life sustaining web."³⁸ Care is a moral theory

---

33 Ibid., 139.
34 Ibid., 141; and Stefanie Wöhl, "Multiple Dimensions of Gender Inequality: Engaging 'the State' in IPE," in *Handbook on the International Political Economy of Gender*, ed. Juanita Elias and Adrienne Roberts (Cheltenham: Edward Elgar, 2018), 171–83.
35 Tiina Vaitinnen, Hanna-Kaisa Hoppania, and Olli Karsio, "Marketization, Commodification and Privatization of Care Services," in Elias and Roberts, *Handbook on the International Political Economy of Gender*, 379–91, at 381.
36 Hironori Onuki, "Transnational Care Work and the 'Care Crisis,'" in Elias and Roberts, *Handbook on the International Political Economy of Gender*, 365–78, at 369.
37 Robinson, "Global Care Ethics," 136.
38 Joan C. Tronto, *Moral Boundaries: A Political Argument for an Ethic of Care* (New York: Routledge, 1993), 69.

that includes virtue, duty, a practice, and a disposition.[39] Care ethics challenges the basic assumptions of liberal theory: that of the private/public divide and that of the individual as a source of moral authority. It relocates moral authority also in the collective political community. This relationality ties citizens to each other and to the state. It steers away from the idea of the individual as a self-determined, self-reliant, and independent self-maximizing atomistic being. This type of autonomy abstracts people from concrete contextual factors to which care is always related.[40]

A feminist care ethic socializes values such as attentiveness (to the care recipient), responsiveness, responsibility, and relationality. Care is something without which humans cannot exist, but its value is continually dismissed.[41] The COVID pandemic has refocused our attention on care, since giving and receiving care became the only ways that humans could survive through the pandemic. A feminist care ethic includes:[42]

- A relational approach to morality—all care is relational and interdependent. Human beings are interdependent.
- Responsiveness to the other—it takes the needs of the other as a starting point and responds to it.
- Context matters—there needs to be an understanding of the unique and particular circumstances of those cared for.
- Crossing moral boundaries—care ethics draws on the notion of "the personal is political" and is not limited to the private sphere; even the political is infused with needs for care.
- Affect/emotion is important for our lives, just as important as rationality.

Given the state of politics in the world, there is an urgent need for care ethics to be taken seriously. Over the past two decades, care manifestos have been written by feminist activists and scholars to invoke a need for a different type of socialization of values. In 2001 the Canadian Charlottetown Declaration on the Right to Care included care as a relational value:

---

[39] Hamington and Flower, *Care Ethics in an Age of Precarity*, 5.
[40] Amanda Gouws and Mikki van Zyl, "Towards a Feminist Ethics of Ubuntu: Bridging Rights and Ubuntu," in *Care Ethics and Political Theory*, ed. Daniel Engster and Maurice Hamington (Oxford: Oxford University Press, 2015), 165–86.
[41] Tronto, *Moral Boundaries*; Selma Sevenhuijsen, *Citizenship and a Feminist Ethic of Care* (London: Routledge, 1998); Virginia Held, *Feminist Morality: Transforming Culture, Society, and Politics* (Chicago: University of Chicago Press, 1993); and Nel Noddings, *Caring: A Feminine Approach to Ethics and Moral Education* (Berkeley: University of California Press, 1984).
[42] Daniel Engster and Maurice Hamington, introduction to *Care Ethics and Political Theory*, 3–4.

> To ensure the right to care, care must be understood as essential, something we must provide as a country. While we have choices about how, when and where to provide care, we do not have a choice about whether to provide care to those who need it. We cannot leave people without necessary care. Care must also be understood as an interdependent relationship. It is not simply about what one person does to or for another but also involves reciprocity.[43]

In the wake of the devastation wreaked by the COVID pandemic, a group of civil society organizations, youth groups, and women from Latin America, Asia, and Sub-Saharan Africa developed the Care Manifesto, which calls for care as a right: "Recognise care as a right ... the public sector should recognise care as a right, enshrined in law, and build a caring economy by addressing the 5 'Rs'—Recognition, Reduction, Redistribution, Representation and Reward for care work, whilst overturning gender-discriminatory norms enshrined in societies and communities."[44] The most important of these manifestos is *The Care Manifesto*, which appeared after the pandemic as a book from Verso Press. The authors call for a "politics that will put care front and centre" and acknowledge human interdependence and relationality.[45]

Relational thinking is "thinking with," not in the abstract.[46] Care ethics can be linked to what is called the affective turn. The affective turn engages the complex relations among power, emotion, affect, and subjectivity and exposes the working of power relations.[47] It also challenges human rights for their inability to reconfigure power relations and create new possibilities for social justice. By allowing space for centering affect and emotions, pain and suffering, rather than abstract notions of justice embedded in the partial and contested claims of human rights, the affective turn exposes the contextuality of care.[48]

Many scholars call for a care ethics to be taken seriously in order to deal with precarity and continuous violence.[49] Postpandemic, David Theo Goldberg, for example, argues that the only way we can push back against dread is

---

[43] The Charlottetown Declaration on the Right to Care, https://thecareeconomy.ca/wp-content/uploads/2021/09/Charlottetown-Declaration.pdf, 3.
[44] "The Care Manifesto," The African Women's and Development Communication Network, Jun. 29, 2021, https://femnet.org/2021/06/the-care-manifesto/, 2.
[45] Andreas Chatzidakis et al. (The Care Collective), *The Care Manifesto: The Politics of Interdependence* (London: Verso, 2020), 5.
[46] Maria Puig de la Bellacasa, *Matters of Care: Speculative Ethics in More Than Human Worlds* (Minneapolis: University of Minnesota Press, 2017).
[47] Bozalek and Zembylas, "A Critical Engagement with the Social and Political Consequences of Human Rights," 37.
[48] Ibid.
[49] See, for example, Engster and Hamington, *Care Ethics and Political Theory*.

through ways of caring that will contribute to life-enabling conditions. He calls for "ecologies of care" that will involve care infrastructures and care cultures that will make living together possible.[50]

In her pathbreaking book *In a Different Voice*,[51] Carol Gilligan has shown that girls' moral development happens differently from that of boys, for girls think relationally and contextually because of their socialization into care. Boys engage more hypothetical and abstract notions of moral dilemmas. From this work, Gilligan developed the notion of a "feminist ethics of care." Care ethics meets the needs of others while maintaining relationships. This type of socialization therefore starts at a very young age for girls, while at the same time it diminishes the importance of a care ethics for boys. Care and autonomy are not mutually exclusive, but autonomy can be reached only through care. The deficit of care-ethic thinking and empathy in most male political leaders was revealed during the pandemic, when countries run by women fared so much better in containing the pandemic and responding to needs of their citizens.[52]

Vivienne Bozalek and Michalinos Zembylas call for socially just pedagogies that will take on board the affective turn that will involve a care ethics,[53] while Colette Rabin and Grinell Smith argue that teaching children care ethics needs to include the notions of "caring about" as well as "caring for," where the latter will make them understand that relationality also extends to strangers, the environment, and the planet.[54] Rabin and Smith argue that affect needs to be integrated into the curriculum, because affect and emotions have become devalued (and linked derogatorily to "emotional" women). A care ethics therefore needs to be juxtaposed with dominance and control. Asha L. Bhandary points out that our understanding of care will be linked to historical trajectories. As she puts it: "practices of care are encoded in cultural norms and narratives, and these narratives are influenced by the particularities of history."[55] In dealing with violent

---

[50] Goldberg, *Dread*, 214.

[51] Carol Gilligan, *In a Different Voice: Psychological Theory and Women's Development* (Cambridge, Mass.: Harvard University Press, 1982).

[52] Greg Orme, "Women Leaders Have Shone During the Pandemic: Men, Take Note," *Forbes*, Aug. 4, 2021, https://www.forbes.com/sites/gregorme/2021/08/04/women-leaders-have-shone-during-the-pandemicambitious-men-should-take-note/?sh=286e729b51c6.

[53] Vivienne Bozalek and Michalinos Zembylas, "Critical Posthumanism, New Materialism and the Affective Turn for Socially Just Pedagogies in Higher Education," *South African Journal of Higher Education* 30, no. 3 (2016): 193–200.

[54] Colette Rabin and Grinell Smith, "Teaching Care Ethics: Conceptual Understandings and Stories for Learning," *Journal of Moral Education* 42, no. 2 (2013): 164–76.

[55] Asha L. Bhandary, *Freedom to Care: Liberalism, Dependency Care, and Culture* (New York: Routledge, 2019), 5.

histories, Virginia Held makes a convincing case that an ethics of care provides a strong grounding to value nonviolence over violence and conflict when children are exposed to a nurturing education.[56]

Why is it that care as a value is not socialized? One of the reasons is that care is considered natural, to the extent that it is not talked about. This coincides with the naturalization of the sex/gender system, which normalizes care as devalued women's work. It is only in the past few decades that feminist scholars have developed thinking about care into moral philosophies and theories of distributive justice. In this regard, the theorization of Carol Gilligan, Joan Tronto, Nel Noddings, Virginia Held, Selma Sevenhuijsen, and Grace Clement[57] blazed a trail for the theorization of care alongside autonomy, independence, responsibility, reciprocity, and responsiveness.

Because care is everywhere, it is taken for granted, and therefore there is the assumption that we all know how to care and how to provide care. Care, however, is socialized through observation and therefore often not considered part of the cognitive dimension of value transmission, but rather related to the emotional or affective domain, something that was undervalued until the recent proposal of the "affective turn." There should be concerted efforts to socialize care ethics as a species activity. The harms of neoliberalism show that human beings are interdependent and that needs are contextual. Even when people draw on rights-based discourses, a conflict of rights shows the interdependencies of people, because conflicts do not arise in vacuums but arise because of people's claims on each other.

Conclusion

In this chapter, I have attempted to show that neoliberalism is harmful to societies because of its emphasis on individualism, independence, and competition to the exclusion of values of a care ethics, such as interdependence and relationality. Under neoliberal conditions, care work is devalued and associated with global care chains that exploit migrant caregivers by not valuing their care. The commoditization of care aggravates conditions for those who cannot afford care. Through the rollback of the state and the shrinking of provision of social welfare, many people now live precarious lives. What is needed is the socialization of an ethics of care that will relate to the individual, the state, the international arena, and the planet.

---

[56] Virginia Held, "Can the Ethics of Care Handle Violence," *Ethics and Social Welfare* 4, no. 2 (2010): 115–29.

[57] Grace Clement, *Care, Autonomy and Justice–Feminism and the Ethic of Care* (Boulder, Colo.: Westview, 1998).

We would do well to heed Michael Rustin's warning: "The world of individualist, acquisitive capitalism has become unsustainable, for many reasons. Its ideology of individual self-interest violates human needs for connectedness and mutual care. Its unseeing and rapacious attitude to the material environment is threatening to destroy the conditions of life on the planet."[58] We ignore a care ethics at our own peril.

---

[58] Rustin, "A Relational Society."

Ethics' Political Imperative: Moving Toward Better Institutions[1]

Andreas Glaeser

This chapter pursues two related arguments about ethics in complex societies. If it is granted that human beings live their lives in and through institutional arrangements, and if institutional arrangements exist in enduring interrelated activities of human beings, then most of the consequences of their actions are mediated by institutions. To be ethical therefore implies a particular care for the quality of the institutions in whose making and remaking human beings are implicated. In other words, one cannot be ethical or act ethically without being political at the same time. This fact raises the further question whether the theory of institutions might not yield general evaluative criteria for the goodness of institutions. I answer affirmatively by offering three such criteria: transparency—to make the consequences of people's actions visible; malleability—to allow them to intervene positively in reshaping the institutional fabric through which they live; and, finally, public goal-conformity—to assess institutions in light of publicly generated and espoused ideals of a good life in the good society.

Introduction

While unfolding these two arguments, I will use a simple example to illustrate my theoretical points. Here it is. A protagonist—a student, perhaps, or a consultant or scholar—is working on a writing project and chances upon a book that has such relevance for her project that she feels she needs to read it right away. She would prefer to work with a print copy but could temporarily also work with an e-book. However, the title is checked out from the library, and her favorite independent neighborhood bookstore does not have a copy in stock. Ordering

---

[1] I would like to thank Piet Naudé and Michael Welker for their kind invitation to develop the following ideas for our Heidelberg conference in May 2022, as well as for being such wonderful hosts. I have benefited greatly from the discussions with all participants and from the critical reactions to a much shorter version of this paper.

it there takes anywhere from two to four weeks. Amazon, however, can get her a paper copy tomorrow and an e-book version right away.

This leaves her with two options. First, she can order the book from Amazon. Yet doing so would produce a plethora of ethically questionable effects. She would make Jeff Bezos richer than he already is, thus contributing to the unabatedly increasing inequality in the United States, which in turn undermines U.S. democracy. She would also deprive her local bookstore of its sustenance, while contributing to the exploitational, union-busting practices at Amazon warehouses and the like.

Second, she can order the book from the local store, thus making a contribution to its survival, while at the same time downloading a pirated digital copy. Here, too, she would produce ethically questionable effects. She would deprive the publisher, a university press, of additional, equally needed income. Plus, she would willingly commit a copyright infringement and thereby contribute to a culture that makes it more difficult for people to live off their writing.

In an instant, this example highlights how the protagonist's ability to *be* ethical or *act* ethically is contingent on a complex assemblage of institutions. The attitudes, values, feelings, and knowledge she brings to bear on the situation are not just hers, but to have them, she has to partake in structured communities of discourse. That is to say, these values are institutionalized—and that on several levels. Her norms and values, feelings and knowledge draw on a particular language and the ways of talking ethics that it provides; they are formed and anchored in an organized public sphere, with particular media of mass communication at her disposal; and they dwell in family and friendship networks, etc. Moreover, the protagonist's knowledge about the consequences of her behavior is contingent on the work of journalists employed by various kinds of news organizations investigating the practices of large organizations like Amazon, as well as on that of social scientists researching the extent, causes, and consequences of income and wealth inequality in the United States. Her knowledge about independent bookstores' precarious situation is likewise mediated through discursive practices.

Of particular ethical concern about situations like the book buyer's is that whichever way she turns (given her preferences for the immediate availability of texts), she produces consequences that she experiences as ethically problematic. Life in complex institutional settings may quickly appear as if it condemns people to choiceless immoral behavior that ultimately draws morality itself into doubt. While the above situation still contains some wiggle room for choices (more on this below), many others do not.[2]

---

[2] Take the use of modern electronic equipment, which is a de facto necessity for participating in normal life in somewhat richer countries. All of it relies on components pro-

One can easily imagine institutional assemblages within which the protagonist's ethical conundrum would never have occurred. If independent bookstores in the United States could rely on an efficient wholesale system, or if Amazon were a different company, there might not be an ethical problem. Of course, the same is true for the ways in which actors bring ethics to bear on their life. The significance of identifying both important dimensions of the ethical situation—not only the actor's habits, beliefs, and values but also the action-environment as institutionalized—is to say that both could be otherwise because they are both generated by actors who could have acted differently.[3] And that points to the fact that actors are implicated in having the ethics they have,[4] and possibly also in in making the environment what it is now and what it will be in the future. If this is so, then actors could possibly make a contribution to changing themselves, the environment, or both.

This possibility has profound consequences for how we might wish to think about ethics. If institutions matter so much, then Kant's question "what ought I to do?" is too narrow and should much rather become "what assemblage of institutions ought we to form, such that we are all more likely to act ethically in the sense stipulated by us together?" This question in turn has consequence for the criteria of goodness we should use to evaluate behavior, because goodness now pertains to institutional fabrics much rather than to individual actions alone. Before I can wonder about useful criteria to judge the goodness of particular institutions within a wider ecology of institutions, however, I need to say more about how best to think about institutions.

Institutions

Sociologically speaking, the concept of institution encompasses all forms of regularized human behavior.[5] The *scale* and *spatial scope* of institutions range

---

duced with rare earths, the mining of which is done mostly under highly problematic environmental and labor conditions.

[3] I discuss the ethical situation in greater detail in Andreas Glaeser, "Analyzing Actually Existing Ethics: A Hermeneutic-Institutionalist Approach," in *The Impact of Academic Research on Character Formation, Ethical Education, and the Communication of Values in Late Modern Pluralistic Societies*, ed. William Schweiker, Michael Welker, John Witte Jr., and Stephen Pickard (Leipzig: Evangelische Verlagsanstalt, 2021), 39–64.

[4] Aristotle, *Nicomachean Ethics*, trans. Robert C. Bartlett and Susan D. Collins (Chicago: University of Chicago Press, 2011), 1103a–1105b.

[5] See Andreas Glaeser, *Political Epistemics: The Secret Police, the Opposition, and the End of GDR Socialism* (Chicago: University of Chicago Press, 2011); and Andreas Glaeser, "Hermeneutic Institutionalism: A New Synthesis," *Qualitative Sociology* 37, no. 2 (2014):

from micro rituals, carried by at least two co-located interactants, to the world financial system, carried by billions of globally dispersed people, and the global climate, carried by all human beings together. Institutions' *temporal scope* ranges from the strategic cooperation of two partners for the duration of a round of cards, to the pre-homo-sapiens (roughly one-million-year-old) knowledge of controlling fire. In spite of the fact that we tend to talk about habits, values, and modes of thinking or feeling as properties of individuals, they are institutions, since they all have to be grounded in ongoing encounters with other human beings and other experiences in the world.[6] Building on the biological endowments of homo sapiens (the capacities to imagine, to form language, to perceive, and to desire, etc.), institutions mediate the particular physical, mental, and emotional dependence of any human being on others as well as on the natural environment. Unlike biological endowments, however—and herein lies their evolutionary advantage—institutions can be reconfigured to reflect some kind of learning that has taken place.[7]

Ontologically speaking, institutions exist in the enchainment of self-similar action-reaction effect flows involving at least two, but often very many, spatially and temporally distributed persons. All who partake in making and remaking an institution can be addressed as its carriers. What this means in the example above is simply this: Amazon is Amazon not only because Bezos and all his

---

207–41. Both works build on Peter Berger and Thomas Luckmann, *The Social Construction of Reality* (New York: Anchor Books, 1966); Alfred Schütz and Thomas Luckmann, *Die Strukturen der Lebenswelt* (Frankfurt: Suhrkamp, 1984); and Max Weber *Wirtschaft und Gesellschaft: Grundriss der verstehenden Soziologie* [1922] (Tübingen: J. C. B. Mohr [Paul Siebeck], 1972).

6   This follows from George Herbert Mead in conjunction with Ludwig Wittgenstein, and it is backed up by empirical psychological research on people kept in isolation. See George Herbert Mead, *Mind, Self, and Society: From the Standpoint of a Social Behaviorist* (Chicago: University of Chicago Press, 1934); and Ludwig Wittgenstein, *Philosophische Untersuchungen/Philosophical Investigations* [1953], German text with English translation by G. E. M. Anscombe, P. M. S. Hacker, and Joachim Schulte (Oxford: Blackwell, 2009). For a detailed account, see Glaeser, *Political Epistemics*, chap. 3.

7   Thinking about the link between human biological endowments and institutional life was pioneered by Helmut Plessner, *Die Stufen des Organischen und der Mensch: Einleitung in die philosophische Anthropologie* (Frankfurt: Suhrkamp, 1928); and Arnold Gehlen, *Der Mensch: Seine Natur und seine Stellung in der Welt*. [1940] (Wiesbaden: Quelle und Meyer, 1997). Their general perspective has become very influential through the works of Berger and Luckmann, *The Social Construction of Reality*. For some contemporary approaches bridging the biological and the institutional with special reference to ethics, see Christopher Boehm, *Moral Origins: The Evolution of Virtue, Altruism, and Shame* (New York: Basic Books, 2012); and Webb Keane, *Ethical Life: Its Natural and Social Histories* (Princeton: Princeton University Press, 2016).

one-and-a-half-million employees do what they do every day, but also because hundreds of millions of people shop on Amazon recurrently, because suppliers sell Amazon the goods it resells, because more than a million vendors use Amazon as a sales platform ("the Marketplace"), because people buy and sell Amazon stock, because government regulators let Amazon do what it does, and so on. That is to say that many millions of people carry Amazon. All of them together make Amazon what it is. Ditto for the independent bookstore.

Institutions do not exist in neatly separable units but in more or less *dense* interrelationships with each other. Amazon, for example, can rely on a huge number of skills and habits that its employees and customers have acquired elsewhere. It can rely on institutionalized forms of communication, transportation, and storage; on governance, law, and law enforcement; on standardized measures of time, weight, volume, money, and electronic payment systems, as well as on ethics of work, keeping promises, etc., none of which it has created. Since Amazon can work only by enrolling these institutions to make itself work, and since these institutions are shared with others, it is suitable to designate them as infrastructural institutions. Of course, Amazon itself has increasingly become an infrastructural institution for the data warehousing, selling, and sourcing efforts of a huge range of other institutions. All institutions rely on such infrastructural environments, and they are often infrastructures for each other.

Precisely because institutions exist in the enchainment of actions that could be altered in manner, force, direction, timing, and so on, they are in principle malleable. Actions can cease to take place altogether, which is to say that institutions can also disappear. If Amazon workers stayed away for good, if customers opted to boycott it, Amazon would cease to exist. Forming, maintaining, and changing institutions intentionally is what politics is all about. At the heart of politics, then, lies the inducement of particular actors, the carriers of an institution, to engage in particular actions in response to other actions. This can be hard and frustrating work because many people need to be enrolled and properly coordinated to achieve desirable effects. The potential for slippage in the translation from political intention to actual institutionalization is considerable.

The means of politics range from joint deliberation to generate a mutually supported transformational goal, to persuasion and incentivization, and to various forms of coercion. The more complex the institutions marked for change are, the more urgent it is to form meta-institutions by charging designated personnel to manage their formation, maintenance, or change. Institution and meta-institution together form an *organization*.[8] Amazon has a professional manage-

---

[8] Understanding the political importance of organization was pioneered by Robert Michels. See his *Soziologie des Parteiwesens: Eine Untersuchung über die oligarchischen Tendenzen des Gruppenlebens* [1911] (Stuttgart: Kröner, 1989).

ment charged with keeping it going; a country has institutions of state to maintain it as an ordered whole. Organization is therefore a means of politics as well as an outcome.

Ethics' Political Imperative

The constitution of institutions in the enchainment of action effects, the scale, spatial, and temporal scope as well as the density of institutions—that is, their complexity—complicates ethics considerably. The more widely acknowledged problem is that the complexity of institutional arrangements makes it extremely hard for actors to track the consequences of their actions to concrete other human beings as well as to the environment.[9] The more densely different institutions interface with each other, and the more widely scoped they are in time and space, the harder it is to track action effects. Yet such complexity defines modern social life.

The much less acknowledged problem is that actions have institution-forming, maintaining, and weakening consequences. While actions often aim to achieve particular effects that actors hold in their minds, actions also make and remake the infrastructural contexts of acting. Blinkered by their intentions (more on this below), actors are rarely aware of the many ways in which they contribute to the formation of institutions. Such institution forming effects are properly called political for two reasons: First they remake the world in and through which a larger community acts and as such they are part of the re publica. Second, if, as I have argued above, politics is the conscious effort to form, maintain, or alter institutions, then the institution-forming consequences could become subject to political effort if actors would be made aware of them. Since many actions have such political consequences, nobody can aim to be or act ethi-

---

[9] Elsewhere I have argued that actually existing ethics are centrally concerned with the social desirability of actions, and that this has ultimately something to do with their effects on self, other human beings, and the natural environment (Glaeser, "Analyzing Actually Existing Ethics"). The didactic classification of types of ethics into virtue ethics, deontology, and utilitarianism can be assimilated to this perspective through the recognition that the consequentialism underlying this sociological perspective is much wider than utilitarianism (the usual stand-in for consequentialism) allows. Virtue ethics is concerned with the habit-forming and thus self-forming (if you wish, the "downward" or "rooting") effects of actions endowing a person with character—a particular type of institution. Deontological ethics is concerned with the ("skyward" or "aspirational") effects on the relation between self and absolute values (divinities, ultimate realities), and finally, utilitarianism is concerned with the ("horizontal") cost and benefits to self and others.

cally without also wanting to consider these political effects. Such consideration then entails the question whether actors can or cannot responsibly stand by the political consequences, given their ethical commitments.[10]

Responsibility matters here in the first instance as accountability for the whole range of effects a person de facto produces.[11] With very large institutions like Amazon, one might think at first that individual contributions to maintaining or altering them are so small (perhaps apart from managers and very large owners who have the power to direct the company) that small effect carriers cannot possibly be held ethically responsible for their contributions. Yet, since most other people's contributions are also very small, and since all of the small contributions taken together make a big difference, the defense of small effect would in many modern contexts be tantamount to erasing the question of responsibility altogether.[12] In other words, institutional complexity would become a generalized excuse—and in fact it has frequently been used in this way. To avoid generalized irresponsibility, then, carriers need to address the consequences of their activities on others (no matter how remote), on the environment, and on the institutional fabric of social life. *The only way out of this general malaise is to band together and build better institutions.* Here responsibility for consequences begins to shade into a second form, namely, generalized responsibility for the institutional fabric of the world in which people live. I will say more below about the institutional preconditions for such a civic responsibility. If the logic of institutions and the fact that human lives are lived in and through them are taken seriously, the very idea of ethics implies a demand to engage in politics. I call this *ethics' political imperative.*

Following the political imperative necessitates the ethical evaluation of institutions. In this wider, politics-including sense, I want to now address the question whether it is possible to articulate general, metaethical principles that

---

[10] The consideration of political effects opens a whole new dimension to the effects considered for ethical evaluation. If these were vertical—up and down (see fn. 4)—as well as horizontal, then the consideration of ethics' political imperative would be concerned with the (recursive) effects of reproducing the conditions of acting in time.

[11] The contemporary literature on responsibility not only moves it into the center of ethics but also differentiates between different types. For an overview, see Ludger Heidbrink, Claus Langbehn, and Janina Loh, eds., *Handbuch Verantwortung* (Wiesbaden: Springer, 2016).

[12] The world climate has, in the Anthropocene, become de facto an institution. Except for climate-change deniers, educated people accept the fact that in spite of their relatively small overall contribution, they could contribute to making a difference. The same holds true for other large institutions resulting from the actions of very many contributors, such as the political, legal, economic, and cultural institutional fabrics of a given country.

can be used to evaluate the ethical goodness of institutions to guide political action.

Transparency

Knowledge about the ways in which institutions transform actions into a plethora of consequences for their own self-maintenance, for the people who carry them, and for others merely affected by them is the condition sine qua non for political action. On the surface, the problem of ignorance is therefore informational. The more fundamental issue is, however, a lack of causal concepts linking actions to effects. Without concepts it is impossible to look systematically for relevant information. Concepts about action-causality are hard to develop where effects are *hidden* either spatially—whether they develop in people's heads, behind closed doors, or in far-removed locations—or temporally, manifesting themselves only in the distant future. Concepts about causality are more difficult to form where effects are imperceptibly *small*, or where causation is *diffused* over many different sources, making causal attribution appear impossible. Finally, actors are less likely to craft concepts of their own efficaciousness in the *absence of incentivizing feedback*, which occurs when effects never accrue as costs and benefits to the actors themselves. Complex institutional assemblages produce ignorance of consequences along all four of these dimensions because they operate across large numbers of people distributed over longer stretches of time and wider spatial expanses while relying mostly on apparently unidirectional, nonreciprocal effect flows.

With the concepts of alienation and commodity fetishism, Marx pioneered two classical concepts to grasp the systematic production of the ignorance of consequences in institutional assemblages. Labor is alienated because the division of labor within and across various sites of production preempts laborers' efforts to assess their place within and contribution to the whole of production.[13] Thus, all cause-and-effect knowledge is extraordinarily stunted—and it is so by design of the institution-forming process itself.

Where markets are spatially, temporally, and personally removed from sites of production and consumption, the conditions of production and consumption become opaque respectively to sellers and buyers, who deal only with the commodities themselves, their quality, and their price instead of addressing the social effects the transaction may have on either production or consumption. Just

---

[13] The concept of alienation characterizes the early work of Marx. See, for example, Karl Marx and Friedrich Engels, *Die Deutsche Ideologie* [1846], in *Marx-Engels-Werke*, vol. 3 (Berlin: Dietz, 1973). Commodity fetishism is developed in the first chapter of *Das Kapital* (1867).

imagine how the act of buying a schnitzel would change if, on the way to the meat counter, the buyer first had to walk through the gloomy, depressing stable in which cute, helpless-looking calves are raised, and then through the pungent odors, the desperate sounds, and the bloody sights of the slaughterhouse, to be guided then through the squalid quarters of the undocumented immigrant workers staffing the operation, with pictures of their home-villages, their children, their partners, and their parents all living in faraway places on the walls. What would change if the slaughterhouse workers themselves had to walk back to their quarters through the dining rooms of their customers, through ordinary apartments and luxury restaurants, on any given day?

Marx's concepts can be generalized to all complex institutional arrangements. One could talk in this context of a *fetishization of institution-forming action*, which simply means that acts are seen *pars pro toto* erasing much of the context in which consequences materialize.[14] Back to the book-buying conundrum presented at the beginning of this chapter: pressing the "buy" button on Amazon's website (it doesn't say "kill the independent bookstore," "make Bezos rich," or "make our democracy weaker"), the buyer can simply persuade herself that she is indeed doing nothing but buying a book. Many linguistic forms at actors' disposal assist in the process of fetishization. Role labels such as "buyer" or "seller" highlight only one kind of effect flow, thus helping to occlude others. Moreover, many languages allow actors to label their activities with the names for their intentions without considering potential "side effects" and irrespective of whether the intentions actually materialize.[15] If the buyer is asked by a friend, "what are you doing," she can simply say, "I am buying a book," abstracting from all the other things she is in fact doing while buying a book.

Knowledge of consequences is central for most understandings of moral accountability. A precondition for moral behavior on the part of individuals is, therefore, that the institutions through which they act are transparent with regard to the consequences they generate on concrete others, the natural environment, and the institutions making up action contexts. One can say, then, that institutional arrangements are the better the less they allow carriers to fetishize their actions, the less they cover up the effects carriers engender on self (in the book-buying example, say, "increased addiction to fast delivery"), on other people ("increased Bezos' net worth by x cents"), the environment ("added a total of x g of CO_2 to the atmosphere"), and the political effects on the institutional fabric ("strengthened Amazon's dominance").

---

[14] Glaeser, *Political Epistemics*, 34.

[15] In the terminology of John Austin's speech-act theory, one could say that in everyday discourses it is acceptable that people identify illocutionary and perlocutionary acts. Of course, his point was precisely that they need to be differentiated. See John Austin, *How to Do Things with Words* (Cambridge, Mass.: Harvard University Press, 1962).

Since institutions beyond a certain scale are rarely transparent on their own, knowledge of effects has to be produced by layering in additional, knowledge-generating institutions into their infrastructural environment. Journalists all over the world have played a significant role in researching the labor conditions of a globalized production regime. The transparency of market transactions has, for example, been increased by a variety of certification processes promising guaranteed "organic" manners of production, "humane" animal husbandry, or "fair trade" goods.[16] Social and natural scientific research can systematically expand human knowledge about the effects of human activities. Fine examples are offered by anthropogenic climate change, the links between nutrition, exercise, and health, and the impact of varieties of parental care on infant development. Much less well understood, and much less well publicized, are effect flows that link consumption patterns to politics in places far afield. This is not to deny that analyzing causal effect chains in complex systems is often difficult and may yield ambiguous or even controversial results. The point is to become better at it and to invest in the institutions that can produce such knowledge.

Institutional fetishism, the institutionally generated absence of knowledge about consequences, can have an immensely stabilizing effect on institutions precisely because carriers do not need to develop qualms about their institution-carrying activity. Amazon benefits materially from buyers' ignorance of how the firm operates, and ignorant Amazon buyers benefit from a certain carefreeness, as convenience does not seem to have a moral cost. One could say that both—in their own ways—enjoy privileges of ignorance. How much of the institutional fabrics within which most people live today owe themselves to privileged ignorance is an open empirical question. But it is probably safe to say that the stabilizing impact of the privilege of ignorance is considerable.[17] Societies are probably built as much on it as they are built on knowledge.

Given the benefits that ignorance conveys, it is no surprise that it is also intentionally produced by rules of secrecy, the mythologizing or branding of institutions, and outright deception. State actors veil, for example what they do with citizens' contributions in money (taxes) and time (military service, campaign assistance), and they deceive the public about the costs and risks citizens are shouldering with their votes for candidates supporting particular policies.[18]

---

[16] For an intriguing study of the history of consumer activism working towards transparency, see Tad Skotnicki, *The Sympathetic Consumer: Moral Critique in Capitalist Culture* (Stanford, Calif.: Stanford University Press, 2021).

[17] The flipside of the privilege of ignorance is that we also often do not know what positive effects we generate. It could be called the handicap of ignorance.

[18] The most blatant examples for systematic government deception in the United States relate to foreign wars in Vietnam (Neil Sheehan et al., *The Pentagon Papers: The Secret History of the Vietnam War* [New York: Racehorse Publishing, 1971]), Iraq (Scott A.

State actors also corrupt knowledge-producing institutions, such as the mass media, by selectively granting or withholding access to information that only they possess. Corporations veil the dangers to which they expose their employees during work. They keep customers in the dark about problematic consequences of their products,[19] and they mislead the general public about the environmental impact of their methods of production while corrupting public opinion with misleading advertising, science by deliberately muddling the picture,[20] and politics through intense lobbying. The opaqueness of institutional dynamics lends itself to myriad forms of abuse.

Pace Socrates, actual knowledge of consequences does not necessarily lead to more-moral actions, especially if culture provides a repertoire of excuses, and the privilege of ignorance is widely enjoyed. But knowledge of consequences surely is the condition for the possibility of recognizing the ethical import of one's behavior. Clearly, it is impossible to make institutions fully transparent. Perhaps it is therefore wiser to refrain from calling institutions good or bad and instead to acknowledge that goodness is a moving target. One could say then that institutions become better the more transparent they are, the more effectively they are tied to infrastructural institutions producing ethically relevant knowledge about them. Institutions also become better by incentivizing increased feedback that inclines them to adjust their activities to the consequences they produce. Where helpful and technologically, organizationally, and economically possible, institutional arrangements providing such feedback can be created. Would carbon-dioxide meters on the dashboards of cars and on heating and hot-water regulators change how people drive or use hot water?

Bonn, *Mass Deception: Moral Panic and the US War on Iraq* [New Brunswick: Rutgers University Press, 2010]), and Afghanistan (Craig Whitlock and the Washington Post, *The Afghanistan Papers: A Secret History of the War* [New York: Simon & Schuster, 2021]), because they involved high bloodshed among citizens and others along with extraordinary material costs at the expense of domestic programs.

[19] The literature is vast. One particularly important example is provided by Robert Bilott, who revealed how DuPont deceived employees, customers, and government regulators about the effects of PFAS (for example, Teflon), one class of "forever chemicals." See Robert Bilott, *Exposure: Poisoned Water, Corporate Greed, and One Lawyer's Twenty-Year Battle against DuPont* (New York: Atria Books, 2019).

[20] See Naomi Oreskes and Erik Conway, *Merchants of Doubt: How a Handful of Scientists Obscured the Truth on Issues from Tobacco Smoke to Climate Change* (New York: Bloomsbury Press, 2010); and Cristin Kearns, Laura Schmidt, and Stanton Glantz, "Sugar Industry and Coronary Heart Disease Research: A Historical Analysis of Internal Industry Documents," *Jama Internal Medicine* 176, no. 11 (2016): 1680–85.

Alterability

Whatever the protagonist in the opening book-buying example would want to do, she should, on account of the consequences of her actions, like to do something that makes the ethical conundrum less acute in the longer run. That, however, can happen only to the degree that she can change the institutional fabric that has created that conundrum in the first place. Politics is the artful practice of changing institutions intentionally. To become more ethical, then, she has to engage in politics with the intention to change institutions for the better.

The problem with politics is that its demands for various kinds of knowledge as well as for temporal and material resources increase with the complexity of the institutions targeted. How could the protagonist change Amazon, the book market, herself? It is therefore necessary to think hard about the point in the institutional fabric where a concerned person following up on the ethical imperative can most effectively intervene to generate desirable results. This requires the availability of a whole slew of institutions that make politics thinkable and doable. To make it thinkable, actors need imaginaries that suggest alternative, indeed better, states of institutions. To assess the realizability of these imaginaries, they need sociological knowledge to map out workable and effective action plans. This knowledge includes an acute analysis of possible obstacles and solutions to circumvent them. And actors need mobilizational knowledge to plan ways to engage the carriers of targeted institutions to change their ways. Finally, these actors will need organizational knowledge to orchestrate all of these activities. In an ethical sense, then, institutional fabrics are preferable that make useful political knowledge and possibilities for political action available for citizens to act on the ethical imperative.

Arguably the easiest kind of intervention available to actors is changing their own habits, beliefs, and feelings, because altering them usually requires the least cooperation from others. Perhaps one could call this a *person-centric response* to ethical problems. In the book-buying conundrum, the obvious candidate for change is the protagonist's perceived need to read without delay. The knowledge about how to do this could come from friends who have already adapted their habits to slow book supplies, and who could provide an encouraging environment for making her efforts successful.[21] Even a person-centric re-

---

[21] Ancient Stoicism (for example, Epictetus, 135 CE) focuses attention on aspects of life that an actor can actually change. The examples usually advanced in Stoicism match what I have just called a person centric approach to ethical problems. For Hannah Arendt, this is a typical response to a historical situation where the possibilities for engaging in politics are blocked for most ordinary citizens—as was the case in the Hellenic and later Roman empires. What is and is not changeable depends on the institutional

sponse, however, may meet many institutional obstacles. In the example, deadlines and productivity expectations can impede the writer's readiness to habituate slow reading.

Social Movements

Person-centric approaches go only so far. While changing their own habits may make actors feel better about themselves for no longer contributing to the reproduction of social arrangements that produce ethical conundrums as a matter of course, the actual problems themselves remain unresolved, as virtually everyone else may continue to replicate them. It may be desirable, therefore, to find a way of influencing the fabric of institutions. Since institutions exist in the interconnected effect flows of many people who together could make more of a difference, the central problem is how to mobilize enough carriers of the institution to participate in effecting changes that, taken together, amount to institutional change.

Unsurprisingly, the solution to the problem of mass mobilization lies in the formation of a particular kind of institution—namely, a social movement organization—that can be charged with this task.[22] The direct power that movements can exert on institutions targeted for reform depends on the movements' ability to destabilize the target's processes of reproduction. A movement's power increases with the damage it can inflict on institutional maintenance. Historically, two approaches have emerged as particularly powerful. In strikes (or boycotts) carriers of the institution simply refrain from engaging in the very acts that have so far maintained the target.[23] The protagonist in the book-buying example

---

environment available to actors. See Hannah Arendt, "What Is Politics," in *The Promise of Politics* (New York: Schocken, 2005).

[22] Founding an organization rather than an institution has many advantages. It allows for degrees of participation thanks to a semiprofessional staff, and it guarantees greater longevity. See Max Weber, "Politik als Beruf" [1919], in *Gesammelte politische Schriften* (Tübingen: J. C. B. Mohr [Paul Siebeck], 1984), 505–60; Gerald F. Davis et al., eds., *Social Movements and Organization Theory* (Cambridge: Cambridge University Press, 2005); and Zeynap Tufekci, *Twitter and Tear Gas* (New Haven: Yale University Press, 2017). Of course, founding an organization also creates a hierarchy of political power in shaping the course of the movement, which has consequences for the degree to which participants may want to organize. See (Michels, *Soziologie des Parteiwesens*; Todd Gitlin, *Occupy Nation: The Roots, the Spirit, and the Promise of Occupy Wall Street* (New York: itbooks, 2012); and Tufekci, *Twitter and Tear Gas*).

[23] For the United States, see, for example, Erik Loomis, *A History of America in Ten Strikes* (New York: The New Press, 2020); Jane McAlevey, *A Collective Bargain: Unions, Organ-*

could, in this vein, organize an Amazon Consumer Union, which would, through selective or general strikes, cajole Amazon to change in morally desirable directions. By forming cooperatives, movements can do even more than temporally withdraw their reproductive support: they can create permanent and morally much more acceptable alternatives to compete with the target institution.[24]

Of course, such an intervention could quickly run afoul of other institutional arrangements. The feasibility of strikes and boycotts, the willingness of movement members to participate, hinges to a large degree on the availability of alternative sources of whatever strikers or boycotters derive from carrying the institution.[25] Once an institution has attained a near monopolistic position—that is, once it has become subjectively indispensable to people—it becomes nearly impossible to fight. People who have structured their lives around Amazon Prime (and more and more do) would have a hard time boycotting it. The feasibility of creating alternatives such as co-ops hinges on factors like start-up costs and barriers to market entry. Suppliers of widely used infrastructural goods and services, such as Amazon, are especially hard to tackle.

In spite of the many impressive successes of social movements, using them as an approach to meet ethics' political imperative faces serious practical limitations. The resources needed to start a movement or to be seriously involved in one are considerable, and the project could easily eat so much time, that it could become a full-time job. With the growing complexity of institutional fabrics, the gap between people's available resources and the movement work that would be necessary to address ethics' political imperative increases. How many movements could people reasonably be expected to join? How many could they reasonably be expected to support financially or even ideally, by at least paying attention to their demands?

The movement approach also faces difficult legitimacy issues. This becomes clear when looking at movements with antagonistic institutional transformation agendas that are in each case meant to rectify moral wrongs. The abortion-rights

---

izing, and the Fight for Democracy (New York: Ecco, 2020); and Philip Dray, *There Is Power in a Union: The Epic Story of Labor in America* (New York: Anchor Press, 2011).

[24] To find out what is strategically more powerful or more realistic, given other institutional constraints, one could play with other ideas. The protagonist could, in extension of the strategy discussed, start a new cooperative bookstore network. Alternatively, she could start something like a "slow scholarship" movement modeled on the one for "slow food." The intention would be to spread her newly acquired habits to many more people, thus creating a favorable institutional environment in which opening and running small bookstores becomes more viable again. In the course of time, this might slowly take some power away from Amazon.

[25] For that reason, labor unions have maintained funds to financially support workers on strike.

and antiabortion movements in the United States are good examples. Social movements have agenda-specific, self-selected memberships. And since their activists represent in almost every case only a very small fraction of all the people either carrying the institution targeted for change or affected by it, the question arises why the activists' demands should hold sway.

The State

The limitations of movements as citizens' agent for reforming institutions toward greater moral acceptability can be overcome, under certain circumstances, by the state. It is noteworthy that while movements have had some success with exercising their direct power as outlined above, the brunt of their success has derived from their indirect power wielded by influencing the state to pass and enforce regulatory laws. [26]

By historical origin and intended function, the state is a *general organization* that facilitates and *authoritatively* regulates the formation of a wide range of institutions within its domain. This includes, on one hand, the direct or indirect provision of infrastructural institutions as public goods for a political community. Examples are the articulation of laws, the adjudication of justice on the basis of these laws, and their enforcement; defense, weights and measures, roads, canals, harbors, and much more. On the other hand, this meta-institutional function includes the provision of templates (usually cast in the form of laws) for forming lower-level institutions, such as individual marriages, inheritances, property relationships, business associations, contracts, and more. [27] The state

---

[26] The labor movement of the nineteenth century vastly increased its success by founding socialist and social democratic parties. And at least in some countries, the environmental movement enhanced its influence by founding green parties, which put competitive pressures on other parties.

[27] The state's meta-institutional function is already apparent in the earliest law codes, dating back to the later third millennium BCE in Mesopotamia: Martha Roth, *Law Collections from Mesopotamia and Asia Minor*, 2nd ed. (Atlanta, Ga.: Society of Biblical Literature, 1997). Roman law, which provided an important foundation for processes of European state formation, is similarly predisposed: Peter Birks and Grant McLeod, *Justinian's Institutes* (Ithaca, N.Y.: Cornell University Press, 1987; and Joseph R. Strayer, *On the Medieval Origins of the Modern State* [1970] (Princeton: Princeton University Press, 1998). I offer this definition of the state based on the theory of institutions presented above as an alternative to the violence centric Hobbesian tradition that has deeply influenced modern theories of state in the social sciences (for example, Weber, "Politik als Beruf" and *Wirtschaft und Gesellschaft*; and Charles Tilly, *Coercion, Capital, and European States, AD 990-1992* (Malden, Mass.: Blackwell, 1990). In its attention to authori-

as the citizens' agent for bettering institutions thus fits right in with the state's well-established and wide portfolio of authoritative meta-institutional functions.[28]

There are several reasons, however, why the state may appear unsuitable to the task. First, as instruments of coercion and ultimately even oppression, the component institutions of the state are often experienced as precisely the ones that need changing. The state has been at least as much of an ethical problem as it has been a part of resolving them. From this perspective, charging the state with moral agency appears akin to putting the fox in charge of the henhouse. Second, modern liberal understandings of the rules that are to govern social life draw a marked distinction between law and morality, where the former is thought to fall into the purview of the state and the latter into the domain of civil society. Breaking a contract may be brought before a judge; breaking a promise is not justiciable. From within this distinction, the state as a purveyor of morally induced institutional change appears at best as unduly paternalistic and at worst as unacceptably authoritarian.[29] Yet if this work were not done by the state, it would have to be done by a set of institutions endowed with the same authority and the same capabilities that the state enjoys as a general meta-institutional agent. That is why revolutions have happened only by taking control of the state first or by creating an alternative state. Apparently, states can be changed only from within their own form.[30]

Moreover, the state can be the citizens' agent of justice only to the degree that all citizens have an equal opportunity to shape the state's institutional change agenda. That is to say that only effective democracies can serve this role. The more authoritarian states are, the more systematically they undermine citi-

---

tative meta functionalities, it is closer to Pierre Bourdieu, yet built on an entirely different logic. See Pierre Bourdieu, *On the State: Lectures at the Collège de France 1989–1992* (Cambridge: Polity Press, 2012).

[28] This does not mean, of course, that the state should or even must exercise this authority in all domains of institution formation. In fact, the modern liberal state has developed in such a way that it can legitimately use its authority only by explicitly ruling out efforts to regulate the formation of certain institutions protected by so-called personal freedom rights.

[29] The history of the modern liberal state is often written as a slow, hard-won extraction of the merely moral from the rightly legal. Notably criminal statutes of religious, sexual, and lifestyle behavior were slowly expunged from the law.

[30] Libertarians might bring markets into play as an alternative form of intermediation between different preferences for ethically inspired social change. Yet even a decentralized market-based solution, which would impose taxes on all moral bads produced by institutions (say on the model of a carbon tax), is nothing but a tool that would have to be constantly adjusted by the state.

zens' ability to act on ethics' political imperative, the more they deprive their inhabitants of full moral citizenship.

It is relatively easy to see what the state could do to reduce the recurrence of the moral conundrum in the Amazon example. It could regulate sourcing and labor practices, wealth accumulation, and the influence of wealth on democratic processes. Yet little of that sort has happened. The question is why? The answer is not that citizens do not want workers to make decent wages and receive adequate benefits; it is not because citizens are not worried about the influence of wealth on politics. Instead, it is because super-wealthy individuals and the representatives of very large corporations have succeeded, in a decades-long campaign, in capturing the United States as an instrument of their own agenda of transformation, thus relegating ordinary citizens, the supposed sovereign, to a minor role.[31]

This example points directly to one of the problems of states as sets of authoritative, generalized, meta-institutional organizations. Precisely because they form the apex of meta-institutional arrangements, they are as such functionally centralized. This makes them relatively easy targets for capture by organized special interests. Indeed, the history of states could be written as a history of capturing, recapturing, and decapturing of states. This would also turn out to be a history of inventing institutions designed to prevent capture and to open the state to citizen programming. Written law, independent courts, successively more inclusive participation, sovereign citizen assemblies, ostracism, elected representative assemblies, constitutions, judicial review, the division of powers, plebiscites—all would be major markers on the way.

No extant approach to changing institutions in a morally desirable direction is perfect. The point is to offer citizens a wide variety of institutional frameworks to follow up on ethics' political imperative. In sum, then, institutions are better the more they are malleable in a desired direction by those who carry them and by those who are affected by them. To accomplish this task, carriers and the affected need political institutions (including political knowledge—imaginaries, sociologies, and rhetorics). These are better the more precisely they allow carriers to alleviate problems without creating new ones. Of course, given the density of

---

[31] See Jacob Hacker and Paul Pierson, *Winner-Take-All Politics: How Washington Made the Rich Richer and Turned Its Back on the Middle Class* (New York: Simon & Schuster, 2010); Alexander Hertel-Fernandez, *State Capture: How Conservative Activists, Big Businesses, and Wealthy Donors Reshaped the American States—And the Nation* (Oxford: Oxford University Press, 2019); Theda Skocpol and Caroline Tervo, eds., *Upending American Politics: Polarizing Parties, Ideological Elites, and Citizen Activists from the Tea Party to the Anti-Trump Resistance* (Oxford: Oxford University Press, 2020); and Kurt Andersen, *Evil Geniuses: The Unmaking of America—A Recent History* (New York: Random House, 2021).

institutions and the generality of political institutions, this is hard to do, and the results will be imperfect, not least because the assessment of consequences is always imperfect too.

Public Goal and Value Conformity

Besides transparency and alterability ethical actors—whether individual persons, movement organizations, or states—need substantive criteria to evaluate institutional fabrics to get ideas for the direction of political change. Since it is impossible to develop a specific vision for all the institutions that actors carry separately and because institutions are interdependent with each, they need *general* criteria that reach their apex in a comprehensive vision of a good life in a good society. Note that it follows directly from the theory of institutions presented here, that the good life and good society are inextricably intertwined. Neither can be considered without the other. Yet the theory of institutions has in itself nothing to say about what a good life is, though it does have something to say about how such an imaginary ought to come about if it were to fulfill certain criteria.

In principle, politics-guiding imaginaries of the good life in the good society have to be developed with well-instituted pathways for all citizens to participate. Here is why. Forming institutions is inevitably a collective effort involving many people as carriers, and potentially many more who are affected by them. Any political effort to change institutions in an ethically more preferable direction can therefore succeed only if a sufficient number of carriers are actually changing their activities in the desired direction.

There are two intertwined issues here. The first is pragmatic. Political changes are much more easily carried out on the basis of mutual agreement, which provides buy-in, motivation, and legitimacy for enacting the change. The second issue goes back to one of the premises of this whole investigation, the institutional enablement of people to act ethically or be ethical. Ignoring any of the carriers deprives them of their ability to act or be ethical in the full sense.

Clearly, neither the state with representative assemblies at its center nor the so-called public sphere in typical liberal democracies is suitable as constituted at present to serve as citizens' moral agent. The liberal state with a parliament at its center has self-consciously abstained from developing visions of the good life in the good society, instead dissipating the question to individual choice. This move was a consequence of the religious pluralities emerging with the Protestant Reformations in Europe. The idea behind the division of church and state is precisely driven by the fear that no agreement can be achieved on ultimate values and pathways to attain them, other than a catalogue of individual freedom rights that allow people to pursue their own vision of the good life, with the consequence that the good society is precisely one that makes the pursuit of divergent visions possible. To all, their own! Since then, pluralism has increased in societies rather than decreased. So there has to be a way to accommodate it.

The problem with this liberal approach is its disregard for the fundamental institution-mediated sociality of human beings who live in and through shared institutions. If they do not work out together which vision of the good life these institutions should conform to, then such a vision will inevitably be imposed by the powerful on the less powerful. In the absence of the state, institutions like markets will determine whose visions prevail. And quickly the freedom to pursue one's own vision of the good life in the good society becomes the privilege of the few rather than the many. Given that most people still spend most of their adult life at work, nothing makes this clearer than the transformation of work (the professions included) in the United States over the past decades, with its shrinking benefits, increasing precarity, lengthening hours, and increasing intensity.[32] Clearly, technology is only one driver in this development, while the other is the politically created, institutionally secured power of the few to impose their vision on the many. Part of this program was indeed a coordinated plan to drive the state out of regulating work, environmental protection, etc., in the interest of "liberalizing" society—the very capture I have talked about in the last section.

The alternative location for working out visions of the good life in a good society is the public sphere.[33] However, the public sphere in most transatlantic democracies has been structured by private, profit-seeking corporations that own the media of mass-communication, first the press, then radio, then television, and now the internet.[34] Even during the heyday of state-run radio and television in Western Europe and Canada, the need for advertising revenue and the market-share logics it entails drove the selection of programming toward favor-

---

[32] See, for example, Louis Hyman, *Temp: How American Work, American Business, and the American Dream Became Temporary* (New York: Viking, 2018).

[33] John Stuart Mill, *On Liberty* [1859] (London: Everyman's Library, 1992); Jürgen Habermas, *Strukturwandel der Öffentlichkeit: Untersuchungen zu einer Kategorie der bürgerlichen Gesellschaft* [1962] (Frankfurt: Suhrkamp, 1990); John Keane, *Civil Society: Old Images, New Visions* (Stanford, Calif.: Stanford University Press, 1998); and Michael Warner, *Publics and Counterpublics* (New York: Zone, 2002).

[34] Habermas, in *Strukturwandel der Öffentlichkeit*, began to outline some of the problems of a public sphere structured by modern mass media corporation. The most famous critique along these lines is perhaps that of Edward S. Herman and Noam Chomsky, *Manufacturing Consent: The Political Economy of the Mass Media* (New York: Pantheon Books, 2002).

ing entertainment in every genre—including news and political debate.[35] The internet has introduced an even more heightened market logic into communication, not just because of capital ownership but because of intrinsic features of the medium, such as "like" buttons and search and suggested link algorithms. The temporal structure of the various media in their historical succession has moreover favored decreasing attention spans. The combined characteristic of markets and media technology have had a profound effect on who gets to participate in discourses of all kinds, what they are about, and how they are presented stylistically.

It is not the case that the question of the good life has had no place in this public sphere. On the one hand, psychologically and stylistically highly engineered paid advertising, and secondary discourses about the quality of products (reviews, reporting on corporations and their newest products) as free advertising, have created a consistent and all-pervasive image of ever more consumption as the pathway to a good life and the growth-driven economy as the blueprint for the good society. Consumerism has been systematically produced not just by consuming individuals, but by corporations whose lifeblood depends on it. On the other hand, there is the enormous success of the self-help and advice genres across all media, which is often connected to the propagation of ascetic practices with regard to spirituality, health, and the environment. All of these visions are rather partial in the sense that they are cognizant of only parts of what makes a life. They are driven by experts and acolytes with entertainment value. And except for discourses on the environment, none of these visions of the good life are systematically connected with the question of the good society.

What is needed, then, is a forum—or better, even, an interrelated set of fora to better accommodate the varying scales and scopes of institutions—in which the question of the good life in the good society can be deliberated equally by all citizens who choose to participate in conjointly developing an authoritative vision against which institutional arrangements can be evaluated. Cues for how to institute such fora can be derived from the many encouraging experiments with the deliberative participation of ordinary citizens in assisting with or even making governmental decisions.[36] Where deliberations are freed from the logics

---

[35] Neil Postman's critique follows Marshall McLuhan's emphasis on the structure of the medium rather than media ownership. The comparative effects of structure and ownership are hard to disentangle. Yet it is not hard to see how they can amplify each other. See Neil Postman, *Amusing Ourselves to Death: Public Discourse in the Age of Show Business* (New York: Viking, 1985); and Marshall McLuhan, *Understanding Media: The Extensions of Man* (New York: McGraw-Hill, 1964).

[36] See Fung Archon and Erik Olin Wright, eds., *Deepening Democracy: Institutional Innovations in Empowered Participatory Governance* (London: Verso, 2003); James Fishkin, *When the People Speak: Deliberative Democracy and Public Consultation* (Oxford: Oxford

of profit-seeking media and polarizing mobilizational politics, while focusing on more concrete matters such as meeting basic needs in food, shelter and health, the characteristics of meaningful of work, fair pay and the quality of personal relationships, broader zones of agreement may come into view which may not satisfy the aesthetic predilections of a philosophical mind, but which may nevertheless provide guidance about the directions in which the institutional fabrics of societies can be improved to allow for more responsible lives.

In sum, then, political institutions used by citizens are the better the more their efforts to change institutions in an ethically desirable direction are informed by citizens' conjointly developed imaginaries of a good life in a good society.

Conclusions: A New Civic Ethos

Seeing humans as living in and through institutions shifts the focus of classical ethics away from individuals to larger social wholes. Kant's question, "what ought *I* to do?" thus becomes, "what assemblage of institutions ought *we* to form such that all citizens have more of an opportunity to act ethically in view of the myriad consequences of their actions on self, others and the environment?" This does not mean that individual actions are no longer ethically evaluated by looking at the effects they directly cause alone or in unity with a few others. Instead, it means that they are to be evaluated more comprehensively in the context of the effects they have through institutional mediation and on institutional reproduction, even where their contribution to the effects is small. The reason why it is necessary to proceed this way is obvious enough. A wide array of ethically significant effects, such as climate change and labor conditions in workplaces at home and on the other side of the globe, are generated by a very large number of people conjointly. If ethics is to mean anything in the complex world in which we live, then those kinds of effects need due consideration, because they account for most of the effects humans produce.

The modern world is morally unhinged, and not because its denizens, tempted by Nietzsche or by fading faith, have become nihilists, but because the privilege of ignorance has made possible the creation of an institutional world in which people not only do not know, but they are kept from knowing what they are doing. At the same time, they can act while feeling morally advanced over their self-righteously, yet still knowingly oppressive (racist, imperialist, classist,

---

University Press, 2009); Jürg Steiner, *The Foundations of Deliberative Democracy: Empirical Research and Normative Implications* (Cambridge: Cambridge University Press, 2012); and Michael A. Neblo, *Deliberative Democracy between Theory and Practice* (Cambridge: Cambridge University Press, 2015).

patriarchal, etc.) forebears. The ethical and political challenges posed by the widening scale, scope, and density of institutions has remained unmet by an ethics that can meaningfully address them.

Ethics viewed through the eyes of an institutionalist shows why this is the case while also pointing to a way out. It entails a call to continuous political action. I have called this ethics' political imperative. To make good of it, societies need to be equipped with better political institutions than those provided by contemporary liberal states and public spheres both of which have come to be captured by special interests. These institutions need to make it possible for citizens to wield meaningful influence on the institutional world which they generate and to whose effects they are exposed. Part of such an institutional fabric of meaningful influence must be a *new civic ethos* that aims to form and, where established, jealously guard these improved democratic political institutions against renewed state capture. These new institutions need to include integrated sets of fora in which citizens conjointly develop visions of the good life in the good society, which can effectively guide the political reform of institutions in an ethically desirable direction. This is a continuous, open-ended process, because institutions change how they operate and what effects they produce in changing institutional environments. And these institutional environments change not least because the consequences of particular institutional arrangements are never fully fathomable and manageable, no matter how hard citizens may try, thus constantly exceeding citizens' understandings. Even if, therefore, institutions will never be simply good, they can always be improved.

Philanthropic Formation at the Intersection of Mercantile and Religious Networks: The Thornton Family in Their Eighteenth-Century Contexts

Roshan Allpress

In 1784 Henry Thornton (1760–1815), youngest son of a wealthy London merchant family, left the well-established countinghouse of his father, John Thornton (1720–1790), and entered into a banking partnership that was soon trading under the name Down, Thornton and Free.[1] Henry's mother felt that the social step from merchant to banker was "to descend in life," but his father was more concerned at the different commercial habits and the "improper company" that would now occupy his son's time, and which he thought would inevitably shape his character.[2] The younger Thornton's subsequent life and career belied these concerns. He emerged as a leading banker of repute, a philanthropist and founding member of the evangelical Clapham Sect, and the political economist who Hayek claimed inaugurated "a new epoch in the development of monetary theory."[3] Reflecting in later life, Thornton ascribed much to his formative experiences in the particular mercantile, family, and religious networks in which he grew up, noting that these had formed in him habits and moral perspectives that set him apart from his peers—many of whom did fail commercially and morally. Writing of his own children, he described raising them with distinctive habits and practices, and hoped that they would come to understand and articulate "the *grounds* of every difference in their practice," and "be instructed to defend their own system."[4]

Henry Thornton and the networks in which he was formed offer a case study in how formation happens in history through participation in commerce and re-

---

[1] Standish Meacham, *Henry Thornton of Clapham, 1760–1815* (Cambridge, Mass.: Harvard University Press, 1964).

[2] Henry Thornton, "Recollections," MS Add. 7674, 1/N, 16, Thornton Papers, Cambridge University Library (hereafter, Recollections, Thornton Papers).

[3] F. A. Hayek, introduction to Henry Thornton, *An Enquiry into the Nature and Effects of the Paper Credit of Great Britain (1802)* (London: Allen & Unwin, 1939), 34.

[4] Recollections, Thornton Papers, 10.

ligious associational contexts. It is a historiographical commonplace to note that participation in globalizing networks of credit and trade during the eighteenth and early nineteenth centuries by groups like merchants in the City of London expanded moral geographies, leading to philanthropic and humanitarian activism, such as that on behalf of enslaved Africans or colonized indigenous peoples.[5] Only a minority of those in these networks became philanthropists or reformers, and it is the particularities of their circumstances that shed light on how their distinctive formation occurred. Of the nearly fourteen hundred mercantile houses operating in the City of London in the early 1760s, fewer than 3 percent were members of the Russia Company, which oversaw much of Britain's trade with northern Europe.[6] Yet more than half of the active committee members of London's philanthropic societies during the 1760s came from that small subset of merchant firms, and Russia Company members were the most prolific set of donors to new philanthropic societies in that decade.

A generation later, during the upswell of reform societies in Britain in the aftermath of the American Revolution, a similarly disproportionate number of the leaders of new philanthropic organizations, such as the Abolition Society, had—like Henry Thornton—spent their childhoods and early careers in families and networks that were closely associated with the Russia Company. Unlike their counterparts, these young men participated in a dense culture of sociability, commercial *habitus*, and intellectual life—increasingly interlaced with the religious innovations of evangelicalism. The distinctive formation that they received shaped their philanthropy—and their characters.

The intent of this chapter is to explore how formation actually occurred in these specific historical contexts—with attention to institutional, associational, intellectual, and cultural particularities[7] and a view to identifying potentials for the formation of character and vocation in the late modern context.

The Russia Company oversaw British trade throughout the Baltic and North Seas—the third-largest British trading sphere after the trans-Atlantic and East India trades, accounting for roughly eight hundred thousand pounds' worth of imports a year during the 1760s, and comparable in scale to East India Company

---

[5] Alan J. Kidd, "Philanthropy and the 'Social History Paradigm,'" *Social history* 21, no. 2 (1996): 180-92; and Hugh Cunningham, *The Reputation of Philanthropy Since 1750: Britain and Beyond* (Manchester: Manchester University Press, 2020).

[6] Thomas Mortimer, *The Universal Director* (London: Mortimer, 1763), 7-78.

[7] See a parallel argument around specificity and causality by Christopher Bayly, "The British and Indigenous Peoples, 1760-1860: Power, Perception and Identity," in *Empire and Others: British Encounters with Indigenous Peoples, 1600-1850*, ed. Martin Daunton and Rick Halpern (Philadelphia: University of Pennsylvania Press, 1999), 22.

(EIC) imports.[8] British traders to this region in the mid-eighteenth century enjoyed unusually profitable credit arrangements, thanks to weaknesses in Russia's domestic credit market and capital outflows from Amsterdam and German cities amid ongoing war and market uncertainties. Further enhancing the profitability of the trade during this period, Russia Company imports of pig iron and lumber were of vital strategic significance to the Royal Navy, especially during the Seven Years' War and the American Revolution, and Russia Company merchants became major creditors to naval procurement projects and intermediaries for investment from the Continent in issues of Navy bills.

Of the major British chartered companies of the mid-eighteenth century, the Russia Company was unusual in that it was a regulated company, not a joint stock company like the EIC.[9] In effect, this meant that rather than being managed by employees, it operated as a trading collective of merchant houses, with its institutional apparatus run by committees of volunteers. Its governing body was not a court of directors, as in the EIC, comprising established merchants looking to wield patronage, but a court of assistants made up of younger men—the average age of first election during the 1770s was thirty-five years—seeking to build reputation, so as to expand the capital they could borrow on credit for their own trading houses.

The context of the Russia Company provided unique circumstances for the establishment of careers, and for formation in commercial *habitus*. A typical career path for an ambitious young man in other major British chartered companies, such as the EIC, involved seeking a patron, who could procur a clerkship or other posting. Once established, advancement and wealth could come through promotion or by private trade on the side, with success leading to a directorship and shareholding returns in London. By contrast, in the Russia Company, an ambitious young merchant would usually take an apprenticeship in a merchant firm, buy membership of the company for the affordable sum of five pounds, and seek to cultivate a reputation for trustworthiness by serving on voluntary committees, such as those coordinating shipping routes or negotiating trade access to Baltic ports. By this kind of voluntary service, younger merchants could work toward becoming trusted to borrow capital from other merchants, by which they might begin to trade on their own account. In this context, Russia Company mer-

---

[8] Elizabeth B. Schumpeter, *English Overseas Trade Statistics, 1676–1808* (Oxford: Oxford University Press, 1960), 18; Arcadius Kahan, *The Plow, the Hammer, and the Knout: An Economic History of Eighteenth-Century Russia* (Chicago: University of Chicago Press, 1985), 207–09; and Herbert H. Kaplan, *Russian Overseas Commerce with Great Britain during the Reign of Catherine II* (Philadelphia: American Philosophical Society, 1995), 57–58.

[9] See Michael Wagner, "Misunderstood and Unappreciated: The Russia Company in the Eighteenth Century," *Russian History* 41 (2014): 393–422.

chants became skilled at collective decision-making—which extended to distinctive practices around taking committee minutes and coordinating volunteer actions. Because access to credit from other merchants was the primary path to commercial success, building networks of interpersonal trust was essential. A strong culture of associational honor predominated, with frequent company dinners held to acknowledge those who had served the merchant community. Comparisons of the diaries of contemporaries show that these merchants were typically spending as much as twice the time per week as their peers in formal and informal socializing—lunches, clubs, and society memberships. Adding to this dense social dynamic were patterns of kinship, with merchant families intermarrying in ways that kept capital within partnerships in the same trade and built dense intergenerational connectivity.

Overlaying this milieu was the expansion of evangelical networks. The nascent religious movement that had emerged in the 1730s spread rapidly through London's mercantile communities from the 1750s, with the Russia Company experiencing some of the highest proportions of conversion. Evangelicalism prioritized particular modes of devotion, such as spiritual journaling, personal and family Bible study, study and prayer groups meeting in private homes, and attendance at multiple sermons and lectures each week.[10] In urban contexts, where social anonymity and religious pluralism were increasingly normative, these practices proved well-suited to shaping individual and community identity, from initial conversion to ongoing religiously motivated activism. In London, evangelicals flocked to increasingly fashionable congregations, with pulpits occupied by popular preachers and lecturers. Evangelicals tended to eschew aspects of popular culture, such as theater—on the grounds of their potential for negative moral formation—but the movement is impossible to code in reactionary terms and was prolific in its cultural creativity. A growing number of printing houses and book societies published and distributed tracts, pamphlets, journals, and magazines that were assiduously read by families. Faced with antipathy by the gatekeepers and structures of the established church to their perceived destabilizing religious "enthusiasm," evangelicals also increasingly pursued their aims through the creation of new charitable organizations—maternity hospitals, Sunday School societies, debt relief associations, and many more. The choice to convert to evangelicalism therefore entailed participation in a dense subculture, in which individuals were encouraged to cultivate an identity through formative religious practices and participation in associational culture, and to live out their faith through various forms of charitable and philanthropic activism.

---

[10] See D. Bruce Hindmarsh, *The Spirit of Early Evangelicalism: True Religion in a Modern World* (Oxford: Oxford University Press, 2018).

The confluence of these two intensely formative cultures created a wave of institutional and cultural innovation beginning in the 1750s, especially in the emerging field of philanthropy. New organizational models combined the entrepreneurial practices and accountability patterns endemic in mercantile networks, with the missional focus and institution-building tendencies of religious charities. Unlike the majority of religious charities in London during the mid-eighteenth century, whose governors tended only to attend annual meetings, the directors of these new philanthropic associations were active on voluntary committees. Immersed in collective deliberation and action for philanthropic purposes, they revealed in their diaries, correspondence, and minutes intense intellectual collaboration and experimentation in organizational practices. Participation or connection to these networks fostered a reinforcing formative culture for the voluntary directors and those close to them.[11]

Henry Thornton's life exemplified the formative dynamics of this context. His father, John Thornton, was a prominent member of the Russia Company who had been converted to evangelicalism around 1754, shortly after marrying Lucy Watson, the daughter of another prominent merchant family. Born in 1760, Henry Thornton therefore grew up immersed in Russia Company networks. He initially entered the countinghouse of his cousin Godfrey Thornton in 1778, before joining his father's firm in 1780. Henry's education and the guidance of his parents led him and his two older brothers through the patterns of preparation for merchant life.

As an evangelical household, the family made rhythms of prayer, study of the Bible, and reading of a wide range of moral and religious literature integral to daily life, alongside multiple church services a week. Henry's parents' involvement in evangelical and philanthropic circles was also deeply shaping. The Thornton household frequently hosted visitors engaged in philanthropy, and the children therefore became acquainted with and sometimes engaged in longer-term correspondence with figures such as the North American indigenous missionary Samson Occom, the enslaved poet Phillis Wheatley, and numerous evangelical ministers and entrepreneurs.[12] The younger Thorntons were encouraged to donate to societies and to attend society meetings and read their annual reports and other literature. For example, John Thornton first donated to the Society for Promoting Religious Knowledge among the Poor in 1761; twelve years later, his eldest son joined, and two years after that, Lucy Thornton and their three other children joined and began attending seminars and meetings of the

---

[11] See Roshan Allpress, "Making Philanthropists: Entrepreneurs, Evangelicals and the Growth of Philanthropy in the British World, 1756-1840" (Unpublished DPhil thesis, University of Oxford, 2015), 41-141.

[12] Milton M. Klein, *An Amazing Grace: John Thornton and the Clapham Sect* (New Orleans: University Press of the South, 2004).

Society.¹³ As an adult, Henry Thornton reflected on the effect that this upbringing had had—in developing lifelong habits of moral self-cultivation and fostering empathy for those in need.¹⁴

Three vignettes illustrate the reciprocal relationship between this context of mercantile, religious, and philanthropic innovation and the personal formation of those involved. During the 1760s, John Thornton became connected with Eleazar Wheelock, who was seeking support for an Indian charity school intended for training indigenous missionaries in North America. Following the disappointment of earlier fundraising attempts by Wheelock and his colleagues, Thornton established an English trust, gathering nine trustees from his commercial and evangelical networks, including the Earl of Dartmouth. Thornton took the unprecedented step of opening accounts for the trust with twelve banks—collaborating with sympathetic partners in those banks to create a remittance network that raised several thousand pounds.

Though the project itself became fraught when Wheelock unilaterally redirected the school's focus from indigenous missionaries to settler education (becoming Dartmouth College), one of its lasting effects was in the relationships that formed among the banking partners who had been involved. The trust that had been built among these bankers bore fruit in a number of collaborations in the subsequent two decades—not least the clearinghouse that was established at Martins Bank in 1773, which marked a turning point for London's financial markets and for the numerous new banking partnerships established during the 1770s and 1780s that led the expansion in paper credit.¹⁵ These bankers recognized in each other a depth of personal character that led to high trust and collaboration among their firms in an age of financial instability. While the historical evidence at the personal level is incomplete, the picture seems to be one in which the recognition of common moral alignment by a group of similarly formed people led to deepening commercial trust, which in turn fed into financial innovation in the City of London. This impression is reinforced by the reality that the lead partners in these banks all shared common formation participation in a small set of London's commercial networks, and—with the exception of Barclays, led by Quakers—all had evangelical partners.

The establishment of the Sierra Leone Company (SLC) in 1791, led by Henry Thornton as chair, provides a second example. During the late 1780s, Thornton had been heavily involved in the unsuccessful political campaign by the Society for Effecting the Abolition of the Slave Trade. Recognizing the unlikelihood of Parliamentary success in the near term, Thornton sought to apply his commer-

---

13 *An Account of the Society for Promoting Religious Knowledge Among the Poor* (London: Thomas Field, 1779).
14 Recollections, Thornton Papers, 34.
15 Hayek, introduction to Thornton, *Enquiry*, 38.

cial experience to the creation of a philanthropic company that would demonstrate the viability of a free-labor economy on the West African coast. Thornton's correspondence and written recollections make it possible to see in detail the close interrelationships between his personal character, moral imagination, and intellectual formation, on one hand, and his evangelical faith and merchant upbringing on the other. Investing and ultimately losing many thousands of pounds in the endeavor, he wrote, "I have in particular learnt to feel for the African race. I hope that my children & any children's children will take up the same cause."[16] Throughout the tenure of his leadership of the SLC, Thornton sought to create both a profitable economic model and a moral community. In his correspondence, single paragraphs included not only directions on the accounting standards he expected to be maintained, but also the books in moral theology that he prescribed for employees to read.

The reciprocity between formation and historical context can also be seen in the intellectual worlds of John and Henry Thornton. By contemporary standards, John Thornton had received an unexceptional education for a son in a wealthy merchant family. However, his trading interests in northern Europe led him to establish relationships and partnerships with local merchants, and following his religious conversion, he began corresponding with ministers and religious writers across a wide geography. Through these networks, he filled the gaps in his formation, becoming widely read in theology and political economy—acting as editor and informal publishing agent for a number of evangelical authors, including John Newton, and forming friendships and collaborating in philanthropy with members of the Blue Stocking Society.

Beyond his evangelical religious upbringing, Henry Thornton's own intellectual formation as a young man was in the world of assocational philanthropy—attending lectures and meetings as diverse as those at the Royal Society and the Lying-In Hospital (a maternity hospital of which his father had been president). On his career shift into banking, Henry read widely in political economy, and his most influential intellectual output was his 1802 *Enquiry into the Paper Credit of Great Britain*.[17] Thornton's original insight in the *Enquiry* was to recognize that the speed of circulation of paper credit reflected not the wealth of the nation, but the net trust of the commercial community. Drawing on two decades of his own formative engagement in banking and merchant finance, Thornton recognized that participation in credit economies was itself a formative practice, and that the long-term stability of any credit economy depended on the extent to which people were habituated to trust the stability of the circulating currency. Along with his friends and intellectual collaborators in the Clapham Sect, Thornton sought to reposition moral theology and political economy in relation to each

---

[16] Recollections, Thornton Papers, 34.
[17] Thornton, *Enquiry*.

other—in response to contemporary writers, such as William Paley—not on the basis of aligning self-interests, but by conceiving of all relationships (including that of people with God) in terms of trust. In this frame, Thornton argued that moral duty and, therefore, moral formation require the cultivation of trust and trustworthiness—and that the basis of the good society and wealthy economy was the cultural accumulation and maintenance of reciprocal trust. Throughout, he explicitly related these insights to his experience in banking. In Henry Thornton's intellectual output, we therefore see the cumulative effects of intergenerational formation—through participation in the market economy, associational philanthropy, and evangelical church and family life—come full circle in articulating what Francis Horner referred to as approaching a "general treatise" on the formation of trust in economies.[18]

In this historical context, the interplay between different formative spheres operated coefficiently. Both contemporary merchant culture and evangelicalism fostered patterns of associational activism that exposed participants to frequent opportunities for voluntary service of the common good or of others. For merchants, their engagement with market forces was not primarily as consumers but as investors and traders—exercising a high level of economic agency, but usually through collective associational means, rather than as individuals or as office-holders in corporate structures. Character traits that facilitated trust and social influence—such as loyalty, humility, integrity, and responsibility—were all preferred and are frequently referenced in the published and private discourse of these networks. The prevalence of these traits translated directly through to one of the hallmarks of emergent philanthropy in the eighteenth century—its collaborative nature. Unlike the later rise of high-profile individual and family benefactors, the earliest dedicated philanthropic organizations comprised groups of donors who developed philanthropic agendas in common, and who personally engaged in the work, sharing responsibility in addition to providing financing.

Especially among those philanthropic entrepreneurs of this period who contributed to multiple successful projects—notably John Thornton, Jonas Hanway, John Howard, and later the members of the Clapham Sect—persistence and creativity were common traits, and these were actively cultivated in young men around the tables of Russia Company dinners and committee meetings and carried through to their leadership in philanthropic societies. This collective formation became increasingly and intentionally cultivated and transmitted. Henry Thornton reflected that his father—while well enmeshed in associations—had nevertheless been too prone to acting on his own accord, without regard for how he might collaborate with others.[19] As a young man in his twenties, Henry ac-

---

[18] Francis Horner, "Review of Thornton's Enquiry," *The Edinburgh Review* 1, no. 1 (Oct. 1802): 172–201, at 174.

[19] Recollections, Thornton Papers, 3–4.

tively gathered around him networks of "associates of his own rank in life to assist him in his labour," and actively sought to ensure that his son formed such a friendship circle at his school and with the sons of other philanthropists.[20] This cultivation of collaborative traits of trust can be seen extending to protégés in business and philanthropy. Thornton, for example, counseled a young Zachary Macaulay—then an employee of the SLC and later a key member of the Clapham Sect—on how developing a habit of regular correspondence with members of the governing committee and returning detailed accounts of affairs he was overseeing would help him stay honest and cultivate a trusted reputation.

For those in this context who had also converted to an evangelical faith, this social formation was overlaid with an intense focus on the cultivation of the inner life. It was not enough that one built social trust and reputation—one must also do so by right means, and for right motives. In the 1750s, John Thornton found himself torn regarding attendance at Russia Company dinners—when he realized that he was enjoying the accolades of his peers and being tempted to indulge in too much wine. Instead, he increased his attendance at other events, such as meetings held by the Royal Society and lectures by evangelical preachers. He made a habit of inviting visiting evangelical clergy to take chapel services for his household, reckoning that he could "muster 40 or more,"[21] and the entire family engaged in regular practices of reflective spiritual journaling. In this way every aspect of life was carefully considered to ensure that not only were they living according to the values they espoused, but that their feelings were also properly aligned—charitable works and integrity in business must be underpinned by a genuine sense of love for the other. Formational practices were remarkably translatable between spheres of religious and economic activity. Many examples exist of evangelical merchants engaging chaplains to minister in their businesses. Inversely, accounting practices could be exactingly turned to the practice of spiritual as well as financial discipline. Diaries of contemporaries contained annotations of time spent in prayer, reading the Bible, self-reflection, and other religiously improving habits, with weekly totals maintained to track spiritual progress.

The dynamic between evangelical self-cultivation and immersion in mercantile culture led to novel attempts to align identity and vocation, with self-conception as a "philanthropist" itself one of the more salient examples. Common to both evangelicalism and merchant networks was an increasing need to consider the globalizing world in which they operated. For merchants, this was driven by an increasing awareness of the impacts of overseas economic conditions on trade, while for evangelicals, their engagement was conditioned by the universal imperative of the Gospel. For those who shared both these perspectives, it in-

---

[20] John Venn, *Annals of a Clerical Family* (London: MacMillan, 1904), 157.
[21] John Thornton to William Richardson, Jul. 1790, Thornton Papers, 1/C fo. 21.

creasingly became obvious that Christ's command to love one's neighbor must extend to global humanity.[22] For evangelicals, business was not merely a means, but must itself be turned to purposes of religious renewal—and so new vocational paths as philanthropists, and philanthropy as a new sphere of activity by which one could make sense of participation in the global world, emerged as a distinct cultural discourse. The formational overlay became so inextricable that historians have frequently noted that philanthropy was inseparably both economic activity and religious expression, with Kirkman Gray famously writing of "the outward symbol of this faith ... [the] subscription list."[23] Underneath the co-option of economic and religious means of formation was a continual wrestling to integrate. Over the span of a generation, the tensions that John Thornton felt between bawdy dinners and serious private devotion became Henry Thornton's intellectual project to integrate the moral bases of economic activity with the conditions of personal faithfulness.

A final element to highlight from the historical case, therefore, is the importance of the intergenerational frame. Formative practices were both inherited and adapted, and in a context of rapidly shifting economic and religious conditions, generational transitions provided a site for intentional enculturation or rejection of prior practices. Further, as can be seen in Henry Thornton's parents' advice on his career path, and his own later comments on his parents' formation, intergenerational perspective sifted the overlay of religious and economic practices, allowing the intentional construction of new patterns of vocational identity. This was especially significant in terms of character formation, with shifts in cultural fashions allowing otherwise invisible norms to be seen and considered. It was in this way that Henry Thornton could lament that his father's early career as a merchant had led him to become too comfortable with speculative risk, and therefore lacking in the discipline to undertake proper diligence later in life. This consciousness of how lived practices had built up character over the course of his parents' and their own lives informed Henry and his wife, Marianne's, own parenting and the domestic formation and educational choices they made for their children.

In considering formation in late modern societies, several themes emerge from this case study. Generalizations about participation in market or religious cultures may inadequately describe the moral formation that occurs. Instead, attention is needed to the formative effects of specific patterns of living within particular contexts. These formational contexts are inevitably multilayered. Henry Thornton was a merchant's son, a banker, an evangelical, a father, a Member of Parliament, a philanthropist, a social reformer, and much more. He lived one

---

[22] David Owen, *English Philanthropy, 1660-1960* (Cambridge, Mass.: Harvard University Press, 1964), 1.

[23] B. Kirkman Gray, *A History of English Philanthropy* (London: King & Son, 1905), 265.

life, shaped deeply by the overlay of religious and commercial spheres. The habits he learned as a Russia Company merchant and those he developed as an evangelical reinforced his character and his vocational and intellectual frameworks as a banker, monetary theorist, and social reformer. The interactions between these spheres were not chiefly oppositional or reactive, but rather constructive of new identities—including the emergent vocation of philanthropy. Most profoundly, perhaps, the story is one of focused and intentional self-formation—of networks of individuals seeking to find ways to live plausibly in a changing world.

Part Two: Integrating Social Systems

Economics, Law, Education, and Religion—Contributions to the Composition of a Good Society

Nicholas Aroney[1]

Introduction

Late modern liberal democracies display a dominant social imaginary.[2] Social problems are understood in a certain way and are addressed through the use of certain tools. Among these tools, three of the most important are economics, law, and education. We think that through growing economies and better distribution of wealth, through better laws and policies, and through improved education and training we can solve social problems, meet human needs, and thereby build a better society. Part of the idea is that law, education, and economics are complementary: each supplies what the others cannot. Law regulates outward behavior, education informs inward beliefs, and economics provides us with our needs and satisfies our preferences.

And yet, there are doubts. Senior jurists question whether we may be placing too much weight on law and regulation.[3] Experienced educators query whether we are relying too much on education.[4] Seasoned economists ask whether we are expecting too much of mainstream economics.[5] There is an "in-

---

[1] My thanks are due Sergio Belardinelli, Nathan Chapman, Andreas Glaeser, Amanda Gouws, Paul Oslington, Jürgen von Hagen, and Michael Welker for comments on an earlier version of this paper. The chapter builds on material presented in "Law, Education and Religion–Pathways to the Good Society?," *St Mark's Review* 252 (2020): 19–37.

[2] Charles Taylor, *Modern Social Imaginaries* (Durham, N.C.: Duke University Press, 2004) identifies three important forms of social self-understanding crucial to modernity: the economy, the public sphere, and the institutions of democratic self-rule.

[3] Lord Sumption, "The Limits of Law," in *Lord Sumption and the Limits of the Law*, ed. N. W. Barber, Richard Ekins, and Paul Yowell (Oxford: Hart Publishing, 2016), 15.

[4] David F. Labaree, "The Winning Ways of a Losing Strategy: Educationalizing Social Problems in the United States," *Educational Theory* 58, no. 4 (2008): 447–60.

[5] Paul Oslington, "Understanding Economic Impacts on Virtue and the Pursuit of Goods," in *The Impact of the Market on Character Formation, Ethical Education, and the Commu-*

cessant stream of lawmaking,"[6] but the social problems persist. Educational reforms come and go, but student achievement stalls or falls.[7] Our economies generate unprecedented levels of wealth and prosperity, but the relationship between income and happiness is ambiguous and variable.[8] Nonetheless, we look to law, education, and economics to deliver the good life, and we invest our hopes in legal, educational, and economic reforms to achieve that outcome. As one commentator has observed, our utopian faith in the capacity of education to solve social and economic problems is "practically a secular religion."[9] Much the same could be said of our hopes for law and economics. Law reform, educational reform, and economic reform have become institutional mainstays of late modern democratic life, instilled with a quasi-messianic sense of mission and purpose. We expect law, education, and economics to deliver us from our failings and lead us to the promised land.

Now it is beyond doubt that good laws, universal education, and growing economies have made important contributions to human well-being. It is better to live in a well-ordered society, where crime and corruption are kept under control. It is better to live in a well-educated society, in which human knowledge is being expanded. It is better to live in a prosperous society, where basic human needs are met and everyone has the opportunity to live a fulfilled and satisfying life. But is there a missing dimension? Is it possible to have good laws, universal education, and growing economies, yet somehow not quite reach the mark?

In an important essay, Jürgen Habermas has recently acknowledged that something is missing in the prevailing social imaginary of the modern secular West. Habermas proposes that enlightenment reason is becoming aware of a "defeatism lurking within it," which is "threatening to spin out of control."[10] Although not a religious believer himself, he suggests that religion is an "unexhausted force" that can awaken "an awareness of what is missing, of what cries out to heaven."[11] His point is that, for all its achievements, the modern secular state cannot from its own resources arouse in its citizens the sense of solidarity

---

nication of Values in Late Modern Pluralistic Societies, ed. Jürgen von Hagen et al. (Leipzig: Evangelische Verlagsanstalt, 2020), 93.

[6] Oliver O'Donovan, "Government as Judgment," *First Things*, Apr. 1999.

[7] Australian Curriculum, Assessment and Reporting Authority, *National Assessment Program: National Report for 2021* (Sydney: ACARA, 2021).

[8] Carol Graham, *The Pursuit of Happiness: An Economy of Well-Being* (Washington, D.C.: Brookings Institution, 2011), chap. 1.

[9] Penny Bender Sebring, "Review of Tinkering toward Utopia," *The Social Service Review* 71, no. 3 (1997): 503–06, at 503.

[10] Jürgen Habermas, *An Awareness of What Is Missing: Faith and Reason in a Post-Secular Age*, trans. Ciaran Cronin (Cambridge: Polity Press, 2010), 18.

[11] Ibid., 18–19.

needed to motivate them to act for the common good. Elsewhere he has observed:

> For the normative self-understanding of modernity, Christianity has functioned as more than just a precursor or catalyst. Universalistic egalitarianism, from which sprang the ideals of freedom and a collective life in solidarity, the autonomous conduct of life and emancipation, the individual morality of conscience, human rights and democracy, is the direct legacy of the Judaic ethic of justice and the Christian ethic of love. This legacy, substantially unchanged, has been the object of a continual critical reappropriation and reinterpretation. Up to this very day there is no alternative to it. And in light of the current challenges of a post-national constellation, we must draw sustenance now, as in the past, from this substance. Everything else is idle postmodern talk.[12]

Ernst-Wolfgang Böckenförde made a similar point when he observed that the modern state is "sustained by conditions that it cannot itself guarantee." While the modern liberal state offers its citizens important liberties, "it can only survive if the freedom it grants to its citizens is regulated from within, out of the moral substance of the individual and the homogeneity of society." This in turn raises the question whether the secular state must, in the final analysis, "be sustained by the inner impulses and binding forces that religious faith imparts to its citizens."[13] If Böckenförde and Habermas are correct, then good laws, universal education, and growing economies may not be enough. The missing element, they say, is religion.

Much depends, of course, on how we define and understand economics, law, education, and religion, and what we expect each of them to contribute to the building of a good society. Definitions are elusive things, however. Scholarship in all four fields is riven by competing definitions of its subject matter. Put schematically, these competing definitions frequently have to do with whether the subject matter is conceived in positive or normative terms. Thus, law is sometimes defined in positive terms by reference to the will and power of the lawmaker and other officials within the legal system, while at other times it is defined by reference to the moral content and ethical purposes of the law. Likewise, education is sometimes defined as the impartation of information, the accumulation of knowledge, and the development of practical skills; however, it

---

[12] Jürgen Habermas, *Religion and Rationality: Essays on Reason, God, and Modernity* (Cambridge: Polity, 2002), 149.

[13] Ernst-Wolfgang Böckenförde, "The Rise of the State as a Process of Secularization" [1967], in *Religion, Law, and Democracy: Selected Writings*, ed. Mirjam Künkler and Tine Stein (Oxford: Oxford University Press, 2021), 152–67, at 167, citing G. W. F. Hegel, *Encyklopädie der philosophischen Wissenschaften* (1830), §552.

can also be defined as the development of character and the inculcation of virtue. Similarly, economics can be defined and pursued in positive, "value free" terms, or it can be understood as a moral science or a branch of moral philosophy directed to moral ends.

In this chapter, I seek to develop these ideas by beginning with contrasting positive and normative definitions of economics, law, and education.[14] My intention is to use each definition to explore the particular ways in which economics, law, and education are understood and how they can contribute to the good society. But having done that, I then seek to show how, when viewed from a religious perspective, they each can be understood in a broader and deeper way, such that they in fact overlap, inform, and shape each other. My suggestion will be that when we view these subjects from the perspective of religion, we can see what the point of law, education, and economics might really be. The things that economics, law, and education can contribute to the formation of a good society are dependent on each domain of human activity doing what it alone can do best, but in a manner that ensures they do not attempt to do what only religion can do best, and that they leave room for religion to perform its unique function within society.[15]

I begin with economics, then turn to law, next education, and finally religion.

Economics

As in any discipline, there are many competing definitions of economics, and these definitions and approaches have varied and shifted considerably over time.[16] While the definitions contain many diverse elements, one important distinction concerns the question whether economics is understood to be a form of moral inquiry or a value-free social science. Many of the major figures of contemporary economics have insisted that the discipline is "fundamentally distinct from ethics" (Lionel Robbins) and that economic analysis is "in principle inde-

---

[14] The definitions I offer are by no means exhaustive or complete; to an extent, I use them schematically to make my wider argument; but I also contend that they fairly capture much of what is meant by their respective subject matters, sufficient at least to ground the wider argument I present in this paper.

[15] I use the terms law, education, commerce, and religion generically. As the argument progresses, the terms become more specific. Readers may judge whether the argument, if sound on its own terms, has application to systems of law, education, commerce, and religion other than those specified.

[16] Roger E. Backhouse and Steven G. Medema, "Retrospectives: On the Definition of Economics," *The Journal of Economic Perspectives* 23, no. 1 (2009): 221–33.

pendent of any particular ethical position" (Milton Friedman).[17] In his Nobel Prize lecture, Gary Becker acknowledged that economics is driven by a "much richer set of values and preferences" than merely "selfishness or gain"; individuals maximize welfare "as they conceive it," he said, whether they be selfish or altruistic in their preferences.[18] While this seems to introduce an ethical element, mainstream economic analysis does not offer an account of what people ought to seek, but only of what they need to do to achieve their objectives. Economics remains what John Neville Keynes called a "positive science," as distinct from a "normative science" concerned with the "criteria of what ought to be."[19]

This does not mean that contemporary economists are not aware of and concerned about the ethical and political implications of their discipline. Adam Smith described political economy as "a branch of the science of a statesman or legislator" concerned with the provision of plentiful revenue and substance for the people and sufficient revenue to the state to provide public services.[20] Lionel Robbins similarly affirmed that economic analysis is always "conjoint with assumptions about the ultimate desirable ends of society."[21] However, most contemporary economists draw a firm distinction between value-neutral economic analysis of the relationship between means and ends, and value-laden determination of what ends should be achieved.[22]

Thus conceived, economics is deployed in contemporary politics in instrumental terms. Economic activity is widely seen as the primary means by which human wants are secured and the well-being of nations is routinely assessed according to their gross domestic product.[23] Bodies like the International Monetary Fund focus on measures of global, regional, and national economic growth as prime indicators of human welfare.[24] The most important event in the parliamentary cycle of most liberal democracies is the passage of the budget—not only

---

[17] See Dotan Leshem, "Retrospectives: What Did the Ancient Greeks Mean by 'Oikonomia'?," *The Journal of Economic Perspectives* 30, no. 1 (2016): 225–38, at 226.

[18] Gary Becker, "The Economic Way of Looking at Life," Nobel Lecture, Dec. 9, 1992.

[19] John Neville Keynes, *The Scope and Method of Political Economy* (London: Macmillan, 1891), 34–35, cited in Milton Friedman, "The Methodology of Positive Economics," in *Essays in Positive Economics* (Chicago: University of Chicago Press, 1953), 3.

[20] Adam Smith, *Inquiry into the Nature and Causes of the Wealth of Nations* [1776] (Oxford: Oxford University Press [Glasgow Edition], 2014), bk. 4, "Introduction."

[21] Ricardo F. Crespo, "Is Economics a Moral Science?," *Journal of Markets & Morality* 1, no. 2 (1998): 201–11, at 207.

[22] Peter J. Boettke, "Is Economics a Moral Science? A Response to Ricardo F. Crespo," *Journal of Markets & Morality* 1, no. 2 (1998): 212–19, at 214.

[23] A. C. Pigou, *The Economics of Welfare* (London: Macmillan, 1932), chap. 1.

[24] See, for example, International Monetary Fund, *World Economic Outlook: Update July 2022: Gloomy and More Uncertain*, https://www.imf.org/en/publications/weo.

because it determines the government's spending priorities for the forthcoming year, but also because it is accompanied by detailed assessments of the economic performance of the nation.[25] Governments claim success when they oversee conditions of sustained economic growth, and fear losing political support during economic contractions and recessions.[26] Thus, contemporary political debates frequently concern levels of economic production and distribution, as well as degrees of inequality and the environmental impacts of economic activities.

This last point brings into view the ethical and political dimensions of economics. On one hand, it appears that most peoples throughout the world have experienced significant improvements in well-being over the long term, measured not only in narrow economic terms but also in terms of health and life expectancy.[27] On the other hand, degrees of material inequality remain significant and have increased in recent decades.[28] This mixed picture brings into focus a further question: even though economic activity and technological advances have contributed to significant long-term growth and unprecedented levels of prosperity for many peoples, it is not clear how much this change is correlated with integral human welfare. There appears to be a broad correlation between objective measures of wealth and subjective measures of happiness within countries, but across countries and over time the evidence is more ambiguous.[29] Relative increases in wealth do not necessarily correlate with happiness over the long term.[30] Indeed, while poor people are less happy on average than wealthy people, very poor people often report that they are very happy.[31] So there is more to happiness than money, and it may be that perceptions of happiness vary. Is happiness to be measured by reference to a Benthamite ethic, which

---

[25] For example, Australian Government, *Budget Documents 2022-2023*, https://budget.gov.au/2022-23/content/documents.htm.

[26] There is some evidence that fiscal discipline and economic growth are correlated with electoral success, at least in developing countries: Adi Brender and Allan Drazen, "How Do Budget Deficits and Economic Growth Affect Reelection Prospects? Evidence from a Large Panel of Countries," *The American Economic Review* 98, no. 5 (2008): 2203-20; and Jeroen Klomp and Jakob de Haan, "Political Budget Cycles and Election Outcomes," *Public Choice* 157, no. 1 (2013): 245-67.

[27] David E. Bloom and David Canning, "The Health and Wealth of Nations," *Science* 287, no. 5456 (2000): 1207-09; and David E. Bloom, "7 Billion and Counting," *Science* 333, no. 6042 (2011): 562-69.

[28] Thomas Piketty, *Capital in the Twenty-First Century*, trans. Arthur Goldhammer (Cambridge, Mass.: Belknap Press of Harvard University Press, 2017), 31.

[29] Graham, *The Pursuit of Happiness*, 16.

[30] Richard A. Easterlin, "Happiness, Growth, and Public Policy," *Economic Inquiry* 51, no. 1 (2013): 1-15.

[31] Graham, *The Pursuit of Happiness*, 3.

aims at maximizing pleasure and minimizing pain? Or is to be assessed by reference to Aristotelian ideas of integral human fulfillment?[32] Other components of well-being, such as friendship and love, good health and a sense of purpose, are also closely associated with reports of subjective happiness and contentment.[33]

Earlier approaches to economics were more explicit about the moral and political objectives of economic analysis. According to Greek philosophers, such as Xenophon, Aristotle, and others, *oikonomia* was concerned with securing sufficient resources not only to provide for life's necessities but also to ensure a "good life," constituted by philosophical inquiry and engagement in political affairs.[34] The Greeks considered economic rationality an ethical disposition, not merely a form of instrumental reason that could be directed to *any* chosen end. For Aristotle, a "luxurious life," in which wealth is accumulated and desires are gratified without limit, is unethical; economic rationality is properly directed only to ethical ends.[35] The medieval scholastics drew on these resources when formulating approaches to economic matters, such as in their condemnations of the vice of covetousness and the sin of usury.[36] Mary Hirschfield has drawn attention to a deep reason why the accumulation of wealth does not necessarily produce increased happiness: as Aquinas put it, while human desire is infinite, "infinite desire can only be satiated when we rest in the infinite good that is God."[37]

Wilhelm Roepke argued that while markets provide substantial benefits through the efficient supply of goods and services, they are "far from generating their moral prerequisites autonomously." A market economy, he maintained, could certainly be defended, but only "as part of a wider general order encompassing ethics, law, the natural conditions of life and happiness, the state, politics, and power."[38] John Milbank and Adrian Pabst have proposed something similar in the idea of a "civil economy" that is a "market economy" framed with-

---

[32] Ibid., chap. 2.
[33] Ibid., 13, 21.
[34] Leshem, "Retrospectives: What Did the Ancient Greeks Mean by 'Oikonomia'?," citing Xenophon, *Oikonomikos*, 2:10, 11:9–10; Aristotle, *Politics*, 1.3 (1256b).
[35] See Aristotle, *Nicomachean Ethics*, 1 (1095b).
[36] See, for example, Thomas Aquinas, *Summa Theologiae*, trans. Fathers of the English Dominican Province (London: Burns & Oates, 1947–48), II.II Q78 and Q118.
[37] Oslington, "Understanding Economic Impacts on Virtue and the Pursuit of Goods," citing Mary Hirschfeld, *Aquinas and the Market: Toward a Humane Economy* (Cambridge, Mass.: Harvard University Press, 2018), 24.
[38] Crespo, "Is Economics a Moral Sciences?," 207, citing Wilhelm Roepke, *A Humane Economy: The Social Framework of the Free Market* (Chicago: Henry Regnery, 1960), 126.

in an ethical context.[39] Without moral constraints, as even Adam Smith recognized, those engaged in commerce are just as likely to conspire against the public interest as they are to contribute to the common good.[40] While Smith was skeptical of the capacity of laws to prevent this from happening, in the social imaginary of contemporary liberal democracies, the primary means by which problems such as market failure, monopolistic practices, and economic exploitation are addressed is through law and government. Governments seek to shape economic cycles, encourage sustained economic growth and maintain full employment through monetary and fiscal policies, and they seek to curb monopolistic practices and protect consumers through antitrust and consumer protection laws enforced by regulatory agencies.

And thus, we turn to law.

Law

As with economics, the discipline of law is characterized by many competing definitions, which, despite the variety, can be distinguished broadly in terms of whether law is conceived in positive or moral terms.

The positivist approach, initiated by Thomas Hobbes and popularized by Jeremy Bentham and especially John Austin in the late eighteenth and early nineteenth centuries, defines law as the command of a sovereign.[41] On this view, law is an expression of the will of the governing authorities. Whatever they command that we should do or refrain from doing *is* the law. The law is effective because the state is sovereign, and it is sovereign because it has the power to enforce its law, and people are in the habit of obeying the law because they are afraid of its sanctions. The renowned American jurist Oliver Wendell Holmes Jr. thought that this approach implies what he called the "bad man" theory of law.[42] This is law seen from the point of view of the person who obeys the law not because it is the right thing to do, but only because that person fears being pun-

---

[39] John Milbank and Adrian Pabst, *The Politics of Virtue: Post-Liberalism and the Human Future* (London: Rowman & Littlefield, 2016), chap. 4.

[40] Smith, *Wealth of Nations*, bk. 1, chap. 10 (Glasgow ed.), 145.

[41] Jeremy Bentham, *On Laws in General*, ed. H. L. A. Hart (London: Athlone Press, 1970); and *John Austin, The Province of Jurisprudence Determined*, ed. Wilfrid E. Rumble (Cambridge: Cambridge University Press, 1995). I deliberately pass over the important contribution of H. L. A. Hart in his highly influential *The Concept of Law* (Oxford: Clarendon Press, 1961), who was highly critical of the "command" theory of law but defended the thesis that law can be conceptually separated from morality.

[42] Oliver Wendell Holmes Jr., "The Path of the Law," *Harvard Law Review* 10, no. 8 (1897): 457-98.

ished for disobedience. I draw attention to this definition, not because I ultimately agree with it, but because it puts into stark perspective what law is capable of doing at its lowest common denominator. Law places a restraint on "bad" people. Perhaps more accurately, law places a restraint on us all, recognizing that in some sense we are all bad people, we are all capable of doing bad things.[43]

Viewed in this way, law can do significant good, but only in a negative sense: it frightens us from doing bad things. However, when viewed in this way, law doesn't seem to be able to do a lot of good in a positive sense. It might coerce us into saying certain things and performing certain actions that appear to be good externally considered, but it cannot determine the content of our internal beliefs, dispositions, attitudes, and motives. It can only compel behavior in the form of a command that identifies what is to be done and what is not to be done. And if a lawmaker wants to eradicate bad behavior entirely, this must be done in increasingly specific detail. The law must command exactly what is to be done and exactly what is not to be done, and it must do so in every significant domain of human life.

Moreover, considerable resources must be committed to the task of enforcing the law. Agencies must be established and invested with powers of surveillance and intervention to ensure compliance and punish disobedience. Without the necessary internal dispositions to support obedience to law, a bad person—which is to say, all of us, in a certain sense—will only do exactly as the law requires, in accordance with what we anticipate the police will actively enforce—and no more than that.

Viewed from this perspective, law is inherently limited in what it can achieve. However, when we forget the inherent limitations of law, when we try to use it to create a comprehensively good society, composed of truly good people, the consequence is this: the enactment of more and more laws, which stipulate in more and more detail exactly what must be done and exactly what must not be done, together with more and more government agencies, armed with more and more intrusive powers, tasked with regulating our behavior and punishing us when we disobey. As Jonathan Sumption, a former justice of the UK Supreme Court, has observed, we live in an age of "unbounded confidence in the value and efficacy of law as an engine of social and moral improvement."[44] Our law books demonstrate the extent to which we have overoptimistic expectations of law and its efficacy. There is not a country in the modern Western world that

---

[43] For a recent discussion of the role of law in a world populated by individuals with different levels of awareness of their ethical and unethical behavior, see Yuval Feldman, *The Law of Good People: Challenging States' Ability to Regulate Human Behavior* (Cambridge: Cambridge University Press, 2018).

[44] Sumption, "The Limits of Law," 16.

has not experienced a tremendous proliferation of laws and regulations enacted by its legislature and executive year after year.[45]

The second definition of law is very different. It maintains that morality and justice are intrinsic to the very nature of law. Law is not merely the command of a sovereign. As Augustine of Hippo pointed out long ago, an unjust law would seem to be no law at all.[46] Thomas Aquinas put it this way: law is an ordinance of right reason directed to the common good.[47] On this view, our understanding of the nature, function, and effectiveness of law will not altogether depend on the crabbed and miserly attitudes of the "bad man," who does only exactly what the law requires and not an iota more. Because morality and justice are inherent in the nature of law, the law itself identifies the good purposes it seeks to achieve. This means, in principle, that the law need not spell out in excruciating detail every particular thing that is to be done and every particular thing that is not to be done. It can rely on an understanding that its rules are there for good reasons, which any rational person can comprehend.[48] This does not mean that a bad person will obey the law in accordance with its spirit and intent. Bad people will still seek to circumvent and avoid the law when it suits them. But it does mean that "good" people—which is to say, potentially all of us—will not need the law to spell out exactly what is to be done and what is not to be done in every possible situation. Rather, good people will understand the good reasons for the law and conform their behavior to it.[49] Consider the simplicity of the Ten Command-

---

[45] Sumption observes that in the decade from 1997 to 2007, more than three thousand new criminal or regulatory offenses were added to the British statute book. Criminal offenses, he says, "appear like mushrooms after every rainstorm": ibid., 16. For Australian examples, see Michael McHugh, "The Growth of Legislation and Litigation," *Australian Law Journal* 69, no. 1 (1995): 37–48; *Rethinking Regulation: Report of the Taskforce on Reducing Regulatory Burdens on Business* (Australian Government, 2006); and Kurt Wallace, "How Bureaucratic Dark Matter Is Swallowing Our Wealth," Institute of Public Affairs, Jun. 14, 2019, https://ipa.org.au/ipa-today/how-bureaucratic-dark-matter-is-swallowing-our-wealth.

[46] *De libero arbitrio*, I.5.11, in Augustine, *The Teacher; The Free Choice of the Will; Grace and Free Will*, ed. The Fathers of the Church (Washington, D.C.: Catholic University of America Press, 2010).

[47] Aquinas, *Summa Theologiae* I–II.90.4.

[48] John Finnis, *Natural Law and Natural Rights* (Oxford: Oxford University Press, 1980), 318: "The law anticipates and seeks to capitalize upon, indeed to absorb and take over, the 'good citizen's' schema of practical reasoning, and to give it an unquestioned or dogmatic status."

[49] Plato put this pithily when he observed that "laws are partly framed for the sake of good men, in order to instruct them how they may live on friendly terms with one another, and partly for the sake of those who refuse to be instructed, whose spirit cannot be subdued, or softened, or hindered from plunging into evil": Plato, *Laws*, trans. Benjamin

ments.[50] Only ten rules! A genuinely good person probably doesn't need much more guidance than this. Consider the two greatest commandments: love of God and love of one's neighbor.[51] A perfectly good person needs nothing more. What a far cry from the reams and reams of legislation enacted by our parliaments every year. Oliver O'Donovan once used a phrase that aptly describes this phenomenon. He called it an "incessant stream of lawmaking."[52]

Is all this lawmaking really necessary to create a good society? Or are we expecting too much of the law? Bad people—which is to say, in a certain sense, all of us—will always find ways to circumvent the law. Like Adam Smith's merchants, it is often in our private interest to conspire against the public interest. However, as Smith also realized, merely increasing the volume and reach of the law does not address the underlying problem.[53] We invest enormous powers on regulatory agencies, but then have to create secondary agencies to ensure that the primary agencies exercise their powers lawfully and ethically. And when those secondary agencies themselves are found to have engaged in misconduct, we see how we are failing to address the underlying problem.[54] Through all of this, the weight of law and regulation places a burden on good people that often gets in the way of their efforts to do good things. And so we realize that we would be better off as a society if we could only generate good, or at least better, people.

And in our social imagination the most obvious instrument to achieve this is education.

Education

What is education? Again, we encounter the question of definition. And again, I propose that we consider the implications of two views.

The first view sees education as primarily concerned with the transmission of knowledge and the development of skills. This is a pragmatic or instrumental

---

Jowett (St. Andrews: University of St. Andrews, 2012), bk. 9, 880d-e (Athenian Stranger).

[50] Exodus 20:2-17; Deuteronomy 5:6-21.
[51] Matthew 22:35-40.
[52] Oliver O'Donovan, "Government as Judgment," *First Things*, Apr. 1999.
[53] Smith, *Wealth of Nations*, bk. 1, chap. 10 (Glasgow ed.), 145.
[54] The Australian States have established special standing commissions charged with responsibility to investigate alleged misconduct and corruption within public agencies. But the commissions themselves are all too often found to have engaged in misconduct themselves. For a recent example (among many), see Tony Fitzgerald and Alan Wilson, *Commission of Inquiry Relating to the Crime and Corruption Commission* (Brisbane, 2022).

view of education. The goal of education is to fill children's heads with facts and equip their hands with practical skills. Education exists to train the next generation of workers. Its focus is on the particular role each person will perform within our society. On this view, education becomes more and more specialized, more and more vocationally oriented. Thus, by the time children are teenagers, we are already expecting them to decide their chosen vocation and to select the subjects they will study at school. Then we send them off to college or university to study accounting, engineering, marketing, or law.

Now, it is not as if this vocational orientation doesn't have its advantages. Occupational specialization enables a division of labor in which each person contributes to the good of society through the application of their knowledge and skills. We are all better off as a result.[55] But if that is all that education is about, then it doesn't grapple with the problem identified earlier. It doesn't necessarily produce good people. It merely produces people who are clever and skillful. Being clever and skillful is good, so long as it is accompanied by good character. Without good character, being clever and skillful can be downright dangerous.

This problem goes very deep. Take this commonplace belief: the better educated you are, or the more intelligent, the more likely you will act on the basis of well-established evidence and careful logical reasoning. Consider also the corollary: the more ignorant, the less intelligent, the more poorly educated, the more likely you will be driven by emotion, prejudice, superstition, and dogma. These are widely shared views. However, the cognitive and behavioral science literature suggests that they simply are not true. Rather, as one author put it, "those who are highly educated, intelligent or rhetorically skilled tend to be significantly less likely than most to revise their beliefs or adjust their positions when confronted with evidence or arguments that contradict their priors."[56]

This is a curious—even shocking—finding. How could it be so? What could possibly explain it? It may be that, at least to some extent, there is a Bayesian-like explanation. Academics have amassed a considerable body of knowledge and understanding. It therefore takes more than a single new observation or a novel claim to overturn their well-founded beliefs. But while this accounts for academic resistance to novel ideas especially within the hard sciences, the cognitive and behavioral science literature suggests a less benign explanation. This alternative explanation is that clever, well-educated people are especially skilled at responding to uncomfortable facts and challenging arguments,[57] espe-

---

[55] This seems to be the underlying perspective of the recent *Report of the Review to Achieve Educational Excellence in Australian Schools* (Canberra: Commonwealth of Australia, Mar. 2018), chaired by David Gonski.

[56] Musa al-Gharbi, "Academic and Political Elitism," *Inside Higher Ed*, Aug. 27, 2019.

[57] Milton Lodge and Charles S. Taber, "The Automaticity of Affect for Political Leaders, Groups, and Issues: An Experimental Test of the Hot Cognition Hypothesis," *Political*

cially by using their highly refined critical abilities to scrutinize others and their beliefs, rather than themselves and their own beliefs.[58] This particularly applies to academics. Despite all our critical abilities, it seems that academics tend to be more ideological, more ideologically rigid, and more ideologically extreme in our beliefs.[59] The literature also suggests that we academics are more likely to form positions on issues, or even change our positions on issues, in response to one-sided, partisan cues of what we are supposed to think based on our political allegiances—to the left or to the right.[60] It also appears that academics are more prejudiced, at least against those who hold views different to their own.[61] While highly educated people may be well versed about contemporary political gossip, dramas, and scandals, they are not necessarily better informed about substantive facts about the world outside their fields of expertise. More generally, beyond academia, there is also evidence to suggest that the level of knowledge about political matters has not appreciably increased over time, notwithstanding massive increases in educational attainment and unprecedented expansion in the quantity and quality of information available to the public generally.[62]

Psychology 26, no. 3 (2005): 455–82, at 476–77; Charles S. Taber and Milton Lodge, "Motivated Skepticism in the Evaluation of Political Beliefs," *American Journal of Political Science* 50, no. 3 (2006): 755–69, at 760–65.

[58] Bruno Latour, "Why Has Critique Run out of Steam? From Matters of Fact to Matters of Concern," *Critical Inquiry* 30, no. 2 (2004): 225–48, at 237–43. While all of us tend to attribute bias to others more than ourselves, this tendency appears to be greater among those with higher cognitive ability: Richard F. West et al., "Cognitive Sophistication Does Not Attenuate the Bias Blind Spot," *Journal of Personality and Social Psychology* 103 (2012): 506–19.

[59] Indeed, the more educated we are, the more we know about politics, and the more we are politically engaged, the less likely it is that we will encounter the articulation of contrary political views in our daily lives: Diana C. Mutz, *Hearing the Other Side: Deliberative versus Participatory Democracy* (Cambridge: Cambridge University Press, 2006), 30–33. Further, those who are inclined to reflect most deeply about issues are more likely to engage in ideologically motivated reasoning: Dan M. Kahan, "Ideology, Motivated Reasoning, and Cognitive Reflection," *Judgment and Decision Making* 8, no. 4 (2013): 407–24.

[60] Bert Bakker, Yphtach Lelkes, and Ariel Malka, "Understanding Partisan Cue Receptivity: Tests of Predictions from the Bounded Rationality and Expressive Utility Perspectives," *The Journal of Politics* 82, no. 3 (2020): 1061–77.

[61] P. J. Henry and Jaime L. Napier, "Education Is Related to Greater Ideological Prejudice," *Public Opinion Quarterly* 81, no. 4 (2017): 930–42; and Toon Kuppens et al., "Educationism and the Irony of Meritocracy: Negative Attitudes of Higher Educated People towards the Less Educated," *Journal of Experimental Social Psychology* 76 (2018): 429–47.

[62] Ilya Somin, *Democracy and Political Ignorance: Why Smaller Government Is Smarter* (Stanford, Calif.: Stanford University Press, 2013), 20.

This is not a very flattering self-portrait. As Alasdair MacIntyre once observed: "a surprising number of the major disorders of the latter part of the twentieth century and of the first decade of the twenty-first century have been brought about by some of the most distinguished graduates of some of the most distinguished universities in the world."[63] How could this be so? And what could possibly be done about it?

Perhaps the answer lies in *better* education. And so emerges a second view, which sees education as primarily directed to the formation of good character.[64] Education, on this view, is not essentially about the acquisition of knowledge and skills. Rather, it is about the inculcation of wisdom and virtue. It is about the formation of good habits. It is about the qualities of honesty, integrity, self-discipline, and generosity. It also involves the development of intellectual virtues such as curiosity, attentiveness, fair-mindedness, honesty, humility, imaginativeness, courage, and perseverance.[65] As Werner Jaeger said of Socrates's teaching: "Education is not the cultivation of certain branches of knowledge. ... The real essence of education is that it enables men to reach the true aim of their lives.'[66] True education is about the pursuit of the good, the true, and the beautiful. It is about the care and perfection of the soul.[67] It means "deliberately moulding human character in accordance with an ideal."[68]

Plato taught that this kind of education—an education for character—requires a conversion of the soul.[69] Our minds, he said, need to be redirected from their

---

[63] Alasdair MacIntyre, "The Very Idea of a University: Aristotle, Newman and Us," *New Blackfriars* 91 (2010): 4–19, at 17.

[64] For a contemporary discussion and defense of this approach, see Kristján Kristjánsson, "Ten Myths about Character, Virtue and Virtue Education–Plus Three Well-Founded Misgivings," *British Journal of Educational Studies* 61, no. 3 (2013): 269–87.

[65] Jason Baehr, *The Inquiring Mind: On Intellectual Virtues and Virtue Epistemology* (Oxford: Oxford University Press, 2011), 21–22. See also Robert Campbell Roberts and W. Jay Wood, *Intellectual Virtues: An Essay in Regulative Epistemology* (Oxford: Clarendon Press, 2007). See also Aristotle, *Nicomachean Ethics*, bk. 6, 1139b15–1143b, and Thomas Aquinas, *Summa Theologiae* I–II.57–58.

[66] Werner Jaeger, *Paideia: The Ideals of Greek Culture, Volume 2: In Search of the Divine Centre*, trans. Gilbert Highet (Oxford: Oxford University Press, 1943), 69.

[67] Plato, *Apology*, 29e.

[68] Werner Jaeger, *Paideia: The Ideals of Greek Culture, Volume 1: Archaic Greece–The Mind of Athens*, trans. Gilbert Highet, 2nd ed. (Oxford: Oxford University Press, 1945), xxii. For an anthology of writings on the tradition of classical educational philosophy, see Richard Gamble, ed., *The Great Tradition: Classic Readings on What It Means to Be an Educated Human Being* (Wilmington, Del.: ISI Books, 2007).

[69] Plato, *Republic*, bk .7, 518b–d. Plato illustrated this in his famous allegory of the cave, in which those accustomed all their lives to living in the murky shadows of the cave are finally released from their intellectual bondage through their escape into the outside

preoccupation with mere appearances to an understanding of the deeper, underlying reality of things. This requires a kind of self-examination. For, as Socrates put it, "the unexamined life is not worth living."[70] But in what does this conversion consist? For Plato and Socrates, it involves the illumination of the soul. Knowledge is the solution to our problems because our essential problem is ignorance. Our salvation lies in enlightenment. No one, on this view, willingly does what is evil. By nature, Socrates taught, human beings pursue that which they consider to be good. Evil occurs, he said, because we are ignorant of the truly good, and so we pursue that which is evil, mistaking it for good. So the remedy lies in acquiring knowledge.[71]

A lot of modern education is premised on this idea. We think that if we give children more knowledge and better understanding, they will embrace what is good and pursue it. But is this true to reality? Think again of that class of people who are the most educated in our society—people with PhDs, people who hold academic positions at universities. Do these people live in a manner that is more virtuous than the less well-educated? It is quite possible that these people are more inclined to overestimate their virtues and underestimate their vices.

Why might this be so? Augustine of Hippo had a word for it. He called it pride. And so we come to religion.

Religion

As with economics, law, and education, it is possible to distinguish two approaches to religion. The first is exemplified in definitions of religion often used in contemporary anthropology, sociology, politics, and law. In these disciplines, we encounter attempts to develop generic definitions of religion that are sufficiently *inclusive*—so as not to exclude any particular religion that should be included—and yet sufficiently *incisive*—so as to identify those features that are specifically characteristic of religion and do not include philosophical beliefs or social practices that lack the features that make religion what it is. The purpose, in other words, is to develop a definition that is objective and neutral as between different religions.[72] Yet a fundamental problem remains. There doesn't seem to be a way to define what is and isn't religion without adopting a particular point

---

world, where, if they will just look up, they will be able to see the source of all light, the sun.

[70] Plato, *Apology*, 28b, 38a.
[71] Plato, *Protagoras*, 352c, 358b-d.
[72] See, for example, Emile Durkheim, *The Elementary Forms of the Religious Life*, trans. Joseph Ward Swain (London: George Allen & Unwin, 1915), 4-5.

of view which is likely to be as controversial as any particular religious standpoint.[73]

The idea that there is a thing that we call "religion" in this sense is a modern invention. And it is associated with an attempt to replace what (are now called) religious interpretations of reality with secular ones. As John Milbank has observed, sociology uses the "category of the social to explain, reduce or redefine all religious phenomena." But it is only able to do so "to the extent that it conceals its own theological borrowings and its own quasi-religious status."[74] The corralling of religion within the theoretical confines of secular thought-forms is thus part of an attempt to confine religion to the private and the personal, limiting or prohibiting its influence in public and social life.[75] In Australian law, for example, religion has been defined as involving belief in a supernatural being, thing, or principle; acceptance of canons of conduct giving effect to that belief; and the existence of an identifiable group of people who adhere to those beliefs and practices.[76] Notice that this definition comes close to treating religion as if it ultimately boils down to a special kind of education (instruction in a set of beliefs) and a special kind of law (adherence to particular canons of conduct).

However, there is a second very different approach to conceiving religion. This second approach focuses on the much older term *religio*, conceived not as a system of beliefs and practices but as a personal virtue or quality of character.[77] As traditionally understood, *religio* is a moral virtue; more specifically, it is a particular aspect of the moral virtue of justice; it is the particular virtue by which due honor or reverence is given to the deity.[78] It is distinct from the theological virtues of faith, hope, and love, but closely associated with them.[79] As Thomas Aquinas put it, *religio* is a special virtue, distinct from all the others, because it involves giving due honor to God, who "infinitely surpasses all things and exceeds them in every way."[80]

This is, of course, a particular understanding of religion, officially Roman Catholic but with roots in earlier Latin usage.[81] However, it is not at all clear

---

[73] For example, ibid., 9–20.
[74] John Milbank, *Theology and Social Theory*, 2nd ed. (Oxford: Blackwell, 2006), 52.
[75] Ibid., 106, 110.
[76] Church of the New Faith v Commissioner of Pay-Roll Tax (Vic) (1983) 154 CLR 120.
[77] Peter Harrison, *The Territories of Science and Religion* (Chicago: University of Chicago Press, 2015), chap. 1.
[78] Aquinas, *Summa Theologiae* II–II.81.2; Catechism of the Catholic Church, §1807.
[79] Catechism of the Catholic Church, §2095.
[80] Aquinas, *Summa Theologiae* II–II.81.4; see also II–II.81.6.
[81] René Gothóni, "Religio and Superstitio Reconsidered," *Archive for the Psychology of Religion* 21, no. 1 (1994): 37–46, at 40: "For Cicero, *religio* was the positive counterpart to

that ostensibly neutral, secular theories are any better at approaching the question of religion than the perspectives of particular religions.[82] Indeed, there is reason to think that people of religious disposition are sometimes much better at understanding, empathizing with, and accommodating other religions than those who claim to be secular in their beliefs.[83] A recent study has shown that, contrary to expectation, Western democracies, despite their secularism, engage in *more* government-based religious discrimination than many countries of Asia, sub-Saharan Africa and Latin America—particularly many of the Christian-majority countries of those regions.[84]

Understanding religion as *religio*—as a virtue, rather than a collection of beliefs—brings it into conversation with approaches to education aimed at the development of character. Socrates and Plato recognized that the development of good character requires a conversion of the soul. But they also thought the central problem to be a deficiency of the mind, not a defect of the will. Augustine begged to differ. For him, "true religion" (*uera religio*), which he associated with "correct piety" (*recta pietas*) and the appropriate "service due to God" (*Deo debita seruitus*), is rendered both outwardly and inwardly, and both corporately and individually, in acts of praise, devotion, sacrifice, and love.[85] True religion consists in us being united with God, for it is in this true union with God that the soul is "filled and impregnated with true virtues."[86] But for this to be the case, Augustine believed that true *religio* requires a conversion of the soul that goes further than anything Socrates or Plato imagined. Augustine put it this way (with a delightful play on words): "Hunc *eligentes* uel potius *religentes* (amiseramus enim *neglegentes*)—hunc ergo *religentes*, unde et *religio* dicta perhibetur, ad eum dilectione tendimus, ut perueniendo quiescamus, ideo beati, quia illo fine perfecti." (Being *attached* to Him, or rather let me say, *re-attached* [for we had *detached* ourselves and lost hold of Him]—being, I say, *re-attached* to Him, we

---

superstitio, because *religio* was a virtue, *superstitio* a vice," citing Cicero, *De Inventione*, II.165; *De Natura Deorum*, I.117-18.

[82] William Connolly, *Why I Am Not a Secularist* (Minneapolis: University of Minnesota Press, 1999), chap. 1.

[83] For a discussion of this theme from a Christian point of view, see John Milbank, "Shari'a and the True Basis of Group Rights: Islam, the West and Liberalism," in *Shari'a in the West*, ed. Rex Ahdar and Nicholas Aroney (Oxford University Press, 2010), 135, at 138-39.

[84] Jonathan Fox, *Thou Shalt Have No Other Gods before Me: Why Governments Discriminate against Religious Minorities* (Cambridge: Cambridge University Press, 2020), 4, 162, 230, 237.

[85] Augustine, *City of God*, X.3.

[86] Ibid.

tend towards Him by love, that we may rest in Him, and find our blessedness by attaining that end.)[87]

This passage brings into focus the one central point on which Augustine rejected Plato's teaching: the human soul, at least in its fallen condition, is *not* naturally moved toward the good.[88] The fundamental problem of human nature is not a deficiency of the mind; rather, it is a defect of the will. The underlying disorder is an inclination to self-justification; a tendency to judge others more harshly than we judge ourselves;[89] to see the small speck in our neighbor's eye, while ignoring the plank in our own.[90] Augustine believed that human pride is our fundamental problem, and that humility must be the first and essential step toward our moral improvement. As Alasdair MacIntyre explained, it is only through a "transformation of the will from a state of pride to one of humility that the intelligence can be rightly directed." For the will "is more fundamental than intelligence and thinking undirected by a will informed by humility will always be apt to go astray."[91]

Augustine offered a striking image of this problem when he wrote of "Pleasure," sitting "like a voluptuous queen on a royal throne," with all the virtues arrayed around her as her attendant handmaidens, ready to do whatever she might command.[92] The image suggests that we might adopt certain virtuous practices—for example, by being wise, moderate, and fair in our dealings with other people—but not out of the goodness of our heart, nor even for the good of those people, but only as means of satisfying our selfish desires. Augustine points out that human pride and the desire for glory work the same way. These motivate us not to do good for its own sake but only to do good—or more precisely, to *appear* to do good—so that others will think well of us, and we will get more out of them. In this way, human pride is the deepest root of our problems, for it infects us even at our very best moments when we appear to be doing good. But because the desire for glory and honor only motivates us to appear to be good, it doesn't motivate us to do what is right when no one is looking, when no one sees, or when we can get away with it. And herein lies the seed of all our problems.

---

[87] Augustine, *City of God*, trans. Marcus Dods, bk. 10, chap. 3 (emphasis added). Source: Philip Schaff, ed., *Nicene and Post-Nicene Fathers, First Series*, vol. 2 (Buffalo, N.Y.: Christian Literature Publishing Co, 1887).

[88] Alasdair MacIntyre, *Three Rival Versions of Moral Inquiry: Encyclopaedia, Genealogy, and Tradition* (London: Duckworth, 1990), 84.

[89] Romans 2:1.

[90] Matthew 7:3.

[91] MacIntyre, *Three Rival Versions of Moral Inquiry*, 91.

[92] Augustine, *City of God*, bk. 5, chap. 20.

St. Basil of Caesarea put it this way:

> To praise virtue in public with brilliant words and with long drawn out speeches, while in private preferring pleasures to temperance, and self-interest to justice, finds an analogy on the stage, for the players frequently appear as kings and rulers, although they are neither. ... [E]very man is divided against himself who does not make his life conform to his words. ... Such a man will seek the appearance of virtue rather than the reality. But to seem to be good when one is not so, is, if we are to respect the opinion of Plato at all, the very height of injustice.[93]

This is a disturbing teaching. But it is the teaching of religion, best understood. Religion in this sense goes further than education, because it forces us to ask deep questions about our motivations. It forces us to self-examination. And it challenges us to confess and to repent—not just to confess the truth about our outward actions and behaviors, but to repent of our darkest inward thoughts and desires. It sets before us a model not of self-justification and self-rationalization, but of candid acknowledgement of our failures.[94] And it presses us to admit that we are in need of forgiveness, and that we need to forgive one another.[95]

Conclusion

Religion is more, therefore, than mere education, law, and economics. Education without religion can only inform the mind and train the hand; it cannot convert the soul. Law without religion can only require outward conformity and punish when there is disobedience; it cannot redirect the heart. Economics without religion provides the necessities of life, but does not give us the good life. Law, education, and economics therefore need to leave room for religion, so that religion can do what it alone is capable of: softening the heart and redirecting the will. An education system that recognizes this will leave room for religion. Public schools will allow religious education to occur on their premises so that the children can, with their parents' consent, learn about the kind of self-examination of which Augustine and Socrates taught. A legal system that recognizes this will also leave room for religious schools to operate according to their religious convictions. The law will acknowledge the freedom of private schools to be religious.

---

[93] St. Basil the Great, "Address to Young Men on the Reading of Greek Literature," in *Renewing the Mind*, ed. Ryan N. S. Topping (Washington, D.C.: Catholic University of America Press, 2015), 107, at 112.
[94] Luke 18:9–14.
[95] Matthew 18:21–35.

This does not mean that there are not important roles for economics, law, and education alongside religion. But if we rely only on laws, education, and economics, how will our people be motivated to obey and act selflessly when disaster strikes? Economics is needed to provide the material resources required for life, health, and the pursuit of the good life. Law is needed to address the bad in us all, and to point us to justice. Education is needed to inform our minds with truths and train our hands for useful work. But more is needed. Religion, properly understood, is what motivates and empowers people to acts that are not only prudentially wise and minimally right, but also heroic and supererogatory.

The fifth-century desert father and Coptic monk Abba Poemen put it best, when he said that it is more important that a teacher be an example to his students, rather than merely instruct them with words and exercises. "[B]e their example [*tupos*]," he said, "not their legislator [*nomothetes*]."[96] In this model of education—in this deeply religious model of education—the role of the teacher is first to be an example or model of character and behavior, and only secondarily someone who is knowledgeable, learned, and an enforcer of rules.[97] Religious education is concerned with something deeper and ultimately more important than knowledge of facts and development of skills. It is about the formation of character, and it recognizes, with Augustine, that a truly good character depends ultimately on our inner motives and the inclination of our wills.

We need a social imaginary that admits the proper roles of economics, law, education, *and* religion.

---

[96] Lillian Larsen and Samuel Rubenson, *Monastic Education in Late Antiquity: The Transformation of Classical Paideia* (Cambridge: Cambridge University Press, 2018), 23.

[97] Ibid., 21.

Social Systems, Moral Individualism, and Education

Sergio Belardinelli

The relationship between social systems and moral individualism is undoubtedly ambiguous. Sociologically speaking, the processes of differentiation and individualization go hand in hand, while taking on different and unpredictable configurations and relationships. However, it is also true that they seem disconnected from each other in the historical moment we are going through. Social systems operate according to systemic codes, while individuals operate according to distinct codes. The former are not interested in the strictly human consequences of their work, nor the latter in the social consequences of theirs. Impressionistically, we could say that our freedom of choice seems primarily concerned with the satisfaction of our individual tastes, interests, or desires, rather than with affecting the functioning of various social systems or with the influence that these various social systems exert on our choices. In fact, when we talk about moral individualism, we rarely refer to the influence exerted on our moral choices by different social systems, such as religion, school, politics, economy, or technology. This phenomenon is rightly emphasized in Michael Welker's project, of which this volume is one part.

As soon as I began to reflect on the relationship of social systems, morals, and education, I realized that I could not avoid thinking about Niklas Luhmann (a disturbing guest at this point). From Luhmann's point of view, as is well known, our problems, the problems discussed in this volume, are problems that modernity produces and solves by virtue of functional differentiation. As for our concerns about the relationship that the different social systems (politics, economics, law, science, education, health care, etc.) have with each other or with moral values and individuals, they appear completely inappropriate. In fact, in Luhmann's opinion, every social system functions in a self-referential way, according to a specific code, which differentiates it from its environment. System/environment is the fundamental distinction. There is no relationship between systems. Whether we are talking about social systems or individual systems (for Luhmann, individuals are also systems), each system always and only refers to an environment, not to other systems. Whatever system you may be talking about, everything else is in its environment. Any social system also has individuals in its environment, just as every individual, as a system, has different social systems in its environment. This is a radical solution to the traditional problem of the relationship between the individual and society. "Man is no longer the measure of society," says Luhmann.[1] Consequently, I repeat, if he were right, our problems would be, at the very least, ill-posed problems.

I'm sure, however, that Luhmann is wrong. But since I have the feeling that our society has really become a society where the different social systems now function as if humanity did not exist, Michael Welker's project appears to me to be even more important. Very briefly, in my opinion it expresses, among other things, the urgency to escape the colonization of the entire social universe by a systemic-functionalist logic and to work instead for a reconciliation between the human and the social. In other words, it is a matter of recovering the human dimension both within each system (it is unthinkable that the economy is only a logic of profit, or that politics is only power), and with regard to society as a whole. Anything but systemic self-referentiality.

This reconciliation between the human and the social is even more important if we consider that the process of functional differentiation of society goes hand in hand with an increasingly radical individualization of the individual. Society functions according to codes that operate behind individuals, and the latter fold more and more into themselves, with the risk that the moral autonomy of each person is interpreted in an emotional way, looking exclusively at individual rights, but neglecting the responsibilities and duties that each of us has toward others. It is a bit as if by dint of insisting on our autonomy and our freedom—mainly understood as emancipation from any social bonds—a certain modern individualism has been paradoxically satisfied: we have conquered a whole series of freedoms that have certainly emancipated us from family, religious, and cultural bonds, but society and social systems function more and more as if individuals did not exist. Hence the singular and worrying symmetry between those who think that the different social systems must follow an exclusively functional/self-referential logic and those who think that individual freedom must be understood as narcissistic/self-referential freedom to do what we like. In other words, the real problem is not so much the "cacophony" of moral, political, or aesthetic points of view that distinguishes our society. Rather, the problem lies in the fact that everyone's sacrosanct right to see things as they like does not always correspond with what Michael Welker rightly defines as the other "aspect" of the issue, namely, the fact that our freedom must always deal with a logic—that of different social systems—which can promote freedom but can also inhibit it. Like it or not, many individual choices that are decisive for the quality of our life depend precisely on the functioning of different social systems. Just

---

[1] Niklas Lumann, *Social Systems* (Stanford, Calif.: Stanford University Press, 1995), 213.

think of how important schools and education are, or politics, economics, and technology. On the other hand, the fact that human life is always conditioned by social context does not mean that it is determined by this context, as if human freedom is simply an illusion.

From a theoretical point of view, we want essentially to avoid both the individualistic and the collectivist drift and to focus instead on a perspective that accentuates the continuous, inevitable interaction between the individual and the system and that is able in some way to indicate a realistic conciliation.[2] In this regard, I believe that the conception of the European man—his uniqueness and dignity, his outward projection, his "social" being, but also his irreducibility to the social and biological conditions of his existence—all this could still constitute a reliable compass to guide us in the complexity of the time in which we are given to live. Others and society are not necessarily a "hell," an unbearable limit to our freedom; indeed, they are the condition that makes freedom possible, that makes an authentic realization of ourselves possible. By holding firm the concept of the person, as a synthetic point of the unrepeatable uniqueness and, at the same time, of the constitutive relationality of each of us and of the society in which we are immersed, it follows that the problem of the individual/society relationship is no longer conceivable, either in the way of a certain individualism, according to which only individuals exist and society is a pure abstraction, or in the way of a certain organicism of the Marxist or Durkheimian type, according to which only social relations are truly real (while individuals are abstract), or in the way of systemic sociology, according to which the individual and society are in a system/environment relationship. Michael Welker's project leads us to look at this problem with the awareness that the individual and society are distinct, but also constantly permeating each other. Neither of the two terms can replace the other, but both are destined, with different variations, to be one within the other. In short, even the functional mechanisms of society must be reflexively traced back to human needs.

I am obviously well aware that one of the most sociologically relevant problems of modernity is represented by the difficulty in adequately addressing the problem of the human in the social. From this point of view, functionalism represents a drastic reduction of complexity and, as such, perhaps the most demanding challenge of our days. But, as Andreas Glaeser's "ethical conundrum" shows, the ethical, and therefore human, dimension must be cultivated not only

---

[2] This reference to realism is important, especially if we consider the simplifications typical of populisms widespread in today's Western political culture. In fact, realism invites us to never lose sight of reality and its complexity, and, as such, it also represents a precious moral instance, a warning not to simplify reality only to obtain consent (See Angelo Panebianco and Sergio Belardinelli, *All'alba di un nuovo mondo* [Bologna: Il Mulino, 2019]).

in terms of the values we care about or the personal consequences that arise from our actions, but also in view of the institution-forming effects of our activities.[3] What I mean is that the one who acts is both inside and outside the social system—not in the systemic sense that considers the actor and the social system in a system/environment relationship, and therefore closed to each other, but in the sense of a continuous interaction between them. In a complex society like ours, the different institutional components are connected to each other, exert a strong and continuous influence on individuals and on different social groups; the latter, in turn, interact, compete, exchange "goods" in a very broad sense, stipulate contracts, try to make the weight of their interests felt on the institutions. Considering that all societies (at least in the West) now tend to take on this complex and differentiated aspect, we need to find a compass that allows us, on one hand, to safeguard the contingency and complexity of the world in which we live (there are no reasons, at least in my opinion, to have nostalgia for the simple societies of the past), and, on the other hand, to maintain the firm distinction between what is right and what is not, between what promotes human freedom and dignity and what instead it inhibits them. There is a normative criterion for our actions, our institutions, and social relations in general, which is given, in very simple terms, by their "human quality." In this sense, again in very simple terms, we can say that there are just actions and unjust actions, just institutions and institutions that are unjust or less just. Wherever human beings are at stake, descriptive and normative aspects come into play. We cannot seriously reflect on society if we lose sight of the subject that is always involved in it. In the words of Edgar Morin, it could also be said that we really need a "restoration of the subject."[4] If it is true that we live in a complex society, whose characteristic features are differentiation, individualization, and, therefore, a widespread pluralism both at the level of social institutions and at the level of the moral convictions of individuals, then I believe that precisely in the human quality of our actions and our institutions resides the idea of a "good" that is compatible with that pluralism. Does what I do promote or inhibit the dignity and freedom of others? Does this institution promote or inhibit the dignity and freedom of citizens? These are the questions we should ask ourselves if we are interested in the human quality, the good, of our individual and social life.

These are questions that do not express a substantial, predefined notion of the good, or a "general will" to which the order of society must be conformed a priori; rather, they express a moral requirement (the primacy of the person and his immeasurable dignity), which, always having to measure itself with concrete reality, remains, so to speak, open to a plurality of outcomes and, as such, generative of an ethos that our liberal and democratic societies urgently need, es-

---

[3] See Chapter 2 in this volume.
[4] See Edgar Morin and Sami Nair, *Une politique de civilisation* (Paris: Arlea, 1997).

pecially if they want to protect themselves from both constructivist and individualistic drifts. Within this ethos, the synthesis of individual interests and social interests, a certain sense of belonging—let us say, solidarity—appears not as a simple rhetorical-moralistic compensation for some unpleasant side effects of modern capitalist society (the "political economy" of society in which we live), but rather as a propulsive element of a human social order which, as the effect of innumerable and unpredictable interactions, is for the most part spontaneous and unintentional.

The Limits of Human Rationality

Keeping in view the centrality of the subject and his continuous interaction with the rest of society helps us not to expect too much from our ability to determine or control the social context within which we move. Too often, as we face the problems of our society, including the question whether we as individuals can affect the social systems around us that deeply affect our individual freedom, we get carried away by the desire to radically change the functioning and course of those systems, simply by virtue of our conviction that it is right to do so. Unfortunately, this conviction is not enough. We can certainly change some things, but, I repeat, none of us are in total control of the complexity of the situations in which we act individually and socially. This is not only because there are so-called unintended consequences of our actions, but also because our rational resources are limited. Not only is our individual rationality limited, but we are not monads—we are social individuals. To our limits as individuals are therefore added those of social systems, limited external resources, and the way in which information flows on a social level. In this regard, new digital technologies, algorithms, and big data can raise the suspicion that we are preparing to live in an increasingly controlled world, but this is not the case. Both those who are enthusiastic about digital technology and those who are afraid of it basically make the same mistake, which is to neglect the role of the unexpected and the uncertainty of our individual and social lives.

I could express the same concept by saying that the intentional character of human actions, human freedom, its "unintended consequences," as well as the limits of human knowledge are what, on one hand, nourish the confidence that no social condition is immutable and, on the other, make the future always uncertain, unpredictable. I believe this is no less true today, in the era of big data and artificial intelligence. There are no algorithms for predicting the future; the more human freedom is at stake and the more we are aware of the limits of our knowledge of that world we call society, the more the algorithms keep pace. They can be very useful, of course, but most of the time to understand social reality we need imagination—let's say wisdom, *phronesis*, as the Greeks called it.

There is no algorithm to manage uncertainty.[5] There are algorithms to manage risks; algorithms that become more and more effective in updating their forecasts as available information increases. But uncertainty and risk are not the same thing. As Frank Hyneman Knight showed over a hundred years ago,

> Uncertainty must be taken in a sense radically distinct from the familiar notion of risk, from which it has never been properly separated. ... The essential fact is that "risk" means in some cases a quantity susceptible of measurement, which at other times it is something distinctly not of the character; and there are far-reaching and crucial differences in the bearings of the phenomenon depending on which of the two is really present and operating. ... It will appear that a *measurable* uncertainty, or "risk" proper, as we shall use the term, is so far different from an *unmeasurable* one that it is not in effect an uncertainty.[6]

In sum, uncertainty escapes our calculations—it is incalculable—but risk can be calculated. If we look to the future, the world of uncertainty is infinitely wider than that of risks.

Algorithms, I repeat it, are based on risk, not uncertainty. In the situation in which we live today, our technological civilization has undoubtedly transformed and continues to transform into risks a myriad of situations that until yesterday belonged to the world of uncertainty. I do not exclude that there are algorithms that allow you to make precise predictions in different fields. Weather forecasts, for example, are making extraordinary progress; they make it possible to establish with almost absolute precision (almost!) whether, in a Formula 1 Grand Prix, it is best for a Ferrari or Mercedes to start with rain tires or dry ones. But while substantial resources are invested in this regard, it is not possible to predict with the same precision what the value of the euro on the dollar will be in ten months. If this were possible, economists would be the richest people in the world.

I am well aware that artificial intelligence and its ability to exploit the enormous amount of data available are designing entirely new scenarios in this regard. The increasingly refined technological use of data by certain economic, political, and other entities suggests that it is possible to predict the behavior of individuals in terms of consumption, electoral preferences, and the like. However, I believe that the Hayekian paradigm about the impossibility for us to

---

[5] See Riccardo Viale and Gerd Gigerenzer, *Routledge Handbook of Bounded Rationality* (London: Routledge, 2021).

[6] Frank Hyneman Knight, *Risk, Uncertainty and Profit* (New York: Houghton Mifflin, 1921), 19–20.

know all the variables of all the possible events that can occur in society still remains valid. At least I hope so, since, as von Hayek teaches, if people were capable of this kind of knowledge, there would be nothing more to be done for our freedom.[7]

What I mean is that, at least as long as there are human beings, we will always have to deal with the unpredictable and the uncertain, and although our knowledge is immeasurable and our calculation tools are very powerful, we will never succeed in keeping everything under control, in knowing in advance all the consequences of our actions. Therefore, not only must we accept the limits of our knowledge and our actions, but we must also refrain from claiming to build a society in the same way we build a car. Society—we can never stress enough—is never the intentional product of our choices, nor can it be configured as the outcome of a human design. Only a fraction of what historically happens depends on our will. Wanting to become masters of history is only a sign of fanaticism, especially in a complex society like ours.

Yet uncertainty and risks are viewed with suspicion, as if everything is reducible to something under our control. In this regard, I would like to recall a further aspect that is usually not adequately thematized when it comes to the society of risks: today's society is risky above all because an increasing number of events depend on our choices, our power, and our freedom. In societies of the past, things were different. Life was then more or less uncertain, as ours is, but it was much less risky; very little of what happened could be attributed to human choices. In short, there is a huge difference between dying of pneumonia because there are no remedies and dying of pneumonia because you have decided not to take penicillin, or because the doctor thought it was a trivial flu. In the first case, our ancestors could only curse God or adverse fate; instead, we can impute our fate to ourselves or to the doctor. It is precisely this new constellation, the result of ever new knowledge, of ever new possibilities of technically dominating the world, that generates the society of risks. Risks grow because our knowledge and freedom grow in some way.

Curiously, however, the growing control that we have gradually acquired over reality has also increased our spasmodic desire for security. We like comfort, and at least in words we also like freedom, but we don't like the uncertainty that freedom always carries with it. We thus experience a sort of schizophrenia, which, on a sociocultural and political level, in the long run, could also produce very serious damage. Above all, it seems to me that uncertainty and insecurity are becoming more and more unbearable; that is, we tend to reject what is most obvious and evident in the human condition. Yesterday, for example, we would have considered a fatal disease or an earthquake as tragedies, for which to blame God, nature, or fate. Today we consider them above all as events attributable to

---

[7] See F. A. Hayek, *The Road to Serfdom* (London: Taylor and Francis, 2014).

human actors: to the doctor who was unable to cure us, to the politician who has not invested more resources in the health system, or who has allowed houses to be built without respecting antiseismic regulations, or to those who did not intervene promptly with help, and so on. This is certainly understandable, given the means we have to deal with both diseases and earthquakes. But it is also true that, by dint of feeding security expectations, the people and institutions that should satisfy those expectations are overloaded with a task that, in a structurally uncertain and risky society, they will never be able to fulfill entirely. Some may even think of promising security in exchange for freedom.

In many ways it is even curious that a society like ours, in which there is so much talk of freedom, is so unwilling to accept the risks and uncertainties it entails. Whether we are talking about individual and social rights, immigration, or the economy, just to give a few examples, what matters above all seems to be security. It is security that is required of the state, which in this way is overloaded with often impossible tasks. The state, however, is happy to take on these tasks, as they greatly increase its power and its claim to be able to control every area of our social and individual life. As I have tried to explain, this is an impossible claim, which often produces, with the consent of the citizens, very serious individual, social, and cultural damage, especially in terms of freedom and responsibility. The result is a sort of populist simplification of the complexity in which we are immersed, countering which requires a real intellectual and moral catharsis, capable of holding together in citizens the love for freedom and the duty of responsibility and of justice, without the expectation that society responds to our designs.

I come to the last point: education.

Education in a Complex Society

Putting together what I said at the beginning about the dense web in which individuals, social systems, and organizations of various kinds find themselves today and the widespread desire to simplify this complexity in the name of often impossible certainties, what should be the purpose of education in such a complex society?

I realize that for our culture, such a question may appear too demanding and even provocative. It is not easy to educate for freedom, responsibility, justice, and uncertainty in a context that wants to be ethically neutral, which is the dominant ethical stance in contemporary Western culture, where, as we know, there are different concepts of "good." Perhaps it is also because of this difficulty that we have turned to educational projects aimed mostly at the needs of the world of work and society in general. But this functionalization of education seems to me too limited and, moreover, not necessarily effective for the goals it aims to achieve.

Let me explain myself briefly. The fact that we live in a social context that aspires to be ethically neutral does not mean that education therefore loses its normative character. Like it or not, an educational process is always a relationship in which someone (the teacher) takes on the responsibility of teaching another (the student) something that is considered good. And while this good certainly lies in the theoretical and practical disciplines that are taught, it also lies in those values—Alasdair MacIntyre would say in those virtues—that are intrinsic to every educational practice: knowledge, honesty, discipline, respect, freedom, solidarity—in short, a certain moral ideal, let's say a certain ideal of humanity.[8]

With this ideal weakened, the educational institutions of Western countries have begun to navigate by sight, without a precise route or a social goal to achieve other than to facilitate entry into the world of work. This is an appreciable goal, of course. But it is too little, and it is not always achieved. The disciplines of study have multiplied, and at the same time there is a widespread loss of the sense of study itself. It is said that children, while studying, must above all have fun, and then we are surprised that they prefer other amusements to school. There is a lot of talk, and rightly so, about a sort of information orgy, in which all of us are immersed, but the school, instead of providing the right tools to extricate ourselves from this orgy, seems to make it a simple sounding board. In the name of a misunderstood pluralism, the substantial issues connected to the values, beliefs, cultural traditions of peoples are avoided, and then we are surprised that young people do not become more open to the "other," but simply more disoriented, more uprooted, and therefore more exposed to the risk of new fanaticisms. The introduction of new multimedia technologies is often presented as the new frontier of education, but, in reality, they only seem to accentuate the disorientation that pervades our educational systems, which are increasingly marked by a worrying superficiality. In short, everything seems to take the form of a sort of alibi to evade the crucial question: what does it mean to educate?

We have forgotten the only real purpose of every educational practice: to help the new generations find its way, feel at home in the world we all live in, and simply become what we are: people, free people, whose unrepeatable uniqueness is rooted in a network of foundational relationships that also encompasses our duties and responsibilities. As Hannah Arendt said, "exactly for the sake of what is new and revolutionary in every child, education must be conservative."[9] Indeed, sooner or later, for each of us comes the time when we say

---

[8] See Alasdair MacIntyre, *After Virtue: A Study in Moral Theory* (Notre Dame, Ind.: University of Notre Dame Press, 1981).

[9] Hannah Arendt, *Between Past and Future* (London: Penguin, 2006), 189.

goodbye to our parents and our teachers and begin to walk alone, to do our own thing. But the way in which this happens, the energy and autonomy that will characterize our journey, and even our desire to make the world a better place, all this will depend largely on how much we feel at home in this world, on how much we feel "reconciled" with it, despite its resistance to our desires.

Fostering this reconciliation is perhaps the most difficult and important task of any educator. We come into this world without having had the choice, and sometimes this happens in families or social or natural settings that do not help us form the view that life is a gift: if we are unloved, abused, or humiliated, or born into a struggle against a hostile natural environment. For psychoanalysis, birth is even viewed as a trauma, a rupture, a loss. So why is all of this overlooked in educational practice? How is it possible that we do not view reality, in its sometimes tragic irreducibility, or resistance to our desires, as the true frame of reference for every educational relationship, and for freedom itself?

Realism and freedom are inseparable bedfellows, more or less happily partnered, but nevertheless forced to be together. If our educational practices seem to care very little about either one or the other, it is only because we love to talk about freedom, especially the freedom to do what we like, but we are much less inclined to face up to the responsibilities and hard work that it entails, not to mention the risks.

The greater freedom we all enjoy, the great tools of domination we have, the old and new media, the network, big data, all would seem to suggest a turning point in terms of awareness of the stakes involved in education. By contrast, instead of focusing on educating young people into the sense of reality, its hardness, its unpredictability, as well as its beauty and its opportunities, we are content with providing information, or some form of professionalizing knowledge, which often does not even respond to the functional needs of the society in which we live. We should teach how to use languages for more effective communication, to translate different points of view, to identify positive potentials in everything that is clearly in transformation, making our students feel an active part of the world we all inhabit. We should educate about uncertainty and complexity, given that a significant percentage of children who enter school today will work at jobs that have not yet been invented. We should get them used to the contamination of knowledge, to the combination of science and ethics, with the hope of having professional leaders capable of interpreting reality in a competent, critical, and responsible way. But, with very rare exceptions, none of this happens.

As Christopher Lasch denounced more than forty years ago, we have become addicted to the idea that "nobody should be asked to learn anything difficult."¹⁰ This is why, by dismissing as "inherently elitist"¹¹ any educational proposal focused on quality, we lose the very meaning of education. Instead of directing the students' attention to what, at first, they may perhaps struggle to understand, but whose charm they could also grasp, we prefer to resort, except in very rare privileged cases, to simplification, leveling, watering down—that is, to attitudes that George Steiner, in a memorable page of his intellectual autobiography, defines not by chance as "criminal," and behind which he sees a substantial contempt for "the capacities unbeknown within ourselves," a "vulgar condescension: towards all those judged a priori to be incapable of better things."¹² In short, there seems to be no more room for education (the famous *Bildung*), that is, for that process through which, with commitment and rigor, individuals critically assimilate a certain universe of values in all the disciplines they study: from arithmetic to grammar, from history to geography, from philosophy to religion. To draw again from Christopher Lasch, any attempt to bring someone closer to a certain horizon of values today risks being considered "an infringement on his freedom of choice."¹³ But precisely if we have this freedom of choice at heart, we need to reverse course.¹⁴

In his chapter in this volume, Rüdiger Bittner asks whether our capitalist model and liberal culture will be able to last much longer. I hope so, but I believe that a lot will depend on how much we invest in education. Speaking of school, it is not a question of finalizing education for religious, political, moral, or professional purposes, at least not directly. Rather, it is about teaching grammar, mathematics, and history very seriously in a way that also helps young people to become autonomous and free people. Unlike closed societies, where educating is equivalent to a sort of automatism, such that those who come after have no choice but to follow in all respects in the footsteps of those who preceded them, open societies are marked by a plurality of options not only on the political level but also on other levels, from the aesthetic to the ethical and the religious. Hence, the tendency to continuously measure oneself against one's own tradition, to have a critical relationship with it, so to speak. This makes educational processes more difficult, less obvious, but for this very reason much more important, in order to avoid, on one hand, the tradition becoming oppressive and, on the other hand, criticism of the tradition becoming destructive in some way, that is, a simple process of negation or emancipation from the tradition itself.

---

10   Christopher Lasch, "Mass Culture Reconsidered," *Democracy* 1, no. 4 (Oct. 1981): 7–22, at 14.
11   Ibid., 13.
12   George Steiner, *Errata: An Examined Life* (New Haven: Yale University Press, 1998), 50.
13   Lasch, "Mass Culture Reconsidered," 14.
14   See Sergio Belardinelli, *La comunità liberale. La libertà, il bene comune e la religione nelle società compesse* (Rome: Studium, 1999).

Instead, we must unfortunately note that, with rare exceptions, schooling seems to have abdicated its critical and formative function. On the other hand, how is it possible to educate in a society that is no longer capable of recognizing the reasons why it is necessary to educate?

In our schools, we speak a lot of imaginative formulas aimed at favoring teaching methods over content, skills over knowledge, and neutrality as the main moral value. We do so because we would like a school more accessible to young people, but instead of promoting their critical thinking, we are only creating themes for their use and consumption. No difficulty, no effort, it all has to be easy and fun. This is a real cognitive standardization that openly contrasts with critical thinking. We are shaping servants, not autonomous and aware citizens.

As for our universities, my belief is that in the coming years it will be precisely those students who have had an education capable of going beyond the rather narrow scope of professional knowledge who will have the best chance of successfully entering the so-called job market. Truth be told, I would make compulsory in all degree courses, even in the more technical ones, a teaching module on the immeasurable function of what has no function, a teaching module that, by making something well known, also ignites passion for truth, beauty, the comparison of ideas, without which there is no, and there cannot be, a university in the proper sense.

Our university system, as is well known, seems to favor other dimensions. But the fact that, at least in principle, it also allows courses of this type to be activated or that lessons are given in this spirit could be proof that even today, the spirit of searching for truth and critical passion—which have always been at the basis of the idea of the university—has not completely disappeared. It is therefore a question of not giving up. The university should take some risks in terms of high-profile proposals and politics, but students as well, as they pay taxes, should support such proposals, all with the confident hope that the market will also be able to reward and benefit from them.

Rüdiger Bittner certainly has some good reason to say that it "is mere theory that the course of people's lives only depends on how well they do, thanks to the education they received, on the various markets they enter. In fact, the rich have found means to give their offspring a hefty advantage on markets, mainly by preserving the right of bequest, which originating in a precapitalist economy and indeed conflicting with capitalist principles, is nevertheless guaranteed in most capitalist countries."[15]

I agree with him about the right of bequest. However, it is not by chance that today education is one of the main tools used by the rich to keep their privileges. The most prestigious schools and universities in the world are accessed mostly

---

[15] See "Our Political Economy's Moral Teaching," herein.

by virtue of the money that families have to pay first for the preparation of the entrance tests and then for the enrollment fees. And given that in an open society like ours, success depends to a large extent, although not exclusively, on education and on equipment we are endowed with to compete and win in the global economy (and this is true for both rich and poor people), it is worth addressing the problem seriously. I believe that we need an education that is certainly attentive to the professional figures required from time to time by the job market, but also capable of arousing a passion for truth, freedom, beauty, the comparison of ideas, respect for all, and human solidarity. In this way, perhaps even certain perverse effects of what Michael Sandel called "the tyranny of merit"[16] could be neutralized. Instead of arrogance, students who reach the top may feel their privilege as something that in some way must be balanced and shared, even with those who have not made it, perhaps also mitigating their sense of frustration in this way. Governments, for their part, should ensure that everyone has the same opportunities to access education, which, again, is the main determinant of success that is not simply economic but also human and, therefore, political and civil.

The moral of what I have been saying so far is quite simple and could be summarized as follows: Contrary to popular belief, liberal democracies and the pluralism that distinguishes them need culture and high culture, not simply to cultivate the tastes or "feelings" of the voting public. I cannot delve deeper into it here, but I believe that the main causes of the growing spread of the so-called cancel culture and the hysterical use of the theme of identity that its protagonists make of it are mainly to be found precisely in the weakening of culture. Otherwise, we would not understand as a priori legitimate the sinister presumption of any expression of will that has made its way into the public debate and above all on social media. Feeling discriminated against, offended, or under attack is enough to put into action the most incredible strategies of intimidation and cancellation, regardless of the rational arguments put forward. Nor would the ostentation of one's tastes (ethical, aesthetic, or cultural) be understood as the affirmation of an identity that must always and in any case have public recognition. A world as a will without truth is hardly compatible with the development of freedom and political institutions worthy of the name.[17]

Yet we must not become depressed. It is true that in the university, "high"[18] education linked to research is becoming a simple option, that is, something that

---

[16] See Michael Sandel, *The Tyranny of Merit: What's Become of the Common Good?* (New York: Farrar, Straus, and Giroux, 2020).

[17] See Sergio Belardinelli, "Cancel Culture: l'identità come volontà senza verità," *Paradoxa* 2 (2022): 25–37.

[18] I am obviously not talking about the education offered by the most prestigious universities, thanks above all to the money required to access them. On this point, I fully agree

can be cultivated in more or less large niches, but which no longer represents the basic inspiration of the university as such. Considering that in most cases the so-called vocational paths do not seem to have particularly satisfactory employment opportunities, I believe that by relaunching a high-level education, we will at worst have more trained and flexible brains, more open also toward others, and perhaps even more capable of success in the economy. It is therefore up to those who believe in taking up the challenge. And it seems to me that, despite all the difficulties, the conditions to do so exist.

---

with Michael Sandel. If it is true that the deepest inequalities of our society emerge precisely at the educational level, these universities seem to be among the main generators of inequalities.

Why Is the Conversation between Theologians and Economists So Difficult?

Paul Oslington

Introduction

The Heidelberg consultation that led to this volume on political economy was a welcome opportunity to highlight the important place of political economy[1] in contemporary culture and its connection to other spheres of culture, such as education, law, and theology. The connection with theology is particularly important, because economics has replaced theology as the master discourse of public policy, especially in the Anglosphere. Discussions of education policy, health policy, and other areas of policy tend today to be conducted in economic language with economic criteria for value.

The relationship between the academic discipline of economics and other disciplines is a question underlying many of the chapters in this volume.[2] My

---

[1] Political economy was the name of the discipline that took shape in Europe in the eighteenth and nineteenth centuries, but since the late nineteenth century it has been known as economics. There have been some recent attempts to revive the old name, political economy—for instance, by economists who, since the 1970 s, have been developing an economics of politics, commonly known as public-choice theory. Another attempt has been the radical political economy movement beginning in the late 1960 s, which has won a place in many universities as an alternative to mainstream economics. Further discussion may be found in Peter Groenewegen, "Political Economy and Economics," in *The New Palgrave: A Dictionary of Economics*, ed. J. Eatwell, M. Milgate, and P. Newman (London: Macmillan, 1987). In this chapter I use "economics" for the contemporary mainstream discipline, and "political economy" for the eighteenth- and nineteenth-century discipline.

[2] The relationship between the disciplines is even more important for this volume about political economy than for the earlier volume in the series about markets, to which I contributed: Jürgen von Hagen, Michael Welker, John Witte Jr., and Stephen Pickard, eds., *The Impact of the Market on Character Formation, Ethical Education, and the Communi-*

contribution in this chapter will be to consider the current state of the conversation between economics and theology, and why it is such a difficult conversation. Scope will be confined to Christian theology, because that is the tradition I know best, but there have been many Islamic engagements with economics in recent decades,[3] a few by Jewish scholars,[4] and an increasing number of Buddhist and other religious engagements with economics.[5]

This chapter offers a brief survey of the current state of the conversation between theologians and economists, then considers various explanations for why fruitful dialogue is so rare, and why it tends to go badly when it does happen. While many of the explanations have an element of truth, I believe that they underplay the role of incentives in the academic disciplines, so I will supplement these with a new explanation inspired by the work of Nobel laureate George Akerlof on market failure in situations of imperfect and asymmetric information. Markets for interdisciplinary[6] research on economics and theology seem to me to work just like Akerlof's famous "lemons" model of the market for used cars.

Conversations between Theologians and Economists

The first task of this chapter is to briefly survey the current state of the conversation. Some of the attempts at dialogue have been initiated by theologians (including Christian ethicists, public theologians, and political theologians), a

---

cation of Values in Late Modern Pluralistic Societies (Leipzig: Evangelische Verlagsanstalt, 2020).

[3] Timur Kuran, *Islam and Mammon: Critical Perspectives on the Economic Agenda of Islamism* (Princeton: Princeton University Press, 2004). I once considered a PhD on Islamic economics, and my first academic publication was on that topic, much to the frustration of the supervisor of the PhD thesis on international trade theory that I had by then enrolled in. This paper was Paul Oslington, "Economic Thought and Religious Thought: Al Ghazali," *History of Political Economy* 27, no. 4 (1995): 775–80.

[4] Aaron Levine, ed., *The Oxford Handbook of Judaism and Economics* (New York: Oxford University Press, 2010).

[5] Clair Brown, *Buddhist Economics: An Enlightened Approach to the Dismal Science* (London: Bloomsbury, 2017).

[6] Throughout this chapter I use the term "interdisciplinary" to cover a wide range of interactions between disciplines, encompassing, for instance, both transdisciplinary ventures by a scholar and multidisciplinary projects. The distinctions are not crucial for my argument, and "interdisciplinary" is a convenient and widely recognized term. Distinctions between various types of interactions are discussed in Julie Thompson Klein, "A Taxonomy of Interdisciplinarity," in *The Oxford Handbook of Interdisciplinarity*, ed. Robert Frodeman, 15–30 (Oxford: Oxford University Press, 2010).

smaller number originate among economists, and some arise in the new interdisciplinary field of economics and theology. I will discuss a few examples that I believe illustrate the strengths and weaknesses of each part of the conversation, with no pretense of a comprehensive survey or full evaluation of the writers chosen as examples.[7] There are, of course, similar conversations between theologians and practitioners of other sciences,[8] especially human sciences like anthropology,[9] sociology,[10] and psychology.[11]

The Conversation in Theology

Although Alasdair MacIntyre identifies as a philosopher rather than a theologian, the vast influence of his work on Christian theologians and ethicists means that his engagement with economics deserves attention. His most substantial engagement with economics occurs in his most recent book, *Ethics in the Conflicts of Modernity*, though this builds on his earlier works *After Virtue, Whose*

---

[7] Several comprehensive surveys are available: Paul Oslington, ed., *The Oxford Handbook of Christianity and Economics* (Oxford: Oxford University Press, 2014); Paul Oslington, Paul S. Williams, and Mary Hirschfeld, eds., *Recent Developments in Economics and Religion*, International Library of Critical Writings in Economics (Cheltenham: Edward Elgar, 2018); Paul Oslington, ed., *Economics and Religion*, International Library of Critical Writings in Economics (Cheltenham: Edward Elgar, 2003); A. M. C. Waterman, "Economists on the Relation between Political Economy and Christian Theology: A Preliminary Survey," *International Journal of Social Economics* 14, no. 6 (1987): 46–68; William Schweiker and Charles Mathewes, eds., *Having: Property and Possession in Religious and Social Life* (Grand Rapids, MI: Eerdmans, 2004); and Devin Singh, "Economy and Modern Christian Thought," *Brill Research Perspectives in Theology* 4, no. 3 (2022): 1–109.

[8] Among the vast number of publications in recent decades on science and religion, I have found the work of John Hedley Brooke and Peter Harrison especially helpful. See, for instance, Peter Harrison, *The Territories of Science and Religion* (Chicago: University of Chicago Press, 2015), which is a revised version of his Gifford Lectures.

[9] For example, J. Derrick Lemons, ed., *Theologically Engaged Anthropology* (New York: Oxford University Press, 2018).

[10] For example, David Martin, *Reflections on Sociology and Theology* (Oxford: Clarendon, 1995); and with a different perspective, Christian Smith, *The Sacred Project of American Sociology* (New York: Oxford University Press, 2014).

[11] For example, Fraser Watts, *Theology and Psychology* (London: Ashgate, 2002); and idem, "Psychology and Theology," in *The Cambridge Companion to Science and Religion*, ed. Peter Harrison (Cambridge: Cambridge University Press, 2010).

Justice? Which Rationality?, and *Three Rival Versions of Moral Enquiry: Encyclopaedia, Genealogy, and Tradition.*[12]

The account of economics that MacIntyre offers in *Ethics in the Conflicts of Modernity* is problematic. He describes economists as "academic protagonists of capitalism" and writes:

> The history of capitalism is in no insignificant part a history of economists. Academic economists have to a remarkable extent educated successive generations to think about the economic order in ways that make it difficult to resist the destructive and inegalitarian tendencies inherent in that order. It was no accident that Marx took it that any effective critique of capitalism would be impossible without an effective critique of economists.[13]

This view is based on the brief account MacIntyre offers of the history of economics:

> Economics took on the form of an academic discipline in a number of European universities in the last decades of the nineteenth century. Its content was principally supplied by the work of equilibrium theorists in Austria, France, England, and elsewhere. The central claim advanced by those theorists and by their successors was and is that it is only through unregulated competition within free markets that scarce resources are allocated efficiently, so that prices express a matching of supply with demand and there is a movement toward a state of equilibrium in which each participant in market transactions fares as well as she or he can under conditions that are optimal for every other participant.[14]

Such an account is seriously misleading for the political economy that took shape in the eighteenth century through British writers such as Josiah Tucker, David Hume, and Adam Smith, Frenchmen such as Francois Quesnay and Turgot, the Neapolitan Antonio Genovese, and the German Cameralists. When MacIntyre writes about Adam Smith, he introduces a series of factual errors that seem to come from a mixture of prejudice and reliance on a strange sample of the secondary literature rather than reading Smith's texts in context. Adam

---

[12] Alasdair MacIntyre, *Ethics in the Conflicts of Modernity: An Essay on Desire, Practical Reasoning, and Narrative* (Cambridge: Cambridge University Press, 2016). I discuss MacIntyre's engagements with economics more fully in Paul Oslington, "Alasdair MacIntyre and Adam Smith on Markets, Virtues and Ends," *Business Ethics* (forthcoming); and Paul Oslington, "Is Alasdair Macintyre Right That Aristotelian-Thomist Natural Law Ethics Is Incompatible with Capitalism and Economics?" (manuscript).

[13] MacIntyre, *Ethics in the Conflicts of Modernity*, 105–06.

[14] Ibid., 101.

Smith's philosophy has much more in common with that of his fellow Scot than MacIntyre realizes, but MacIntyre seems blinded to this similarity by Marx's description of Smith as a "vulgar" political economist, as well as by the late twentieth-century mythology of Smith as an advocate of unbridled capitalism. MacIntyre's reference in the quotation above to equilibrium theorists seems to be to the economics of William Stanley Jevons in England, Léon Walras in French-speaking Switzerland, and Carl Menger in Austria in the 1870 s. But he seriously misunderstands their work, as there were no full models of the existence and efficiency of competitive equilibrium until Kenneth Arrow and Gérard Debreu in the 1950 s. And MacIntyre's statement that the outcome is optimal for every participant is just wrong as a description of Arrow and Debreu's equilibrium theory. Further examples of basic errors could be provided. It is hard to take seriously the negative opinions MacIntyre offers on contemporary economics when their basis is so shaky.

David Bentley Hart is an excellent and influential contemporary theologian, who has written various articles in recent years on capitalism and its ideological companion, economics. The title of his article "Mammon Ascendant: Why Global Capitalism Is Inimical to Christianity"[15] doesn't leave readers guessing about his views. Bentley Hart writes, "As a cultural reality, late capitalism is not merely a regulatory regime for markets, but also a positive system of values," seemingly with economics in mind, and he concludes that "the claim that capitalist culture and Christianity are compatible—indeed, that they are not ultimately inimical to one another—seems to me not only self-evidently false, but quaintly (and perhaps perilously) deluded."

Just as with MacIntyre, though, there are serious questions about the accuracy of the portrait of contemporary economics that is the basis of the views expressed. Bentley Hart runs together criticism of capitalism and economics, and assumes that economists are simply ideological lackeys of capitalism. Even if we accept that many of his criticisms of capitalism have force, the thinness of his engagement with economics leaves the opinions he expresses about economics as little more than that.

Another excellent and influential theologian who has written on economics is Kathryn Tanner. Her *Christianity and the New Spirit of Capitalism* is based on her 2016 Gifford lectures and follows her earlier exploration of economics, *Econ-*

---

[15] David Bentley Hart, "Mammon Ascendant: Why Global Capitalism Is Inimical to Christianity," *First Things*, Jun. 2016, http://www.firstthings.com/article/2016/06/mammon-ascendant. The quotation is from page 9. See also David Bentley Hart, "What Lies Beyond Capitalism? A Christian Exploration," *Plough*, Aug. 2019, https://www.plough.com/en/topics/faith/discipleship/what-lies-beyond-capitalism.

omy of Grace.[16] She writes, "my own Christian commitments as I hope to show are inimical to the demands of capitalism," and "the Christian religious project differs fundamentally from a current capitalist one." Just as in David Bentley Hart's essay, economics is guilty by association with capitalism. This view hardens even before she gets to actually engage with economics in chapter 6, where her account of economics is painfully ignorant, especially of Smith's invisible hand, the economics of competition, and positional goods. How can a theologian who does careful and insightful work with other texts make such a mess of economics?

John Milbank's argument in *Theology and Social Theory*—that governing assumptions of modern social theory are modifications or rejections of orthodox Christian positions—includes a chapter on political economy.[17] After summarizing the thought of several important eighteenth- and early nineteenth-century political economists, including Adam Smith and Thomas Malthus, Milbank concludes that political economy is a "heretical theodicy" in its stronger versions, while "agnostic" and "pagan" in weaker versions. There is again too much reliance on questionable secondary literature and numerous errors with the details (for instance, confusing Smith's contemporary James Steuart with his biographer Dugald Stewart) that should have been picked up if Milbank had taken the trouble to engage with any competent economist or historian of economic thought.

Serious engagement with the discipline of economics is reasonable to expect of Christian ethicists writing on economic issues. D. Stephen Long has written a great deal on economic issues and is a representative example.[18] His introduc-

---

[16] Kathryn Tanner, *Christianity and the New Spirit of Capitalism* (New Haven: Yale University Press, 2018), with quotations from page 7 and page 213. It follows her earlier *Economy of Grace* (Minneapolis: Fortress Press, 2005). My "Review of Christianity and the New Spirit of Capitalism by Kathryn Tanner," *Colloquium: The Australian and New Zealand Theological Review* 55, no. 1 (2021): 131–35, sets out more fully the problems with Tanner's account of economics.

[17] John Milbank, *Theology and Social Theory: Beyond Secular Reason*, 2nd ed. (Oxford: Blackwell, 2006 [1990]). The quotations are from page 37. For discussions of Milbank's approach to economics, see Jennifer Herdt, "The Endless Construction of Charity: On Milbank's Critique of Political Economy," *Journal of Religious Ethics* 32, no. 2 (2004): 301–24; Steven McMullen, "Radical Orthodox Economics," *Christian Scholar's Review* 43, no. 4 (Summer 2014): 343–64; and Paul Oslington, "Radical Orthodoxy Encounters Economics; Deeper Engagement Needed," *Journal of Markets and Morality* 24, no. 1 (2021): 195–205 and 13–15.

[18] D. Stephen Long, *Christian Ethics* (Oxford: Oxford University Press, 2010); idem, *Divine Economy: Theology and the Market* (London: Routledge, 2000); and idem, "The Theology of Economics: Adam Smith as Church Father," *The Other Journal*, no. 5 (2005). Further

tion to *Christian Ethics* does not discuss or cite any economists or historians of economics, despite his writing about the importance of economic issues and emphasizing the importance of dialogue and a historical perspective. His earlier book on economics, *Divine Economy: Theology and the Market*, shares these weaknesses, though various economists do get a mention. Claims there about marginalist economics, and that Keynes was alone among economists in recognizing that economics was a moral science, are bizarre. Long relies on Milbank's account of political economy (even repeating the confusion of Steuart and Stewart), which itself relies on questionable secondary literature. This is a revealing example of the way Christian ethicists operate—large claims made about economics without bothering to study the literature of economics or engage with economists.

Stanley Hauerwas has strongly criticized American capitalism for many years.[19] Yet unusually among Christian ethicists, Hauerwas has taken the trouble to engage seriously with economists (including supervising PhD theses at Duke University jointly with economists). In a contribution to an interdisciplinary symposium on economics, he distinguishes between capitalism and economics, and concludes more moderately than many Christian ethicists that "we cannot avoid antagonisms between Christianity and modern economics because both want all."[20]

Biblical studies is an area where we might expect a fruitful engagement between economists and theologians, given the seemingly large amount of economic material in the Christian scriptures. This isn't the case, however, as biblical scholars engage very little with contemporary mainstream economists, and when they draw on social science it is usually anthropology or sociology. In the rare cases where they draw on economics, it tends to be varieties of Marxian economics.[21]

---

detailed criticisms on Long's work may be found in Paul Oslington, "Review of Divine Economy by D. Stephen Long," *Journal of Markets and Morality* 4, no. 1 (2001): 136–41.

[19] Examples from his recent writing include Stanley Hauerwas, "Can Greed Be a Good?," *ABC Religion and Ethics*, Oct. 3, 2010, https://www.abc.net.au/religion/never-enough-why-greed-is-still-so-deadly/10101110; and "The End of Charity: How Christians Are (Not) to 'Remember the Poor,'" *ABC Religion and Ethics*, Feb. 10, 2014, http://www.abc.net.au/religion/articles/2014/02/10/3941760.htm.

[20] Stanley Hauerwas, "Economics and Antagonisms," *History of Political Economy* 43, no. 2 (2011): 413–15, at 415.

[21] I discuss this curious avoidance by biblical scholars of contemporary mainstream economics in Paul Oslington, "Economics and Biblical Studies," *Oxford Bibliographies*, ed. Christopher Matthews (New York: Oxford University Press, 2020).

Roland Boer is a leading biblical scholar who has more recently turned to writing (with Christina Petterson) on the history of economics.[22] While the prose of the book *Idols of Nations* is sparkling, there is a staggering ignorance about the historical context of the political economists discussed, and it is hard to believe that Boer and Petterson have actually read the economic texts they discuss. Many of the arguments are preposterous—for example, that Adam Smith's invisible hand is the penis of either Adam Smith or God, based on a possible pun in the Hebrew between hand and penis. No evidence is presented for Smith's knowledge of the Hebrew language or motivation for introducing such a pun. Nor is there any attempt to engage other possible interpretations of Smith's invisible-hand passages. Examples could be multiplied from Boer's work.

This is a sample of the writing on economics of eminent contemporary theologians who have done otherwise excellent work. Common threads in their engagement with economics include running together criticism of capitalism and criticism of economics, strong prejudices against both, ignorance of the context of economists they discuss, reliance on secondary sources rather than primary texts of the economists they discuss, and seeming not to have taken the trouble to engage with economists or historians of economics whose criticism they might have benefited from. Writing by less eminent theologians about economics is often more extreme and even less well-informed.

It is worth noting that these sorts of problems are not unique to theologians critical of capitalism and economics—they are shared by the smaller number of theological enthusiasts for capitalism and economics. Many of these are Americans and are associated with think tanks. Here, strong prejudice for capitalism plus uncritical reception from their tribe render serious engagement unnecessary.[23]

---

[22] Roland Boer and Christina Petterson, *Idols of Nations: Biblical Myth at the Origins of Capitalism* (Minneapolis: Fortress Press, 2014). The argument about Smith's invisible hand is at 99–100. Further discussion of the book may be found in Paul Oslington, "Review of Roland Boer and Christina Petterson *Idols of Nations: Biblical Myth and the Origins of Capitalism* and Roland Boer, *The Sacred Economy*," *Australasian Pentecostal Studies* 19 (2017): 129–41. Also see Paul Oslington, "Review of *Time of Troubles: A New Economic Framework for Early Christianity* by Roland Boer and Christina Petterson," *Australasian Pentecostal Studies* 20 (2019): 154–57.

[23] Examples are Gary North, *An Introduction to Christian Economics* (Nutley, N.J.: Craig Press, 1973); Jay Wesley Richards, *Money Greed, and God: Why Capitalism Is the Solution and Not the Problem* (New York: HarperOne, 2009); and Victor Claar and Greg Forster, *The Keynesian Revolution and Our Empty Economy: We're All Dead* (New York: Palgrave Macmillan, 2019).

Problems with theological engagement with economics are not new.[24] Denunciations from theologians and other religious figures began as soon as political economy took shape as a discipline in nineteenth-century Britain. The emerging discipline was demonized by the poets Samuel Taylor Coleridge and Robert Southey and the art critic John Ruskin. Thomas Carlyle famously described it as the "dismal science" because it undermined social hierarchies, and in particular because it undermined the arguments for the subjugation of African American slaves in the West Indies.[25] Karl Marx wrote of the "vulgar" political economy of Smith, David Ricardo, and Malthus, reserving particular scorn for "parson" Malthus.[26] Later in the nineteenth century, English Christian Socialists, such as F. D. Maurice, J. M. Ludlow, and Charles Kingsley, attempted to build an alternative religious economics. In late nineteenth-century America, an alternative religious economics was also advocated by the social gospel movement.[27]

Examples of Economists Who Have Entered the Conversation

In contrast to the large and growing theological literature on economics, there is little interest among contemporary economists in engaging with theology and theologians. Interest among mainstream economists has been not rising but steadily falling. By contrast with contemporary economists, those who built political economy in the eighteenth century, including Adam Smith, were theologically literate, and their writing was shaped by their theological context. A prime example is Smith's "invisible hand" language, which Peter Harrison has shown

---

[24] The general phenomenon of humanities scholars' ignorance and antipathy toward economics has been described by William Coleman, *Economics and Its Enemies: Two Centuries of Anti-Economics* (Basingstoke: Palgrave, 2002). Donald Winch describes the romantic reaction to economics in *Riches and Poverty: An Intellectual History of Political Economy in Britain, 1750–1834* (Cambridge: Cambridge University Press, 1996); and *Wealth and Life: Essays on the Intellectual History of Political Economy in Britain, 1848–1914* (Cambridge: Cambridge University Press, 2009). Deirdre McCloskey traces what she calls the clerisy's rejection of economics in *The Bourgeois Virtues: Ethics for an Age of Commerce* (Chicago: University of Chicago Press, 2006).

[25] Peter Groenewegen, "Thomas Carlyle, 'the Dismal Science,' and the Contemporary Political Economy of Slavery," *History of Economics Review*, no. 34 (Summer 2001): 74–94.

[26] Karl Marx, *Contribution to the Critique of Political Economy*, trans. Nahum Isaac Stone (New York: Progress Publishers, 1970 [1859]).

[27] Bradley W. Bateman and Ethan B. Kapstein, "Between God and the Market: The Religious Roots of the American Economic Association," *Journal of Economic Perspectives* 13, no. 4 (1999): 249–58.

beyond dispute is the providential hand of God.[28] Early nineteenth-century political economists, such as Malthus, Thomas Chalmers, Richard Whately, and William Whewell, were concerned to reconcile their work with Christian theology and engaged with theologians over issues such as theodicy.

An exception, perhaps, to the falling interest by economists in theology is the recent surge of interest among historians of economic thought in the religious background of the discipline.[29] However, it is hard to argue this is really an exception, because historians of economics are peripheral at best to the contemporary economics profession. The history of economics is no longer part of the graduate training of economists and is little read by mainstream economists.

The dominant view among contemporary mainstream economists is that engaging with theologians is a waste of time. This reflects economists' general disdain for other disciplines, believing that their discipline is superior to the other social sciences and may eventually replace them.[30] For example, Nobel laureate Gary Becker espouses the view that economics is a universal science of human action, based on rational-choice theory, that has no need of other disciplines (not even psychology, when dealing with preferences of the actors).[31] Economists prefer to speak about other fields rather than engage meaningfully with them.

---

[28] Peter Harrison, "Adam Smith and the History of the Invisible Hand," *Journal of the History of Ideas* 72, no. 1 (2011): 29–49; and Paul Oslington, "God and the Market: Adam Smith's Invisible Hand," *Journal of Business Ethics* 108, no. 4 (2012): 429–38.

[29] Much of my own work in recent years has been on the religious background of the rise of economics as a discipline in the eighteenth and nineteenth centuries, and in particular on the key figure of Adam Smith. See, for instance, Paul Oslington, *Political Economy as Natural Theology: Smith, Malthus and Their Followers* (London: Routledge, 2018); and Paul Oslington, "The New View of Adam Smith in Context," *History of Economics Review* 71, no. 1 (2019): 118–31. This builds on earlier work by distinguished historians of economics, such as Jacob Viner and Anthony Waterman. A sample of this literature is Jacob Viner, *Religious Thought and Economic Society*, ed. J. Melitz and D. Winch (Durham, N.C.: Duke University Press, 1978); and A. M. C. Waterman, *Revolution, Economics and Religion: Christian Political Economy 1798–1833* (Cambridge: Cambridge University Press, 1991).

[30] Marion Fourcade, Etienne Ollion, and Yann Algan, "The Superiority of Economists," *Journal of Economic Perspectives* 29, no. 1 (2015): 89–114.

[31] Gary Becker, *The Economic Approach to Human Behavior* (Chicago: University of Chicago Press, 1976); and his Nobel lecture, "The Economic Way of Looking at Human Behavior," *American Economic Review* 101, no. 3 (1993): 385–409. See also the discussion of preferences in George Stigler and Gary Becker, "De Gustibus Non Est Disputandum," *American Economic Review* 67, no. 2 (Mar. 1977): 76–90.

A good illustration of this attitude of economists is the rise in recent decades of the subdiscipline of economics of religion.[32] It attempts to model religious behavior and religious institutions by using the tools of contemporary mainstream economics. Relations are poor with sociologists of religion, who resent economists' incursion into territory they have traditionally occupied, and believe with some justification that the economists of religion expect to supersede their field. Economists of religion have had considerable success in explaining some aspects of religion, but they tend to be weakest when dealing with the aspects of religion that require detailed knowledge of religious institutions and ideas. In these areas, economists' sophisticated mathematical models and empirical techniques yield a limited return, and there is no alternative to engaging deeply with the literature of religious studies and theology. Economists of religion these days are reading more theology and history than in the early years of the subdiscipline, but deeply ingrained habits from their disciplinary training, reinforced by the career incentives in the discipline, are hard to change.[33]

The Emerging Interdisciplinary Field of Economics and Theology

Recent years have seen the emergence of a new interdisciplinary field of economics and theology, which seeks to overcome the shortcomings of the engagements within the disciplines of economics and theology. It is about conversation for mutual benefit of the disciplines, and for cooperation between economists and theologians in dealing with issues that involve both disciplines. An example is the area of financial regulation, where theology has over two thousand years of experience (under the category of usury) in dealing with financial exploitation, and this experience can assist economists in framing the problem and highlighting dimensions of financial exploitation that are neglected by standard economic models.

Institutionally, the interdisciplinary field is marked by several associations of Christian economists that were founded in the 1970 s, though these tend to be dominated by the concerns of economists and have sometimes been seduced by

---

[32] Laurence Iannaccone, "Introduction to the Economics of Religion," *Journal of Economic Literature* 36, no. 3 (1998): 1465-95. As a Chicago PhD student, Iannaccone was much influenced by Becker's approach.

[33] For the changing nature of economics of religion, see the symposium "What Do Economists and Theologians Have to Say to Each Other," *Faith and Economics* (Fall 2011): 1-30. A more recent survey of the subdiscipline is Sriya Iyer, "The New Economics of Religion," *Journal of Economic Literature* 54, no. 2 (2016): 395-441.

a dream of creating a distinctively Christian economics.[34] There are a growing number of specialized conferences, journals, and books.[35] However, informal networks of scholars working across disciplinary boundaries have probably been more important than the formal associations for progress in the field.[36]

It is a difficult conversation. Geoffrey Brennan and Anthony Waterman, who have led many attempts to get theologians and economists together, describe one conference that went spectacularly wrong, where the economists ended up in one corner of the room talking among themselves about how stupid and irresponsible the theologians were, while the theologians in the other corner were unable to believe that such heartlessly evil persons as economists existed.

---

[34] An important assessment of the state of the associations of Christian economists was J. David Richardson, "Frontiers in Economics and Christian Scholarship," *Christian Scholars Review* 17, no. 4 (1988): 381–400. He obtains this assessment in J. David Richardson, "Interface and Integration in Christian Economics," in Oslington, *The Oxford Handbook of Christianity and Economics*, 282–304. Robin Klay discusses the Christian economists' groups in "Where Do Economists of Faith Hang Out? Their Journals and Associations, Plus Luminaries among Them," *Econ Journal Watch* 11, no. 2 (2014): 106–19. Paul Heyne, one of the few members with doctoral qualifications in both economics and theology, wrote insightfully on the issues, and his work is collected in *Are Economists Basically Immoral, and Other Essays on Economics, Ethics and Religion*, ed. with introduction by Geoffrey Brennan and A. M. C Waterman (Indianapolis: Liberty Fund, 2008). I have discussed the project of creating a distinctively Christian economics in "The Kuyperian Dream: Reconstructing Economics on Christian Foundations," *Faith & Economics* 75 (Spring 2020): 7–36.

[35] Journals include *Faith & Economics* (published by the U.S. Association of Christian Economists), *Journal of Markets and Morality* (Acton Institute for Religion and Liberty in the United States), *Journal of Economics, Theology and Religion* (Erasmus Economics and Theology Institute in the Netherlands), *Journal of Catholic Social Thought* (Villanova University), *Catholic Social Science Review* (Franciscan University of Steubenville), and the *International Journal of Public Theology* (Global Network for Public Theology, with the journal based at Charles Sturt University in Canberra). Among books, a model of interdisciplinary conversation is Jürgen von Hagen and Michael Welker, eds., *Money as God?: The Monetization of the Market and Its Impact on Religion, Politics, Law and Ethics* (Cambridge: Cambridge University Press, 2014).

[36] A sample of the informal networks I am involved with includes an Australia-based group that meets every year or so in Canberra hosted by the Australian Centre for Christianity and Culture; an online discussion group organized by the American economist Robert Tatum; a group that calls itself Economic Humanists and emphasizes modelling; and the religion and economy group of the American Academy of Religion.

Brennan and Waterman write of the difficulties they have observed with the conversation[37]:

> Economics ... is an imperialist beast, claiming the relevance of its general approach—including specifically its model of man embodied in the (predominantly selfish, entirely rational) homo œconomicus—to a very wide range of human activities. And Theology, with its transcendent, cosmic aspiration, is no less inclined to consider its picture of the human condition as definitive and metaphysically prior. In other words, Theology might accept homo œconomicus as a possibly useful abstraction in certain contexts—but not concede that the Christian conception of the human condition is a "model" in the same way.

There is also a clash of styles. Theology is textual and historical, while "economics is largely a-historical and is so self-consciously." Economists believe their discipline has progressed. Theologians tend not to think that way, and recovering the past and connecting proposals to past thinkers are frequent moves in the theological literature. Nevertheless, Brennan and Waterman believe genuine conversation is possible. "Often, however, the experience of conversation between Theologians and Economists is that of people talking past one another; and this is partly because basic attitudes towards epistemic and methodological issues are so different."

A different type of interdisciplinary exchange occurs when a theologian and an economist work together on a particular issue—for example, the recent work of Piet Naudé and Stan du Plessis on inequality, which, despite some progress in interdisciplinary understanding, concludes that "This bi-disciplinary journey is challenging."[38] Another example is the attempt of the economist David Richardson and the theologian Jamie Smith to work on globalization, an effort that did not end well.[39]

When an economist or a theologian becomes qualified in the other field, the personal and practical difficulties of cooperation are at least taken out of the interdisciplinary exchange. An example is the work of Ben Cooper, an Oxford economist who studied theology and drew on his background in both fields in

---

[37] Geoffrey Brennan and A. M. C. Waterman, "Christian Theology and Economics: Convergence and Clashes," in *Christian Theology and Market Economics*, ed. Ian R. Harper and Samuel Gregg, 77-93 (Northampton, Mass.: Edward Elgar, 2008). Geoffrey Brennan and A. M. C. Waterman, eds., *Economics and Religion: Are They Distinct?* (Boston: Kluwer, 1994) describe the disastrous conference in their introduction.

[38] Piet Naudé and Stan du Plessis, "Economic Inequality: Economics and Theology in Dialogue," *International Journal of Public Theology* 12, no. 1 (2018): 73-101, at 100.

[39] James K. A. Smith and J. David Richardson, "Economists, Theologians and Globalization: An Exchange," *Faith & Economics* 56, no. (Fall 2010): 1-64.

writing about happiness and game theoretical models of biblical interpretation.[40] Another example is the work of Andy Hartropp on economic justice, informed by doctoral study in both economics and theology,[41] or Mary Hirschfeld, with a Harvard PhD in economics and a Notre Dame PhD in theology, who has written on the economic dimensions of Thomas Aquinas's work and other topics.[42]

I know of more economists who have undertaken advanced degrees in theology than theologians who have done the same in economics. An exception is Paul Heyne, who followed theological study with advanced study of economics at the University of Chicago, and then became a legendary teacher of economics at the University of Washington. Another is Anthony Waterman, an Anglican priest who was sent by his bishop to Australian National University to undertake a PhD in economics, so as to advise the Canadian bishops on economic issues. Unfortunately for the Canadian bishops, he returned with views on economics that they found unpalatable, and he eventually resigned his orders.

Why Is the Conversation So Difficult?

There are systematic problems with the conversation between economists and theologians. With some notable exceptions, theological writing on economics is of poor quality. Economists tend not to be interested in theology, and the conversation within the discipline is thin. Those who have initiated interdisciplinary conversations have found the enterprise very difficult.

Various explanations have been offered for the difficulty of the conversation between economists and theologians:

- The mathematical and statistical form of contemporary mainstream economics makes it hard for theologians to read the literature and engage with economists. This may be true, but it is also true of sciences like physics, with which theologians have engaged much more competently. It also does not account for the antipathy that theologians displayed for political economy long before economics became so mathematical.

---

[40] Ben Cooper, Cecilia Garcia-Penalosa, and Peter Funk, "Status Effects and Negative Utility Growth," *Economic Journal* 111, no. 473 (2001): 642–65; Ben Cooper, "Chasing after the Wind: The Pursuit of Happiness through Economic Progress," *Kategoria* 13 (2000): 9–24; and Ben Cooper, "Adaptive Eschatological Inference from the Gospel of Matthew," *Journal for the Study of the New Testament* 33 (2010): 59–80.

[41] Andy Hartropp, *What Is Economic Justice? Biblical and Secular Perspectives Contrasted* (London: Paternoster, 2007).

[42] Mary L. Hirschfeld, *Aquinas and the Market: Toward a Humane Economy* (Cambridge, Mass.: Harvard University Press, 2018).

- The literary and historical form of theology, along with the linguistic skills needed in biblical studies, are barriers for economists. This is undoubtedly true, but the barriers for theologians are at least as great, and do not discourage them from writing on economics, though mostly badly. Why the asymmetry of outcomes?
- Differences in terminology between the disciplines of economics and theology make communication difficult. For example, mainstream economics has a particular conception of rationality as individual maximization based on preferences, subject to income and other constraints, while theologians tend to have quite different conceptions of rationality. Conceptions of scarcity are also very different. These differences mean that interdisciplinary conversations can become bogged down in endless debates about terms, or that economists and theologians talk past each other until frustration with the failure of communication ends the conversation.[43] There are also terminological difficulties in conversations with other sciences, such as biology and physics, but in the other sciences technical language intersects less with the language of theology, so confusion is easier to avoid than with terms like rationality and scarcity.
- The disciplines ask different questions. Economists are trained to think about the properties of large impersonal systems, whereas Christian ethics tends to ask questions about individual actions and to be more comfortable dealing with small-scale communities.[44] Just as with the language explanation, the difficulty here is magnified for the economics-theology conversation by superficial similarities, that economics and theology both deal with human nature and human society.
- Jealousy divides the disciplines because political economy has replaced theology as the master language in Western societies.[45]

---

[43] Brennan and Waterman's essay discussed in the last section emphasizes language, especially the key concepts of rationality and scarcity, as a barrier to conversation.

[44] Paul Heyne emphasizes this difference as a barrier to communication and sees theological ethics as incapable of addressing markets. This is why he saw his Christian vocation as teaching economics, abandoning any attempt to combine his earlier theological training with his economics. Heyne was of course influenced by Frank Knight's approach to these questions—as discussed in Brennan and Waterman's introduction to Heyne's work cited in the last section. The authority on Knight is Ross Emmett, for instance, in "Frank Knight: Economics Versus Religion," in Brennan and Waterman, *Economics and Religion: Are They Distinct?*, 103–20.

[45] A. M. C. Waterman, *Political Economy and Christian Theology since the Enlightenment: Essays in Intellectual History* (London: Palgrave Macmillan, 2004).

- The intensely political nature of economic policy makes theological engagement with economics much more complex than engagement with a less politically charged science like physics.

All of these explanations have an element of truth, but none is a complete explanation of the problems identified with the conversation. A missing element may be the career incentives that participants face when they consider engaging in dialogue.

Example of an Incentive Problem

I will now briefly describe an example of an incentive problem that undermines interdisciplinary writing, including on economics and theology. The example draws on the economics of incentives under imperfect information, a branch of economics that considers individual behavior in different institutional and contractual settings, with a view to identifying inefficiencies and inequities generated by these settings, and suggesting remedies. Imperfect and asymmetric information is common in the settings studied in this literature.

Consider the situation where an economist, Bridget, sees some benefit in engaging with theology, perhaps because of its relevance to the policy issue she is writing on. When she approaches the theological literature, however, Bridget sees a vast array of papers on economics, and has great difficulty knowing where to start and how to distinguish low-quality from high-quality research. She will read a paper by a theologian on economics if the expected value to her of reading the paper, which depends on the quality of the research, exceeds the cost of reading. Bridget has a flourishing academic career, and she could spend her time reading and writing on other topics—the main cost of reading a theological paper is the value of alternative uses of her time, especially as her tenure review is coming up.

Consider now the theologian Bruce, who is interested in economics. Bruce's dean encourages writing on economic topics, as it seems a way of making theology relevant in an academic environment where theology is less and less honored. Colleagues and students think it is really cool that Bruce is bravely taking on capitalism, and Bruce always has a ready audience in the theology common room whenever he talks about his research—certainly a larger audience than for his common-room discourses on the nature of the Trinity. At the American Christian college where Bruce works, grants are available for Christian scholarship, including for theologians like Bruce, to do interdisciplinary work on economics. None of these rewards depend on the quality of what Bruce writes, for Bruce's dean and the director of the institute at the college who allocates grants know even less about economics than he does. When Bruce considers writing on economics, there are also rewards that depend on the quality of the paper he writes—for instance, being cited and esteemed by knowledgeable colleagues in his discipline and beyond, perhaps even by economists like Bridget, who might read his work. However, writing a high-quality paper means reading the dreary economics literature and talking with economists. Bruce will write a high-quality paper if the total rewards of writing, including both the component independent of quality and the quality-dependent component, exceed his costs of writing. If Bruce decides it is not worthwhile to write a high-quality paper, then he may still write a low-quality paper if the rewards of a low-quality paper on economics and theology, which are mostly independent of quality, exceed the minimal costs of writing such a paper.

A well-functioning academic market is one where papers are written by the theologian Bruce and read by the economist Bridget to the benefit of both and to the benefit of society.

This situation of imperfect and asymmetric information about the quality of research is analogous to a famous incentive problem studied by the economist George Akerlof.[46] When buyers cannot easily judge the quality of used cars, there is an incentive for sellers to flood the market with poor-quality cars (known as lemons), so that good cars are not offered for sale, and the market collapses. This means that even though there may be potentially mutually beneficial trades for sellers of good-quality cars and car buyers, the collapse of the market means these do not occur.

The poor-quality used cars that flood the market are analogous to the low-quality papers that theologians like Bruce have an incentive to produce under these circumstances of reader ignorance of quality. Our economist, Bridget, will rationally choose not to read any papers by theologians on economics, and the academic market in theological papers on economics will collapse. This may be the case, even if there is a potential high-quality paper that would be in Bruce's interests to write and that Bridget would gain by reading. Both Bruce and Bridget, and wider society, lose out because of the asymmetric information related market failure.[47]

---

[46] George A. Akerlof, "The Market for 'Lemons': Quality Uncertainty and the Market Mechanism," *Quarterly Journal of Economics* 84, no. 3 (1970): 488–500. The significance of Akerlof's work is discussed by Karl-Gustaf Löfgren, Torsten Persson, and Jörgen W Weibull, "Markets with Asymmetric Information: The Contributions of George Akerlof, Michael Spence and Joseph Stiglitz," *The Scandinavian Journal of Economics* (2002): 195–211.

[47] I have chosen an example of where a theologian writes a poor-quality paper about economics, but the argument applies equally to economists writing on theology.

Conclusions

We need a better conversation between economists and theologians because of the cultural importance of economics, and because so many policy issues involve both disciplines. The problems identified with the quality of theologians' treatment of economics, and the current lack of participation by economists in the conversation, suggest that the new interdisciplinary field of economics and theology is the best site for a more fruitful conversation.

If so, investment in the new interdisciplinary field of economics and theology is needed, but to be effective such investment must be made with careful scrutiny of the difficulties that have been encountered in the past, together with an awareness of the incentive issues that shape the conversation.

Wise investment might include:

1. Sponsoring theologians and economists who are willing to seriously study and write in the other discipline. Such work outside one's own discipline brings both greater knowledge of the other discipline and exposure to the culture of the other discipline.
2. Investing in mechanisms that enable quality of interdisciplinary research to be better assessed. An example would be having both economists and theologians at the table when the other discipline is being discussed (along the lines of Wilfred Cantwell Smith's famous dictum for interreligious dialogue that descriptions of another religion should be recognizable to participants in that religion, even if there are different evaluations of that religion). Including properly qualified representatives of the other discipline would go a long way to correcting some of the fanciful descriptions of economics and readings of economic texts by theologians that were discussed earlier in this chapter. It should apply to conferences and to editorial boards and referees of journals and books that aspire to high-quality contributions to the conversation. The more of these sorts of assessments that are easily accessible to researchers in other disciplines, the better.
3. Supporting study of the history of the disciplines of economics and theology. History is common ground between the disciplines, and historical study is especially useful for understanding fruitful and unfruitful interactions between the disciplines in different contexts.
4. Investing in a university research center somewhere in the world that can be a focus for the new interdisciplinary field. Such a center would be a place where skills in facilitating conversations and collaboration across disciplinary boundaries can be nurtured. It would provide a base and the necessary support for launching new research projects, which are inherently riskier for scholars, especially young scholars, than research in one's own discipline. A center would also be a place where PhD students who will be the

future of the field can be trained. Critical mass matters in enterprises such as this.

Appendix

This appendix describes the Akerlof "lemons" model and discusses formal analogies between this model and the situation of academic paper writers and readers.

George Akerlof's model[48] was seminal for the economics of imperfect information and a large part of the award of the 2001 Nobel Prize to Akerlof, Michael Spence, and Joseph Stiglitz "for their analyses of markets with asymmetric information." Akerlof considered the market for used cars, where sellers know the quality of cars and buyers do not, and showed that under certain conditions the market will collapse, becoming flooded with poor-quality cars—"lemons"—so that good-quality cars will not be traded, even though there are potential trades that would make both buyers and sellers better off.

However, rather than present Akerlof's original model, I present here a simplified version developed by the some of the economists involved in his Nobel award ceremony.[49] This simplified model omits derivations of buyer and seller demand functions from their utility functions and works with two discrete qualities, high and low, rather than a continuous distribution of quality.

This is the simplified model: There are two qualities of a product, low and high, available in proportions λ and $(1-\lambda)$. Quality is hidden from the buyers, but sellers know the quality. For buyers, low quality is worth w^L and high quality is worth w^H. For sellers, low quality is worth $v^L < w^L$ and high quality is worth $v^H < w^H$.

If the markets for high- and low-quality products are separated, then any price between v^L and w^L will support a market for the low-quality product, in the sense that buyers and sellers will participate, and any price between v^H and w^H will support a market for the high-quality product.

If the markets are pooled, and $v^H > \hat{w}$ where $\hat{w} = \lambda w^L + (1-\lambda) w^H$, then sellers withdraw their high-quality products from the market. The market for high-quality products collapses. Only low-quality products will be offered to the market by

---

[48] Akerlof, "The Market for 'Lemons.'"
[49] Löfgren, Persson, and Weibull, "Markets with Asymmetric Information." There are various other simplified versions of the Akerlof model—for instance, Donald E. Campbell, *Incentives: Motivation and the Economics of Information*, 3rd ed. (New York: Cambridge University Press, 2018), 299–300; and A. Mas-Colell, M. D. Whinston, and J. R. Green, *Microeconomic Theory* (Oxford: Oxford University Press, 1995), 724.

sellers, and will be traded at a price between v^L and w^L. This means that potential welfare gains from trade in high-quality products are lost.

Note that the market is more likely to collapse if there is a high proportion of low-quality products λ. It is also more likely to collapse if there is a small gap between the seller and buyer valuations w and v.

The situation of academic paper writers and readers is similar to this. Readers are like buyers of used cars who cannot easily assess quality before reading a paper and must make decisions about whether or not to read on the basis of the average quality of papers in the market. Writers are like used-car sellers who have an incentive to upsell the quality of their work and to flood the market with poor-quality papers that are less costly to write than high-quality papers. Under certain conditions, the market collapses, and high-quality papers cease to be written and read. Trade in papers either ceases or continues in a diminished manner with only low-quality papers. Potential welfare gains from high-quality papers being written and read are lost.

While the situations in the used-car and academic-paper markets are similar, they are not exactly the same. One difficulty is that there is no explicit price paid by readers of academic papers to writers. If readers, rather than their institution, do pay a monetary price, it goes to the academic publishing house rather than directly to the writer. There are nonmonetary transfers somewhat akin to a price, such as the reader citing a paper she has read, or esteeming the author in ways that are valuable to the author's academic career. Both these types of nonmonetary transfer are relatively costless to the reader, though potentially very valuable to the writer of the paper.

Another difficulty is that in the Akerlof model, there are fixed supplies of the product of particular qualities. In the case of the production and reading of academic papers, the choice by the writer whether to produce a low-quality or high-quality paper means that the production process for papers really should be modelled.

Despite these difficulties, which would seem to be remediable, the analogy between the two situations suggests that the Akerlof conclusions about market collapse and the loss of potential gains from trade in high-quality products are likely to apply to the case of the production and reading of academic papers. Such a suggestion, of course, would have to be borne out in an appropriate and fully developed model.

Part Three: Evaluating Liberal Capitalism

Our Political Economy's Moral Teaching

Rüdiger Bittner

By "political economy" I understand the basic political and economic framework within which a society's members live together. "Political economy" used to refer to one branch of inquiry, the one of which Adam Smith's *Inquiry into the Nature and Causes of the Wealth of Nations*[1] is the classic example, but more recently the expression also has come to mean the thing investigated in that inquiry, and this is the usage adopted here. A country's political economy thus comes close to what John Rawls called its basic structure, the set of fundamental institutions in which citizens live together.[2] While it may comprise written laws too, it is basically a set of regularities, expectations, and customs evident in people's dealing with each other. As such, it has, contrary to what is often assumed, no normative import in itself. It is just "how they do things here"—whether they do right in doing them this way is a different matter. However, it can sensibly be asked whether their doing things this way helps or hinders the growth of certain conceptions as to what is right to do. A political economy may be hospitable to one kind of moral outlook and hostile to another. This invites the question of the present chapter: is our political economy fertile ground for particular moral conceptions or, indeed, misconceptions?

The political economy in which we live is that of liberal capitalism, meaning by "we" not humans in general, but only those living in what is vaguely called the West. The vagueness here I shall not try to overcome, and neither shall I try, lacking the requisite knowledge, to characterize the political economies of countries outside the West. I shall be concerned just with life around here. Still, around here the political economies are remarkably similar: Western countries run pretty much the same way, and that way is liberal capitalism.

The term "capitalism" misleads, though. Capital is something that people, individually or collectively, hold, and there are different accounts of when peo-

---

[1] Adam Smith, *An Inquiry into the Nature and Causes of the Wealth of Nations* (1776), ed. R. H. Campbell et al. (Oxford: Oxford University Press, 1976).
[2] John Rawls, *A Theory of Justice* (London: Oxford University Press, 1972), §2.

ple's holdings should be considered capital.³ However, to say that our political economy is capitalist is not to say that most or the most important of people's holdings are capital in one of these senses. It is to describe the way in which people predominantly gain access to goods and services, to the extent that they do. Under capitalism they gain such access by buying goods and services on competitive markets, in exchange for things they to a large extent in turn acquired on markets, for instance by selling their labor power on labor markets. A better term for this type of political economy would thus be market economy, but capitalism, probably just because of its various polemical uses, has become the standard expression.

Liberal capitalism differs from mere capitalism in that the markets distributing goods and services are regulated and limited by a state whose operations in turn are regulated in the form of law and limited by legally and effectively guaranteed liberties of individuals. The set of these liberties varies among countries, but a widely shared list includes freedom of speech, of movement, of political activity, of religion, of association, and of contract, and the guarantee that any government interference with one's liberties will be held to the principles of *Rechtsstaat*. In addition, these liberties are weighted differently in different countries. Freedom of speech, for instance, holds a much higher position in the United States than it does in Germany, say, where certain false historical statements already can get you into prison. Finally, countries differ over whether they consider one's liberty to be diminished by poverty, some following the libertarian line and denying any connection between income and freedom, and others following the social-democratic tradition and considering poverty an abridgement of one's liberty that a liberal state, precisely as liberal, must at least mitigate, if not eliminate.

Evidently, however, under liberal capitalism not all goods and services get allocated through markets. Families, for instance, form a large pocket of givings and receivings that take place outside markets, and so do charitable donations and provisions of the welfare state. Furthermore, the rich have found means to give their offspring a hefty advantage in entering markets by preserving the right of bequest, which, originating in a precapitalist economy and conflicting with capitalist principles, is no less guaranteed in most capitalist countries. Still, disregarding these large exceptions, for most people in Western countries, the way to move through life has become to try to improve one's position through participating in markets.

---

[3] See, for instance, Karl Marx, *Das Kapital* (1867), in *Marx Engels Werke* (hereafter MEW), ed. Institut für Marxismus-Leninismus beim ZK der SED, vol. 23 (Berlin: Dietz, 1969), chap. 4, sect. 1. See also Max Weber, *Wirtschaft und Gesellschaft. Grundriss der verstehenden Soziologie* (1922), 5th ed., ed. J. Winckelmann (Tübingen: Mohr, 1972), chap. 2, § 11.

Liberal capitalism is a product of the last few centuries. As for capitalism in particular, both the rise of the market to become the dominating institution in the allocation of goods and services and especially the worldwide expansion of markets are quite recent developments. For the longest time in human history, people mostly consumed what they themselves or their family produced, only the smallest amount being exchanged or bought and sold on competitive markets. As for a liberal political order, to restrain by law what in the name of political collectives or their rulers may be done to their members or subjects, so that certain liberties of individuals can be relied on to remain untouched, is an achievement pretty much unheard of in human history.

Aware of the historical contingency of liberal capitalism, social theorists have also envisioned a political economy that could eventually replace it. Thus, Karl Marx anticipated a state in which production would have become fully social, so that people could receive a share of the common product proportionate to their needs, not to their contributions, and markets would lose their function.[4] Essentially the same is already true in Thomas More's Utopia, where there are markets in name only—that is, places where people just pick up what they need, without payment;[5] and an invitation to socialism worth pondering was put forward in contemporary terms by G. A. Cohen recently.[6] Capitalism, in contrast both to the old subsistence system and to the envisioned socialist systems, makes an individual's share of goods depend not only on his or his family's productivity or on the size of the entire social product and the extent of his needs, but also on how one's product compares both to what others produce and to what others desire. In this way it makes individuals' lives depend on the vicissitudes of markets.

Still, owing to the unprecedented quantity and quality of goods available under liberal capitalism,[7] this type of political economy saw a remarkable success worldwide in the twentieth century. Its success, however, appears to be basically economic, which is to say that people are largely satisfied with the goods provided under liberal capitalism, in contrast to its success being founded on people's conviction that liberal capitalism is under current circumstances the best way of living together. Hence, there is reason to wonder, especially in view of recent developments, whether liberal capitalism is going to last.

---

[4] Karl Marx, *Randglossen zum Programm der deutschen Arbeiterpartei* (1875), MEW 19: 21.

[5] Thomas More, *De optimo reipublicae statu deque nova insula Utopia* (1516), in *The Complete Works of St. Thomas More*, ed. E. Surtz, SJ, and J. H. Hexter, vol. 4 (New Haven: Yale University Press, 1965), 136.

[6] G. A. Cohen, *Why Not Socialism?* (Princeton, NJ: Princeton University Press, 2009).

[7] See Deirdre McCloskey, *Why Liberalism Works* (New Haven: Yale University Press, 2019), chap. 6.

For one thing, people's appreciation of the rule of law and the guaranteed liberties of individuals seems to be waning. Busy to improve their position by all sorts of exchanges, including selling themselves into subordination, whether temporally and materially limited or not, they apparently do not care all that much about safeguarded liberties and "an empire of laws, not of men," to borrow James Harrington's phrase,[8] and so the liberal element of our political economy seems to be in retreat. What is essentially the Chinese model—capitalism with its economic success but without liberal guarantees; a political system ruled by a self-sustaining party elite, perhaps with a charismatic figure at the top; and a system that curtails the range of individuals' activities and obstructs their pursuit of political alternatives—is gaining ground in the West as well, both in Europe and in the United States.

For another, capitalism may owe its economic success to the ruthless exploitation of natural resources, and with that treasure to a large extent squandered and restrictions becoming unavoidable, capitalism may no longer be in a position to fulfill its alluring promises. Indeed, some observers claim that a capitalist economy is constitutionally incapable of preserving to a sufficient extent its natural basis.[9] Others doubt this, but if it is true, then capitalism is doomed, or perhaps large numbers of humans are. Still, I shall pursue neither of these worries here, serious though they are. I shall stay with liberal capitalism, this being at the moment our political economy, and ask whether and, if so, how it shapes people in a moral respect.

Liberal capitalism differs from the political economy preceding it, which in Europe was feudalism, in that it does not recognize some people's holding a higher rank and thereby being entitled to an income not attained through market exchanges, but procured unilaterally by the people of lower rank. Individuals under capitalism come shorn of status and dignities, whether these are held by birth or conferred on them by spiritual transactions; they meet on markets in principle on the same footing. True, some are rich and powerful, others live in poverty, and indeed massive income differences have accompanied capitalism from its very early stages right to the present. Still, under capitalism the rich and powerful differ from the poor and weak only in the quantity of what they have or can marshal, not in principle in how they acquire goods. The rich are not human beings qualitatively apart, as the nobles and, for different reasons, the priests were supposed to be, and are not for this reason above the need to buy and sell and thereby to secure or improve their position.

---

[8] James Harrington, *The Commonwealth of Oceana* (1656), in idem, *The Commonwealth of Oceana and A System of Politics*, ed. J. G. A. Pocock (Cambridge: Cambridge University Press, 1992), 8.

[9] See, for instance, Klaus Dörre, *Die Utopie des Sozialismus. Kompass für eine Nachhaltigkeitsrevolution* (Berlin: Matthes, 2021).

Accordingly, the rich and the poor alike do not find a course of life simply set for them, they build one up for themselves in uncounted steps and exchanges. Anybody is constantly directing and redirecting his boat, even though no one ever becomes fully master over the effects of what he does, since these at the same time depend on what others want and do. To be sure, the rich stand a much better chance of arranging a satisfying life for themselves. The point is, however, that no matter whether rich or poor, one's life is something resulting, in part, from one's choices, whether those are clever and lucky or the opposite. Under liberal capitalism we are all, to a larger extent than ever before, self-made men and women.

This gives rise to the need for education, a need that became pressing precisely when capitalism took over. Under capitalism there is no path through life for which people are destined by their origin, so they have to acquire the ability of dealing with the world at large without as yet knowing where in particular they will end up. Under capitalism people therefore must be educated for an entire range of positions so as to increase—especially in the case of those not cushioned by inherited wealth—the probability of their having, once they enter markets, sufficient capacities to sell their labor at a price allowing them a decent life.[10] Indeed, the idea of *Bildung*, of a rich individuality familiar with and receptive to all manner of worldly concerns—an idea powerful in the classical German tradition, in Johann Wolfgang Goethe, say,[11] and, via Wilhelm von Humboldt[12] and John Stuart Mill,[13] highly influential in liberal thought—can be understood as an answer to that modern predicament. There being no place in the world in which individuals can consider themselves to be coming into their own, they must find in themselves the wherewithal from which to build a meaningful course through the world.

Therefore, under capitalism general, state-run, or at least state-controlled and obligatory schooling got introduced everywhere. The demands of a capitalist economy having become so large and so diverse, it took a comprehensive system of education with professionally trained teachers to give everybody a chance to achieve a reasonable price on the labor market. Like cattle, you may object, but

---

[10] Johann Heinrich Pestalozzi saw this clearly; see his *Lienhard und Gertrud*, vol. 3 (1785), in *Sämtliche Werke*, ed. A. Buchenau et al. (Berlin, 1927-), 3:15. See also Pestalozzi, *Sämtliche Werke*, 25:35.

[11] Johann Wolfgang Goethe, *Wilhelm Meisters Lehrjahre* (1795/96) (Munich: dtv Verlagsgesellschaft, 1962), esp. book 8.

[12] Wilhelm von Humboldt, *Ideen zu einem Versuch, die Gränzen der Wirksamkeit des Staats zu bestimmen* (1792), in *Humboldt, Werke in fünf Bänden*, vol. 1, ed. A. Flitner and K. Giel (Darmstadt: Wiss. Buchgesellschaft, 1980), sect. 2.

[13] John Stuart Mill, *On Liberty* (1859), in id., *Utilitarianism*, ed. M. Warnock (London: Collins, 1962), chap. 3.

keep in mind that the institutions devoted to making people fit for being sold on labor markets have thereby not only extended the knowledge but also fostered critical thinking in the general population to a degree unknown before the advent of capitalism. By extending knowledge and critical thought, they also formed people's behavior and, hence, their character. Thus, liberal capitalism through its educational institutions, chiefly the school, is certainly involved in character formation and the transmission of values, and its contribution in this respect is certainly to be welcomed, since it made people less dependent on external guidance, better capable of figuring out a good path for themselves.

Note that it is not through ethics as a special subject in the curriculum, through an extra virtue class, that schools morally benefit students. The help they provide lies simply in introducing the young carefully and responsibly to the world as it is today. For nowhere but in dealing with our present world is virtue to be learned. Teachers need not throw an extra dose of morality into their brew, nor are they well advised to do so, and we should not worry whether the morality inevitably informing their teaching is precisely the one we consider right. Students will run into people with odd moralities in any case in the course of their lives. If teachers help students attain a clear view of where they are and what the world around them is like, they will have done them the good they need. What direction to take is then for the students to decide; they just have to acquire the capacity and the courage of deciding this responsibly and with an open mind. How well this or that school system is doing in this respect is not part of the present topic. Here the point is only that liberal capitalism, through its schools, benefits—and under current conditions irreplaceably benefits—individual character formation and the transmission of values in society at large.

However, this may not be the disputed point. Perhaps it will be granted on all sides that under liberal capitalism schools have an important function in helping the next generation find their way in the world they face. Perhaps the point at issue is rather that liberal capitalism all by itself, with or without schools, is already a moral teacher, and one whose teachings may be suspected of being pernicious. In fact, many writers argue that capitalism has a corrosive influence on people's moral valuings.[14]

One of these writers is Michael Sandel, who presented this view forcefully and to wide acclaim. Explaining that his discontent with markets is not only founded on their distributing goods unjustly, he writes: "Even in a society without unjust differences of power and wealth, there would still be things that money should not buy. This is because markets are not mere mechanisms; they em-

---

[14] Jason Brennan and Peter Jaworski, *Markets without Limits* (New York: Routledge, 2016), offer a comprehensive survey of, and defend a distinct position within, this debate.

body certain values. And sometimes, market values crowd out nonmarket norms worth caring about."[15]

So markets as such, regardless of the distributions they bring about, sometimes have a corrupting influence. However, the statement that markets—after all, mere collections of people's doings—embody values is difficult to understand. Perhaps what Sandel means is just that people, when engaging in market transactions, ascribe to the goods bought or sold not only a certain value, which would be trivial, but a certain kind of value, and that there are goods, such as human beings themselves or parts of them or sexual activity with them, that do not actually have the kind of value that would make them suitable objects for buying and selling. On this reading, however, people subjecting these goods to market transactions would merely be in error, and Sandel is clearly aiming at a more serious kind of going wrong. As he puts it two paragraphs earlier, market treatment is degrading for such goods—it *is* degrading, which must mean that market treatment actually makes the goods have a lower sort of value from what they had before. (A degraded officer does actually hold a lower rank than before, and is not just by error ascribed a lower rank than he has.) How can buying and selling things do that, though? If the goods in question have a value of a sort that makes them inappropriate objects of market transactions, then they must be supposed to keep this value even when inappropriately subjected to such transactions. Were they to lose it when so treated, market treatment would be self-justifying, since with that value lost, market treatment would not be inappropriate after all.

A similar problem—the paradox of demeaning, as it was called—arose with reference to human dignity. A number of contemporary writers claim that human beings as such have dignity. However, if by a demeaning treatment we understand, as is natural, a treatment violating somebody's dignity, there cannot be such a treatment once it is assumed that humans as such have dignity: however abominably you treat people, their dignity stands unaffected.[16] The same sort of mistake is at work here as with the allegedly nonmarketable goods. The friends of human dignity, trying to be very good boys and girls through their theory, protect human beings from demeaning treatment by ascribing to them a dignity that puts them in principle out of the reach of such treatment, with the unwelcome consequence that so to treat them becomes not wrong, but impossible, because they will keep that dignity however treated. (Note Sandel's waver-

---

[15] Michael Sandel, *What Money Can't Buy* (New York: Farrar, 2012), 113. Debra Satz, *Why Some Things Should Not Be for Sale* (Oxford: Oxford University Press, 2010), chap. 4, offers a similar argument.

[16] Avishai Margalit, *The Decent Society* (Cambridge, Mass.: Harvard University Press, 1996), chap. 7. See also Ralf Stoecker, "Menschenwürde und das Paradox der Entwürdigung," in idem, *Menschenwürde* (Vienna: öbv, n.d).

ing between speaking of what "money should not buy," as in the quote above, and what "money can't buy," as in the title of his book.)

The cure is the same in both cases. No, human beings do not just as such have dignity. It is true only that they are sometimes treated very badly. But that it is bad to treat them so does not derive from their having in themselves a dignity making them inaccessible to such treatment. We can drop human dignity and still ask that no human being be so treated, that no human being be tortured, for example. In the same way, there is no degrading of goods by buying and selling them, since goods do not have a natural property, a kind of sacredness, that puts them above having this done to them. It is true only that for some goods there may be reason not to distribute them through markets. Such a reason, though, needs to be laid on the table. Just general talk about the degrading effect of markets will not do.

Now if markets are not demeaning, because things do not come with the sort of inherent value that could be desecrated by market transactions, then they are the mere distributive mechanisms that Sandel denies them to be. Hence, markets do not teach any morality, whether right or wrong. Neither does capitalism when it allocates goods by means of this mechanism.

Neither does, in particular, liberal capitalism, which subjects market transactions to the laws of a state guaranteeing individual liberties. Having such a state may well be advantageous, but it is not for moral reasons recommendable or even required.[17] True, a large number of contemporary writers have argued on broadly Rawlsian lines[18] for the moral superiority of liberal political regimes,[19] but summarily speaking, these arguments suffer like Rawls's own from relying on overly strong idealist assumptions about the citizens of these regimes, and therefore cannot be trusted to be even relevant for the ordinary people among whom we live.

Liberal capitalism, then, does not come with any moral message. In particular, it does not come with the advice, contrary to true morality, to live a life of self-seeking, narrow-minded greed. Liberal capitalism does change the ways in which people are shaped, but it does not determine into what they are shaped. Having to find for themselves the best path to take on the various markets they enter, and assured of being in important respects free in determining their course, they indeed outgrow being predominantly shaped by custom, received

---

[17] Following Richard Arneson's democratic instrumentalism, defended in his article "The Supposed Right to a Democratic Say," in *Contemporary Debates in Political Philosophy*, ed. T. Christiano and J. Christman (Oxford: Wiley, 2009), 197–212.

[18] Rawls, *Theory of Justice*; and John Rawls, *Political Liberalism* (New York: Columbia University Press, 1993).

[19] Anita Horn, *The Human Right to Democracy* (Berlin: de Gruyter, 2019), provides a comprehensive survey of the discussion.

tradition, shared belief, and community values. More than in centuries past, people form themselves, indeed cannot avoid doing so, and less than in the past they follow spiritual superiors or exemplary figures like heroes or saints.[20] Materially, however, no moral option is thereby foreclosed or even made less attractive. Doing what are truly good things is as much on offer in the practical landscape of liberal capitalism as doing the mean and the horrendous. Conversely, to become one who does what is right and good, one does not need to be lacking in the rationality that is trained under capitalism, in the careful calculation of what works best in the situation at hand. Indeed, it is a point already to be found in Aristotle that virtue requires prudence and thus also cleverness.[21]

To hold that liberal capitalism teaches people the wrong morality is in fact curiously self-refuting. Where, after all, did you come to know the true morality whose disregard or positive suppression under liberal capitalism you deplore? Under liberal capitalism of course, since that is where you grew up. You might claim to have access to seeing what is right to do that is not owed to the world around you and the present political economy—an access by intuition, pure reason, or revelation—but in that case your pronouncements are likely to meet with disbelief outside the circle of your friends. If, however, you did learn true morality right here under liberal capitalism, liberal capitalism cannot be such a bad teacher. As you managed to take in the right lesson at its knees, so may anybody else. The political economy under which we live, liberal capitalism, thus does not narrow the range of moral learning. Good paths can be found here too.

And bad news it would be if they could not. Political economies, though they are just sets of what people do and thus could do differently, do not allow themselves to be changed at will. That at least is what historical experience shows. Liberal capitalism grew into being the political economy of Western countries; it was not introduced by anyone's so deciding. In the twentieth century a memorable attempt was made to skip liberal capitalism. It was decided to set up a different, more reasonable political economy, socialism. The attempt failed, however, and capitalism returned, though not a liberal form of it. So if liberal capitalism were indeed hostile to true morality, we would be stuck. Fortunately, it is not.

It may well be asked at this point why it is so widely believed that a market economy undermines true morality. Here are a number of explanations. One is that determining one's own path by choosing what to buy and what to sell on the various markets fosters people's independent judgment as to what is good to do and makes them more resistant to guidance by representatives of a traditional

---

[20] For an attempted revival, see Linda Zagzebski, *Exemplarist Moral Theory* (Oxford: Oxford University Press, 2017).

[21] Aristotle, *Nicomachean Ethics*, VI, 12–13.

morality, which gives the appearance, especially to these representatives, of their having put aside moral concerns altogether.

A more interesting source of the assumption that markets are hostile to morality is the conviction that rational agents are bound to be selfish. This conviction in turn may arise from confusing rational agents' following their own judgment about what is good to do with their doing only what they expect to be good for themselves. Put so blandly, the confusion here is evident. To be the one who judges and the one who profits are clearly two things. So the conviction that rationality entails selfishness may be suspected to stem from a deeper, more insidious supposition—the Christian, in particular protestant, belief in humans' thorough sinfulness. Immanuel Kant, for instance, found everywhere "the dear self" lurking behind the seemingly noblest actions,[22] a judgment he must have learned from the pulpits, as on his own view we do not know people's hidden motives. With that supposition in place, it easily follows that people left to their own devices in determining their path cannot but open the gates to immorality. Still, the assumption that humans are fundamentally sinners, or radically evil, as Kant later put it,[23] must be given up, merely based on an old myth as it is,[24] and on a badly misunderstood myth to boot.[25] Not that man is good instead. Rather, people need to be supposed to be as capable of fine as of base action, thus of the whole mixed bag that we find them producing, both under liberal capitalism and under other conditions.

A third source of the judgment that markets are destructive of true morality may be the old Platonic contempt, evident in the class structure of Plato's republic, for those who earn their living by working with material things and selling their products on the market. This intellectual prejudice persisted right down to Theodor Adorno, say, who spoke of words "sullied by commerce" (*mit dem vom Kommerz besudelten*, sc. *Wort*).[26] In the same spirit, people currently complain about "the economization of health services," apparently suggesting that help bought is no longer helpful, and that medical personnel should be working from mere charity, without pay. In fact, there is nothing wrong with buying help from, and selling help to, others. There is nothing wrong with providing support

---

[22] Immanuel Kant, *Grundlegung zur Metaphysik der Sitten* (1785), in *Kants gesammelte Schriften*, ed. Kgl. Preußische Akademie der Wissenschaften (Berlin: Reimer, 1902–) (hereafter AA), 4:407.

[23] Kant, *Über das radikale Böse in der menschlichen Natur* (1792), AA, 6:19–53.

[24] Genesis 3:1–24.

[25] See, for instance, Thomas Krüger, "Sündenfall?," in *Beyond Eden*, ed. K. Schmid and C. Riedweg (Tübingen: Mohr, 2008), 95–109.

[26] Theodor W. Adorno, *Zur Schlußszene des Faust* (1959), in idem, *Noten zur Literatur II* (Frankfurt: Suhrkamp, 1961), 8.

to people unable to support themselves should it even be motivated by a worldly concern to make money.

None of these lines of thought proving defensible, then, we rest with the conclusion that there is no such thing as an ethos of liberal capitalism. Our political economy does not teach us any morals, either good or bad. It does invite us to cast off the merely given ones of old, but which to adopt it does not say. The observation is often heard that people, especially the young, are disoriented today, and in a literal sense this may be true, because the orient, an allegedly natural point of reference by which to determine how to go on, is no longer available, since those given values and distinctions of former times have lost standing. However, this means only that people today cannot avoid figuring out for themselves how to go on, from the bits and pieces they collected when watching others or themselves trying to find suitable paths. They cannot avoid learning how to live through life alone. Which is fine, though: life's teaching morals must, and also does, suffice.

It will be objected that thus to become reconciled to our present political economy with regard to moral matters is to close one's eyes to the material and to the moral devastation that liberal capitalism has brought to the West. Uncounted human deaths, massive poverty, and the destruction of much of our life's natural basis have been its material effects, and morally it has dissolved people's sense of belonging to, and being respected in, a community that gives meaning to their lives. These momentous losses forbid making our peace with the current political economy. Perhaps it cannot be changed at will. Yet we must keep alive at least the awareness of what was lost so as to preserve the vision, for now perhaps utopian, of a truly human life.

Two replies. As regards, first, the material losses humans suffered and still suffer under liberal capitalism, they are indeed staggering, but it is not clear that liberal capitalism is to be blamed for them. Yes, under liberal capitalism people killed and subdued people on a massive scale and often without qualms, and they destroyed with unprecedented speed the natural resources by which we live, but perhaps it was not a consequence of liberal capitalism that they did this. At the least, a convincing argument for laying the horrendous destructions of the past few centuries at the door of liberal capitalism has not been made. These destructions may well be considered, relative to the framework of our political economy, mere mistakes, though enormous ones. For it is part of the story of liberal capitalism that people, determining their paths by what they buy and sell on markets, can also, perhaps through error or habit, choose unwisely and make themselves or others worse off. (Philosophers often prefer to idealize away this liability.) However, as we can make mistakes, so we can learn from them and do better in the future. The jury is thus still out on liberal capitalism's performance with respect to the material issues mentioned. Things went terribly wrong, no doubt, but we may still try to find better paths. Try, since it may be difficult to leave behind the errors and habits that caused our going wrong before.

Matters are different with regard to the alleged moral losses, for these are not losses really, but traditional misconceptions happily shed. If people under liberal capitalism lack a sense of belonging to a community in which their lives acquire meaning, that is fine, since actually such communities no longer exist, if ever they did. Yes, liberal capitalism does away with the domes of meaningful life under which people find themselves united. Individuals need to put together such a life themselves from whatever they come across. In particular, the political collective of which you are a member is not a community to which you belong in any stronger sense of belonging than that of being one of their number, so there is no reason why it should form a substantial content of what you do. Substance is not given or found, but only put together within the particular life whose substance it is. The essential political unity of a people—in the past invoked by Johann Gottfried Herder[27] and Georg Wilhelm Friedrich Hegel,[28] and still clung to by contemporary authors like Charles Taylor[29] and Ernst-Wolfgang Böckenförde[30]—got in fact dismantled under liberal capitalism, so that a realistic understanding of democracy today has to dispense with the notion of the demos, the people. Welcome, then, to the uprooted individuals, as they are called, who no longer depend on the presumed objective meaning-providers of the past, but just examine with interest and open eyes which of the possibilities on offer to go for in their lives.[31] Like consumers, true, but there is nothing contemptible about that.

To prevent misunderstanding, this defense of liberal capitalism is not intended to protect from critique specific political and economic developments in Western countries, it is rather to direct such critique to its proper target. People suffer, within these countries and beyond, but their suffering is not owed to liberal capitalism. It is owed to what is currently done within liberal capitalism and

---

[27] See, for instance, Johann Gottfried Herder, *Briefe zu Beförderung der Humanität. Fünfte Sammlung* (1795), in *Herders Sämmtliche Werke*, ed. B. Suphan (Berlin: Weidmann, 1881), 17:285–89, 319.

[28] Georg Wilhelm Friedrich Hegel, *Grundlinien der Philosophie des Rechts* (1821), 4th ed., ed. J. Hoffmeister (Hamburg: Meiner, 1955), §§ 257, 258, 260, 264, 268.

[29] Charles Taylor, "Wieviel Gemeinschaft braucht die Demokratie?" (1992), in Taylor's volume of that name (Frankfurt: Suhrkamp, 2002), 11–29.

[30] Ernst-Wolfgang Böckenförde, "Demokratie als Verfassungsprinzip," in *Handbuch des Staatsrechts*, vol. 2, 3rd ed., ed. J. Isensee and P. Kirchhof (Heidelberg: Müller, 2004), 26–28.

[31] The figure was variously depicted in novels. Noteworthy is the portrait Robert Musil gives of the protagonist of his novel *Der Mann ohne Eigenschaften* (1930), ed. A. Frisé (Hamburg: Rowohlt, 1952), chap. 5.

done in preference to other things that could as well be done within liberal capitalism. That is to say, the critique of what happens around us should be political as opposed to systemic. With the terms that used to be current on the left, it should be reformist, not radical, and it should forget about utopian visions. It is not the system under which we live that is at fault, it is what we do within it. Besides, as mentioned earlier, for all our critique, liberal capitalism is not likely to budge in the foreseeable future.

To conclude, then, it is not through our political economy that characters are formed and values transmitted. Liberal capitalism is morally neutral, for as long as it is liberal it presents to people a whole range of courses to take. What makes them think of good and bad the way they do is not liberal capitalism, but the particular experience they go through within liberal capitalism. In response to the human beings they meet and the events through which they live, they come to see things this way or that way and direct their steps in the future. So if we want to improve character formation and value transmission, we should not worry about liberal capitalism. We should see to it that within liberal capitalism people find sufficient space to appreciate or to reject, as they think fit, the human paths that our culture offers.

The Devaluing of Virtue: The Global Financial Crisis of 2007–10 as a Test Case of the Effect of Moral Formation

David McIlroy[1]

> The poorest man I know is the man who has nothing but money.
> —John D. Rockefeller

Introduction

Prior to the coronavirus pandemic of 2020–22, the global financial crisis of 2007–10, triggered by the collapse of an asset price bubble in housing, was the greatest economic shock to the West since the Great Depression. The devastating ramifications of the crisis were caused by the amount of leverage (debt) that banks had taken on to finance their trading in financial instruments and by the mechanisms through which they had transferred liabilities (often sliced and packaged) to other actors in the financial markets (including public authorities, pension funds, and others). Instead of being economic shock absorbers, banks had become, according to the doyen of investors, Warren Buffett, sellers of "financial instruments of mass destruction."

Alan Brener was one of many commentators who identified individualistic factors, including greed, hubris, and amorality, as contributing causes of the global financial crisis, the manipulation of the London Interbank Offered Rate

---

[1] This chapter draws on material previously published in David McIlroy, "What Effect Does Regulation Have on the Culture of Banks?," in *Law and Economics: An Anthology*, ed. Kim Østergaard, Jacob Lyngsie, and Bent Ole Gram Mortensen (Copenhagen: Jurist- og Økonomforbundets Forlag, 2016); McIlroy, "From Captain Mainwaring to Gordon Gekko: Why Bankers Need to Be a Law unto Themselves," *Crucible*, Jan. 2017, https://theologyoflaw.org/wp-content/uploads/2020/07/Crucible-Article-From-Captain-Mainwaring-to-Gordon-Gekko-David-McIlroy.pdf; and McIlroy, "Time for a Financial Reformation?," *Cambridge Papers* 26, no. 2 (Jun. 2017): https://static1.squarespace.com/static/62012941199c974967f9c4ad/t/620e8171ee1c3961aea815ee/1645117814838/CP+Vol26+no2+Time+for+a+financial+reformation.pdf.

(LIBOR), and other scandals.[2] The Group of Thirty named "a culture of individualism and short termism" as among the major causes of the crisis.[3]

The global financial crisis was not, however, caused by lone wolves, rogue agents, or isolated rotten apples. The incentives of self-interested individuals were aligned with those of banks seeking to deliver short-term profits to their shareholders.[4] The problems with banking culture were widespread in the Anglo-Saxon world. The financial crisis was caused by the cumulative effect of decisions made by people (mostly men, mostly white) who were told by their shareholders and boards of directors that all that mattered were quarterly and annual profits, to be achieved regardless of whether customers and counterparties were being sold products which were necessary, suitable, or beneficial. Both the Australian Royal Commission investigating the banking industry[5] and the *United States Financial Crisis Inquiry Report*[6] identified poor culture as the major factor behind almost all the instances of bank misconduct they investigated.

The widespread antisocial cultures in banks were the result of an assumption that personal and corporate morality were not mission-critical. This assumption was taught by a school of economics which: (1) claimed that economics was a science, and therefore that its account of human nature was factually accurate; (2) declared that wealth (in the form of shareholder value and executive remuneration) was the sole measure of success; (3) made it an article of faith that markets are self-regulating; and (4) endorsed the outsourcing of ethics to governments and regulators. A major reason for the catastrophe of the global financial crisis and the fall in the reputation of banks which accompanied it was

---

[2] Alan Brener, "Developing the Senior Managers Regime," in *Research Handbook on the Law and Ethics of Banking and Finance*, ed. Costanza A. Russo, Rosa M. Lastra, and William Blair (Cheltenham: Edward Elgar, 2019).

[3] The other two were "a weak culture of oversight among board members" and "a weak risk culture": Group of Thirty, ed., *Banking Conduct and Culture: A Call for Sustained and Comprehensive Reform* (Washington, D.C.: Group of Thirty, 2015), 19.

[4] A recent survey of employees in three financial institutions found that a culture that implicitly condones self-interested behavior was more likely to lead to unethical pro-organizational behavior than any other factor: Elizabeth Sheedy, Patrick Garcia, and Denise Jepsen, "The Role of Risk Climate and Ethical Self-Interest Climate in Predicting Unethical Pro-organisational Behaviour," *Journal of Business Ethics* 173 (2021). 281–300.

[5] Australian Royal Commission, "Final Report of the Royal Commission into Misconduct in the Banking, Superannuation and Financial Services Industry," Royal Commissions, Feb. 4, 2019, https://www.royalcommission.gov.au/banking/final-report.

[6] *The Financial Crisis Inquiry Report: Final Report of the National Commission on the Causes of the Financial and Economic Crisis in the United States* (Washington, D.C.: Govt. Printing Office, 2011), 180, 207, 265, 273.

an approach that regarded markets as intrinsically amoral and affirmed no value other than money.

The Scientific Claim of Economics That Rational Individuals Are Self-Interested

The culture of profit-seeking at all costs was given a scientific justification by the Chicago School of Economics. One of the distinctive features of some modern definitions of science is the assertion that science "does not consider issues of 'meaning' and 'purpose' in the world."[7] Approaches to economics that aspire to this scientific status therefore sought to describe human behavior as it actually is, rather than to prescribe how human beings ought to behave in order to maximize human welfare, flourishing, and goods. Many members of the Chicago School presented their models as based on verifiable assumptions about how people, on average, behave.

The origin of this approach is to be found in the claim of the eighteenth-century moral philosopher and founder of economics, Adam Smith, who famously said, in *The Wealth of Nations*, that "It is not from the benevolence of the butcher, the brewer, or the baker that we expect our dinner, but from their regard to their own interest." The average butcher, Smith seems to assert in this passage, gives us good quality meat because he wants our repeat business, not because he has an active interest in seeing our families well-fed. The Chicago School of Economics argued that this meant that the invisible hand of the market will deliver outcomes that are good for most people most of the time, even if some people are acting selfishly and disregarding the interests of others.

The dominant model for human behavior as described by the Chicago School was that of the rational self-interested person (*homo economicus*). *Homo economicus* is "a calculating, rational, freely choosing, egoistic individual, endowed with perfect foresight and pursuing [their] interests in perfectly free, perfectly competitive markets."[8] Avner Offer traces the rise of this model from discussions in early game theory in the 1940 s to the status of (almost) unquestioned orthodoxy by the 1970 s.[9]

---

[7] Kitzmiller v Dover Area School District, 400 F. Supp. 2d 707 (M.D. Pa. 2005). In contrast, Aristotle understood scientific inquiry as considering not only the questions of material cause (*what?*) and efficient cause (*how?*) but also the questions of formal cause (*what shape?*) and final cause (*why, for what purpose?*).

[8] David Marquand, *Mammon's Kingdom: An Essay on Britain, Now* (London: Allen Lane, 2014), 77.

[9] Avner Offer, "Regard for Others," in *Capital Failure: Rebuilding Trust in Financial Services*, ed. Nicholas Morris and David Vines (Oxford: Oxford University Press, 2014).

The economists and sociologists of the Chicago project "made it a fundamental assumption that *all* human behaviour is driven by self-interested economic rationality; that is, people invariably choose actions which offer the greatest surplus of positive benefits over the costs of the actions."[10] Even within its own terms, the assumption leads to unethical and antisocial behavior in cases where the short-term benefits are visible and certain but the long-term costs are invisible and uncertain (even if catastrophic), or where the actor is the one who will receive the benefits but the costs will be largely borne by others.

While this model is now widely recognized as flawed, failing to depict how most people behave most of the time, it became normative for those most likely to have been exposed to it through their study of economics, business, or related disciplines. By pretending not to offer a normative account of good human behavior, economics in fact endorsed the standard of rational self-interest as both necessary and desirable. David Marquand concludes that the Chicago School's message—"that altruism and public spirit are surplus to requirements"—led to "money worship, selfishness and callousness."[11]

In an age of fragile personal relationships, in which a popular expression talks of middle-aged men "trading in" their wives for a younger model, the model human being (*homo economicus*) imagined by economics was an isolated, materialist individual with no social or moral connections. Such a "man"[12] was meant to be a description of human nature as it is, on average, having smoothed out the extremes of heroism and malice. As Robert Nelson points out, the approach of the Chicago project normalizes (and therefore implicitly legitimizes) self-interested behavior in family life, including breaking up a family in order to pursue a more attractive love life.[13] The rationality to which the Chicago School appealed was not only descriptive but also prescriptive, a "substitute for 'good.'"[14] *Homo economicus* became a justification for those who choose to live self-centered lives—if necessary, at others' expense.

In the financial sector in particular, the pursuit of profit for shareholders quickly became the pursuit of short-term profit for shareholders (financial prod-

---

[10] Donald A. Hay and Alan Kreider, eds., *Christianity and the Culture of Economics* (Cardiff: University of Wales Press, 2001), 168.

[11] Marquand, *Mammon's Kingdom*, 87.

[12] As Eve Poole has pointed out, *homo economicus* displays distinctly masculine traits and is not shaped to any meaningful extent by attitudes (stereo-)typically regarded as more feminine, such as cooperation, protection, and nurturing: *Capitalism's Toxic Assumptions: Redefining Next Generation Economics* (London: Bloomsbury, 2015).

[13] Robert H. Nelson, "Economic Religion Versus Christian Values," paper presented at conference of the American Association of Christian Economists, Jan. 5-6, 1998, Chicago, Ill.; and Poole, *Capitalism's Toxic Assumptions*, 64.

[14] Marquand, *Mammon's Kingdom*, 83.

ucts and services being ones which, by their nature, allow significant profits to be recorded if their risks are not adequately provided for). The result was both a collapse in ethical standards[15] and a loss of any sense that banking had a purpose beyond the generation of profits. David Knights and Maria Tullberg[16] studied financial services in the UK and Sweden and found that the banking crisis arose partly because of a narrative of the "masculine autonomous self"—the notion of the self-interested, self-sustaining individual—which led to "poor ethical standards [that] stemmed from the conditioning of individuals to not recognize their social interdependence" or their social responsibilities.

Wealth Replaces Other Markers of Respect

The Chicago School's model of *homo economicus* was not the same as Adam Smith's tradesman. Smith thought that self-interest was tempered by our desire for respect from others. In *The Wealth of Nations* (1776) and *A Theory of Moral Sentiments* (1759), he placed a heavy emphasis on the influence of our peer group on how we act. He thought that one of the major reasons why the baker would not sell us substandard bread was because of how he thought his behavior would be viewed by other bakers.[17]

In what is still the most famous sociological essay of all time, Max Weber explained the success of European capitalism in achieving unprecedented levels of prosperity and improvements to human lives on the basis of what he identified as the Protestant work ethic. People worked hard, saved money, and accumulated wealth not as an end in itself or because they were insatiable consumers, but because they saw work as a meaningful activity of service to others and God. Respectability depended on industriousness, thrift, and self-restraint.

In the mid-twentieth century, popular culture provided examples of the altruistic banker at the heart of their community. In the 1946 film *It's a Wonderful Life*, George Bailey, the managing director of a savings and loan association, is the hero who has funded a modern housing development and who thwarts the ambitions of the rack-rent landlord Henry F. Potter. In Britain, the local bank manager was typified by Captain George Mainwaring in the popular sitcom

---

[15] Instances of which are discussed in McIlroy, "What Effect Does Regulation Have on the Culture of Banks?," 69–75.

[16] David Knights and Maria Tullberg, "Managing Masculinity/Mismanaging the Corporation," *Organization* 19 (2012): 385–404.

[17] John Milbank and Adrian Pabst, *The Politics of Virtue: Post-Liberalism and the Human Future* (Lanham, Md.: Rowman & Littlefield, 2016), 122, point out that Smith drew distinct limits to the effects of sympathy and therefore already placed most of his faith in amoral, neutral market mechanisms.

Dad's Army. The comedy, which ran from 1968 to 1977, was set during the Second World War. Captain Mainwaring, pompous but sincere and well-meaning, was responsible for a troop of local volunteers, who represented Britain's last line against invasion by the Nazis. George Bailey and Captain Mainwaring served their communities, whether behind their desks at the bank or in their spare time.

Adam Smith thought that the idea that we measure our behavior by how we think others will see it was a force for morality in the world.[18] But the principle can work in the opposite direction. Groupthink can be a force for ill as well as for good. If a banker thinks that other bankers would see nothing wrong in laundering money, why shouldn't he launder money? LIBOR, a benchmark rate used in many transactions, was supposed to reflect the truth about the average rate at which major banks were borrowing from one another. In fact, for much of its history, traders, sometimes colluding between different banks, provided false data so that they could make profits by distorting the level at which a supposedly independent benchmark was set.[19] The banks' actions in manipulating LIBOR demonstrated how the banks continued to act like a club against the interests of their clients. As Paul Downes QC puts it: "It is clear that from at least 2005, there was a cultural acceptance that LIBOR was simply a variable, to be managed just like any other variable, to maximise the returns being generated by individual traders, for their own personal financial benefit, and to bolster the banks' trading revenue."[20]

If the sense of any purpose in banking beyond the manufacturing of shareholder value is lost, then money ousts all other registers of respect and esteem. From the 1980 s onwards, bankers ceased to be pillars of respectability, known for their good works and proud of their success in supporting businesses and community. Instead, they became flashy, superrich individuals, driving fast cars and displaying ostentatious wealth. The change was signaled by their move from their traditional buildings to new glass-fronted, skyscraping corporate headquarters. Another development that promoted the cult of the individual was the change from paying bonuses to a whole team to paying bonuses to individuals. This weakened the sense of the good of the organization as a whole[21] and encouraged high-flying traders and executives to think of themselves as "self-made men."

---

[18] Offer, "Regard for Others," 155.

[19] McIlroy, "What Effect Does Regulation Have on the Culture of Banks?," 65–87.

[20] Paul Downes QC, "LIBOR: More to LIBOR Than *Graiseley?*," *Butterworth's Journal of International Banking and Financial Law* (2014): 83–85.

[21] Catherine Cowley, "How the Financial Institutions Dug the Hole We're In," in *Christian Perspectives on the Financial Crash*, ed. Philip Booth (London: St Pauls Publishing, 2010), 39.

The poster boy for money as the measure of success and esteem was Gordon Gekko, the financier played by Michael Douglas in Oliver Stone's 1987 film *Wall Street.* Gekko's slogan was, "Greed, for lack of a better word, is good. Greed is right. Greed works." The irony is that *Wall Street* was intended to be a satire. Many people on Wall Street and in the City of London didn't see the joke: they thought Gordon Gekko was the role model to aspire to be. In 2005, *Fortune* magazine announced on its front cover that hedge funds were the new apostles of the idea that greed is good, and that "if Gordon Gekko were on Wall Street today, they'd eat him for breakfast." The bankers responsible for the global financial crisis were described by Australian Prime Minister Kevin Rudd in a speech on October 8, 2008, as the "the 21st century children of Gordon Gekko."[22] Gekko's "children" were a generation of highly paid, mostly white males who grew up admiring his ruthlessness, his lack of hypocrisy about his motives, and, perhaps above all, the money he made.

In his investigation into the culture at Barclays Bank, Anthony Salz concluded that "Elevated pay levels inevitably distort culture, tending to attract people who measure their personal success principally on compensation."[23] Pay, promotion, and prestige were all dependent on an individual's performance in making money, at all costs. Salz found that "the culture that emerged tended to favour transactions over relationships, the short term over sustainability, and financial over other business purposes."[24] Instead of the culture among bankers providing a restraint on selfish behavior, it now rewarded that behavior beyond any reasonable expectations.

The Chicago School of Economics offered a model for "normal" human behavior, and popular culture provided, in Gordon Gekko, an exemplar for the successful banker to copy. The result was a significant change in the behavior of market participants "guided by market values, ... [which] are quite different in character from the moral values that are supposed to guide the behaviour of people as members of society."[25] The expectation of bankers was that the markets would nonetheless deliver beneficial social consequences, because that was what the efficient-market hypothesis predicted.

---

[22] Kevin Rudd, edited extract of speech, "The Children of Gordon Gekko," *The Australian*, Oct. 6, 2008, https://web.archive.org/web/20090116120126/http://www.theaustralian.news.com.au/story/0,25197,24450662-7583,00.html.

[23] Anthony Salz, *An Independent Review of Barclays' Business Practices* (Apr. 2013), 11.16. Available online at http://online.wsj.com/public/resources/documents/SalzReview04032013.pdf.

[24] Ibid., 2.13.

[25] George Soros, "Capitalism Versus Open Society," *Financial Times*, Oct. 30, 2009; Robert H. Franks, Thomas Gilovich, and Dennis Regan, "Does Studying Economics Inhibit Cooperation?," *Journal of Economic Perspectives* 7, no. 2 (1993); 159–71.

Markets Are Self-Regulating

The efficient-market hypothesis is the bowdlerized version of the idea that greed is good. Adam Smith, the founding father of economics, ascribed a quasi-divine status to the invisible hand of the market. Smith's invisible hand is a secular substitute for the Christian doctrine of providence, for the idea that God, by his Holy Spirit, is at work behind the scenes in human affairs, working toward God's good purposes. Smith recognized, however, the need for regulation (particularly of banks) because

> those exertions of the natural liberty of a few individuals, which might endanger the security of the whole society are, and ought to be, restrained by the laws of all governments. ... The obligation of building party walls, in order to prevent the communication of fire, is a violation of natural liberty, exactly of the same kind with the regulations of the banking trade which are here proposed.[26]

The market's ascent to godhood was completed by the efficient-market hypothesis. The efficient-market hypothesis comes in a number of different forms, but its essence is captured by the slogan "You can't beat the market" (at least not consistently).[27] Devised by Eugene Fama, of the University of Chicago, the efficient-market hypothesis is the belief that markets always know what they are doing, even if individual investors within them don't, and therefore the market price for assets is an accurate reflection of their real value.

According to the efficient-market hypothesis, the market always knows best, and therefore the best thing that governments can do is to deregulate the market as much as possible. The invisible hand of the market will do the rest. Putting the efficient-market hypothesis into practice, neoliberal governments deregulated financial services, abolishing the restrictions put in place after the Great Depression. With the passing of the Gramm-Leach-Bliley Act in the United States in 1999, the process was complete. The result was herd-like behavior by banks engaging in ever more leveraged speculation in order to grow larger and to deliver shareholder returns.

The popular interpretation of Fama's ideas was that, provided there are certain minimal basic rules in place, the individual motives of market participants are irrelevant, because the invisible hand of the market will sort everything out. The efficient-market hypothesis promoted a "thin" notion of rational self-interest which is individualistic and atomistic, and in which my rational self-interest causes me to act in ways which are at best indifferent to the interests of anyone

---

[26] Adam Smith, *The Wealth of Nations* (Oxford: Oxford University Press, 1998), 188.
[27] Adair Turner, *Between Debt and the Devil: Money, Credit, and Fixing Global Finance* (Princeton: Princeton University Press, 2016), 37.

and everyone else. The efficient-market hypothesis says that there is no need for government to intervene to restrain this selfish approach to self-interest, because the consequences of such selfishness will be miraculously transformed as a result of the work of the invisible hand of the market. Bankers were taught, in effect, that they did not have to have a personal conscience about their activities at work, because issues of social benefit would be handled by the market itself.

The bankers who grew up in the shadow of Gordon Gekko had been taught that the single-minded pursuit of their own interest by delivering short term profits for the bank's shareholders was normal, that their success in doing so was properly rewarded through bonuses that grew larger as their leveraged transactions enabled them to squeeze large profits out of small movements in the financial markets, and that the social consequences of their actions would be addressed through the autocorrecting and invisible providence of the market.

The new motto was: let's make a profit at all costs and by all means. A striking feature of the defenses of their actions mounted by Tom Hayes (convicted in the UK for manipulating LIBOR), Kweku Adoboli (whose fraudulent trading cost UBS 1.4 billion pounds), and Jerome Kerviel (whose fraudulent trading lost Société Générale 4.9 billion euros) was their insistence that their bosses knew what they were doing and tacitly approved it, so long as they seemed to be making money, regardless of whether they were breaking the rules. Junior bankers were inculcated into a culture in which customers were treated as counterparties and were sold products they did not need, and whose fears and ignorance not only could, but should, be exploited.

The official teaching was that the personal morality of bankers was irrelevant. The markets were amoral. The practical result was immorality, law-breaking, and the infliction of harm on millions of people who ended up carrying the costs of underpriced risks.

The assessment of the financier and philanthropist George Soros was:

> It has been extensively analyzed by economists, but they look at it exclusively in terms of contracts and incentives and they largely disregard questions of ethics and values. Yet if you leave out ethical considerations the problem becomes pretty well intractable. Values like honesty and integrity lose their grip on people's behavior and people become increasingly motivated by economic incentives. By claiming to be value free, market fundamentalism has actually undermined moral values.[28]

With classic British understatement, Adair Turner said: "The pre-crisis policy orthodoxy reflected overconfidence in the power of free financial markets to de-

---

[28] George Soros, "Capitalism Versus Open Society."

liver optimal results."[29] What Joseph Stiglitz called the religion of market fundamentalism was lauded,[30] but its legacy was a disaster. More trenchantly, John Talbott listed the claim that "free-market capitalism works best with no regulation and no interference from government" at number seven in his *The 86 Biggest Lies on Wall Street.*[31]

Jeffrey Sachs, writing in the *Financial Times* on January 18, 2012, titled his column that day, "Self-Interest, Without Morals, Leads to Capitalism's Self-Destruction." Will Hutton, economic and political commentator, declared that the dominant intellectual ideology of the past twenty years—free market fundamentalism and the way it was applied in the financial markets, the efficient-market hypothesis—was the biggest intellectual mistake this generation has ever witnessed, arguably the biggest that the world has ever witnessed.[32] Even the doyen of the law-and-economics movement, Richard Posner, said, following the global financial crisis, that "the movement to deregulate the financial industry went too far by exaggerating the resilience—the self-healing powers—of laissez-faire capitalism."[33]

Ethics Can Be Outsourced to Government

The most famous articulation of the idea that business ethics is a matter for governments, not for companies or their executives, came in a magazine interview given by Milton Friedman in 1974. He stated, "Do corporate executives, *provided they stay within the law*, have responsibilities in their business activities other than to make as much money for their stockholders as possible? And my answer to that is, no they do not."[34]

The single-minded pursuit of rational self-interest by businesses was, according to Friedman, to be achieved by the single-minded pursuit of profit for their shareholders. The business of business was to deliver shareholder value, nothing more and nothing less—that was the beginning and the end of corporate

---

[29] Turner, *Between Debt and the Devil*, 242.
[30] Joseph Stiglitz, *Globalization and its Discontents* (London: Penguin, 2002), 134.
[31] John R. Talbott, *The 86 Biggest Lies on Wall Street* (London: Constable & Robinson, 2009).
[32] Will Hutton, "Thanks to the Credit Crunch All Bets Are Off," *The Guardian*, Feb. 27, 2009, https://www.theguardian.com/commentisfree/video/2009/feb/27/will-hutton-capitalism-crisis.
[33] Richard Posner, *A Failure of Capitalism: The Crisis of 2008 and the Descent into Depression* (Cambridge, Mass.: Harvard University Press, 2011), xii.
[34] Milton Friedman, interview with John McLaughry, contributing editor of *Business and Society Review*, "Milton Friedman Responds," in *Chemtech* (Feb. 1974), 72, cited at Bartleby.com, https://www.bartleby.com/73/143.html.

social responsibility. Business people had no need for a personal moral compass; they could outsource their conscience to the government. The common good was the sole concern of the government (which could serve the common good most effectively by enlarging the arenas in which markets operate). Business leaders made their contribution to the common good through pursuing shareholder value ruthlessly but (in an important but subsequently neglected proviso) within the law.

Increasingly prescriptive regulation was the way in which governments exercised their role as the outsourced conscience of banks. As deregulation allowed banks to carry out an ever-wider variety of financial services, so the rules seeking to ensure that they did so safely and in ways that were not antisocial grew ever-more-lengthy and -detailed. The project was doomed from the start. Since the 1970s, banking has been regulated by a vast edifice of ever-more complicated and technical rules. The way in which banking transactions are carried out has become controlled by detailed prescriptive rules, but this approach "has undermined rather than enhanced ethical standards, by substituting compliance for values."[35] As early as 2002, the warning signs were already apparent to Alistair Alcock. He criticized the increasing emphasis on rules as meaning that whereas in the 1980s people in the financial services sector asked themselves whether what they were doing was right, in the 1990s they asked themselves whether what they were doing was within the rules.[36] The attempt to control people's behavior through external laws rather than instilling in them personal morality was, as the Hebrew scriptures should have taught us, doomed to failure.[37] Regulators need to rip up the rulebook, replacing many of the detailed rules with clear principles that bankers are required to internalize and to live by.[38]

In his report on Barclays, Anthony Salz said, "Barclays was sometimes perceived as being within the letter of the law but not within its spirit."[39] Although the UK did not experience any scandals on the scale of WorldCom in the United

---

[35] John Kay, *Other People's Money: Masters of the Universe or Servants of the People?* (London: Profile Books, 2015), 273.

[36] Alistair Alcock, "Are UK Financial Services Over-Regulated?," public lecture at the Institute of Advanced Legal Studies, Oct. 31, 2002.

[37] David McIlroy, *A Biblical View of Law and Justice* (Carlisle, UK: Paternoster, 2004), chap. 7.

[38] One suggestion by ResPublica is a bankers' oath: http://www.respublica.org.uk/disraeli-room-post/2014/08/07/bankers-oath-honesty-integrity-ethics/.

[39] Salz, *Review of Barclays' Business Practices*, 2.18.

States,[40] basic standards of honesty and transparency were lost within a forest of detailed rules.

"A Report on the Culture of British Retail Banking," by New City Agenda and Cass Business School,[41] identifies a widespread and aggressive sale culture as one of the central reasons for the numerous failures of banking in the UK between 2007 and 2014—problems that were particularly prevalent in the biggest banks. Bankers were forced, by both the promises of bonuses and the threats of dismissal, to sell customers products they did not need. In many cases, the products offered customers no real benefit, but transferred risks to customers that they did not understand and were not equipped to cope with.

As the rules became more detailed, the trend for bankers to concern themselves *solely* with the question "is it within the rules?" became more pronounced. However, on top of this, the major banks also began to engage in patterns of widespread breaches of the detailed rules when the rules got in the way of making a profit, as well as flagrant defiance of basic standards of honesty and transparency.

The Chicago School asserted that market discipline and regulatory oversight would keep banks in line. Market discipline turned out to mean that all banks were forced to engage in similar mis-selling, the practice of "originate and distribute" (where poorly assessed loans were quickly sold on secondary markets and the money recycled to make further loans), and other aggressive tactics in order to generate the quarterly profit figures shareholders came to expect. Regulatory oversight was minimal: staff at the regulators were either too inexperienced and overstretched to understand what was happening in the marketplace or were caught in the revolving door between the regulators and the banks. Former employees of Goldman Sachs and other major banks ensured that regulatory capture was nearly total. Even if they could see what was happening, regulators lacked the confidence and the gravitas to challenge the dominance of Chicago School orthodoxy. Oversight by regulators proved to be no substitute for the mutual self-control of bankers, who knew that they would be personally ruined if their bank were to fail.

Revaluing Virtue

Numerous studies conducted in the United Kingdom following the global financial crisis found that the decline in banking standards had been caused by a

---

[40] Where many of the accounting maneuvers were within the letter of American accounting rules, but their cumulative effect was to present a picture of the company's finances, which was misleading to the tune of nine billion dollars!

[41] http://newcityagenda.co.uk/wp-content/uploads/2014/11/Online-version.pdf.

change in the culture at banks, in what bankers regarded as right and wrong, and in what bankers thought the purpose of banking was. In one of the most telling exchanges, Bob Diamond, the CEO of Barclays, was called to give evidence before the UK Parliament's Treasury Select Committee in 2012. He was asked by John Mann MP to name any of the three founding principles of the Quakers who set up Barclays. He could not do so. Honesty, integrity, and plain dealing all seemed to have become wholly alien to the culture of the banks in the run-up to the great financial crisis.[42]

Eight hundred years earlier, Thomas Aquinas had said that "the common good of a political community can be rightly disposed only if its citizens, at least those to whom its ruling belongs, are virtuous."[43] What the global financial crisis of 2007–10 revealed was that the common good of a bank can be rightly disposed only if its senior managers, traders, and customer relationship managers are virtuous. Viewing markets as amoral and profit as the sole business value was a fundamental error. The antidote lies in four E's: Education, Empathy, Example, and Enforcement.

Education

Education because virtues have to be taught. Instead of the normalization of selfishness implicitly endorsed by the Chicago School, business virtues need to be expressly inculcated. The virtues required of bankers need to be taught in universities and in induction and training courses at banks, and need to be repeated following each promotion. What is needed is a new education for business leaders and management consultants, one that recognizes that issues of character are key for those who will be in future leadership positions in banks and other large companies. Character needs to be understood as the demonstration of a rounded set of virtues that are central to the mission of the bank, rather than side-constraints that equality, diversity, inclusion, and other forms of virtue-signaling risk becoming.

There is a place for a return to something like the Banking Code, a short statement of fundamental rules of fair dealing, agreed upon by the banks themselves, applied in the first instance by the industry, but then subject to an appeal to a body representing the public interest. Yet uptake in the UK for postcrisis initiatives, such as the Financial Services Culture Board (FSCB) and the Char-

---

[42] These three virtues are listed in Robert Barclay's 1678 book, *An Apology for the True Christian Divinity*. Kenneth Hopper and William Hopper, in *The Puritan Gift: Reclaiming the American Dream Amidst Global Financial Chaos* (London: I. B. Taurus, 2009), suggest how those virtues could once again transform the way in which business is done.

[43] Aquinas, *Summa Theologiae* I-II.92.1 ad.3.

tered Banker Professional Standards Board, has been low.[44] In Eleanore Hickman's assessment, it remains the case "that profit trumps professionalism," that banks still have not aligned their interests with those of the community more generally, and therefore that "the cultural issues that brought us the [2007–10] financial crisis" have not been effectively addressed.[45]

But in the end, bankers need to be people who do the right thing even when no one else is looking.[46] Ethical persons are a law unto themselves: they act justly not because they are following a rule for fear of a sanction but because they have internalized the fact that acting justly is the right thing to do. Businesses need to teach this, and bankers need to earn respect on the basis of the quality and extent of their service to their customers.

Empathy

Empathy because, as Adam Smith saw, to the extent that we allow our capacity for sympathy and our desire for friendship to inform our understanding of our self-interest, we grow in wisdom and learn to control our selfishness and greed. Finance should be understood as a service industry, one whose value and profitability lie in the quality of the services it provides to companies, individuals, and public institutions. As Anthony Salz concluded, "transforming the culture [in banks] will require a new sense of purpose beyond the need to perform financially."[47]

In 2014, one of the most successful toy companies in the world, Lego, produced one of the most successful animated movies, *The Lego Movie*. The villain in the movie is Lord Business. Lord Business is the villain because, unlike the company that makes Lego, he does not exist for any higher purpose other than business. He is the embodiment of the idea that the business of business is business. Is this supposed to be postmodern irony, in which adults see the joke in being told by a major corporation that major corporations are the enemy? Or is the message actually more profound? What has made Lego such an enduring success? Lego bricks are fun to play with. Lego is a successful business because it produces goods that serve the essential human good of play. Lego succeeds as

---

[44] Eleanore Hickman, "Is the Senior Managers and Certification Regime Changing Banking for Good?," *Modern Law Review*, Jul. 25, 2002, https://onlinelibrary.wiley.com/doi/full/10.1111/1468-2230.12752, at 14–15.
[45] Ibid., 15.
[46] David T. Llewellyn, Roger Steare, and Jessica Trevellick, *Virtuous Banking: Placing Ethos and Purpose at the Heart of Finance* (London: Res Publica, 2014).
[47] Salz, *Review of Barclays' Business Practices*, 2.20.

a business because it is effective at enhancing human flourishing by enabling children (and adults) to enjoy playing.

There are two very different conceptions of a bank: one sees banks simply as financial businesses, while the other sees banks as providers of financial services. In the conception of banking as merely a financial business, there is no deeper purpose to banking: it exists purely for the sake of making money. Yet, conceived of as nothing other than money-making institutions, banks are problematic: on one hand, they benefit from an implicit or explicit government guarantee, which means that the full rigors of capitalism do not apply to these most capitalist of institutions, and, on the other hand, they have the capacity to generate enormous external costs for everyone else in the economy. In the conception of banking as a financial service, however, the purpose of banking is to serve the common good indirectly by serving customers directly, providing opportunities for liquidity and risk transfer that benefit customers in ways that are sustainable because the bank charges a reasonable profit for its services.

Banks need to get closer to their customers, to understand what the small businesses as well as the big businesses need. This is particularly important because many of those with whom banks deal do not have access to any alternative sources of information and advice about the banks' products. Even if human beings do behave consistently in the way the Chicago School assumed, its predicted outcome that "contracting will only take place if it is to the net advantage of both parties"[48] is false if there is significant information asymmetry. A bank and a customer may both *believe* that the contract is to their net advantage, but if the customer lacks the knowledge, legal advice, accountancy expertise, and economic analysis to be able to understand the risks to which they are exposed, what will result is a contract significantly skewed in favor of the bank.

The primary focus of banks ought to be on offering products and services that customers and counterparties would want even if they were in possession of the same information as the bank. It is from the provision of good quality services in the customers' and counterparties' best interests that the profits of the banks should flow.

Example

Example because, as Adam Smith realized, our self-interest includes a strong desire for approbation or esteem. Gordon Gekko was a compelling character, the

---

[48] Hay and Kreider, *Christianity and Culture of Economics*, 169.

embodiment of an ideal. What is needed are alternative heroes[49] and institutional cultures that remember them, nurture them, and promote them. The desire for approbation and esteem is a powerful factor in the construction of popular morality and other social conventions: we behave in certain ways because we believe that our actions will be approved of by those whose opinion we value. A company's true values are not those recorded in its mission statement, they are the ones lived out in the promotions and bonuses. Bankers need to see that those who try to do the right thing and who win and maintain the respect of their customers are promoted and rewarded.

The tone that is set at the top of a bank is a signal to the lower levels of the bank about what the bank really values, and how much of a price it is prepared to pay to live up to its rhetoric.

Enforcement

Enforcement is also essential. After the global financial crisis, few bankers were jailed, lost their license to be a banker, or had their bonuses and pension entitlements clawed back. The collective responsibility of boards of directors meant that, as the UK's Parliamentary Commission on Banking Standards put it, "a buck that does not stop with an individual stops nowhere."[50]

The UK sought to address this by introducing the Senior Managers and Certification Regime (SMCR), which is specifically designed to ensure that an individual senior manager becomes personally accountable for every aspect of a firm's regulated activity.[51] Banks now have to provide regulators with a management responsibility map accompanied by a statement of responsibilities for each senior manager, so that the regulators know exactly whose door to knock down in the event of regulatory breach. Senior managers are seen as responsible for

---

[49] Though here, too, we need to be careful not to replicate the myth of the self-made man, the rugged individualist, who is a solo success. We need instead to celebrate communities whose shared values and collaboration lead to sustained achievements.

[50] Arnold Martin, "Two HSBC Directors Quit in Protest over New Conduct Rules," *Financial Times*, Oct. 7, 2014, http://www.ft.com/cms/s/0/a237eb26-4e12-11e4-bfda-00144feab7de.html#axzz3UBk5QiFw.

[51] The Prudential Regulation Authority (PRA) lists twenty "prescribed responsibilities" and the Financial Conduct Authority (FCA) twenty-seven "key functions" that need to be allocated to a senior manager who will be required to perform one or more of eighteen senior management functions. Significantly, there will be a need to appoint a senior manager with personal responsibility for implementing the new regime—to ensure that the firm is fully compliant with it and personally accountable to the regulators if it is not.

setting a bank's culture and are therefore placed under express duties both to ensure that all staff are fully aware of what is and what is not acceptable conduct for their specific function and to monitor and gather evidence that staff actually comply with these standards in their everyday interactions with customers, markets, colleagues, and regulators.

I predicted, in a 2016 article,[52] that the introduction of the new SMCR by the UK regulators was unlikely to be sufficient, in itself, to see positive changes in the culture in UK banks. Recent research by Eleanore Hickman has found that the effectiveness of the SMCR has been compromised by inconsistent messaging and a failure to enforce it robustly.[53]

Banks need also to hold their staff accountable to high standards. Regulators cannot be expected to see everything or act on everything, but if those who cheat their customers are dismissed, and those who build long-term relationships are promoted, then others will copy their example.

Conclusion

The global financial crisis of 2007–10 shows the disastrous effects of taking ethics out of the financial markets. A culture emerged in which self-interested behavior (by both banks and their key employees) was normalized, and in which profits and bonuses became the sole meaningful markers of success and respect, justified by the claim that markets are efficient and self-regulating and the lip-service paid to the idea that the regulatory framework imposed by government would be sufficient to protect the common good.

Markets are not purely natural phenomena. Markets are dependent on, sustained by, and shaped by the existence of social attitudes, accepted standards of behavior by market participants, and the enforcement of laws that reinforce those attitudes and behaviors. Banks need to rediscover the importance of serving their customers and the intentional pursuit of the common good. Stephen Green, formerly chairman of HSBC, has rightly pointed out that regulation and legislation "are not and cannot be, sufficient without a culture of values," not only for individuals but also for the "institutions of capitalism—businesses, banks and other institutions of the financial markets."[54]

---

[52] McIlroy, "What Effect Does Regulation Have on the Culture of Banks?"
[53] Hickman cites how, in the five years since the SMCR came into force, there have been only thirty-seven investigations conducted by the FCA, only two of which resulted in regulatory action. See Hickman, "Is the Senior Managers and Certification Regime Changing Banking for Good?"
[54] Stephen Green, *Good Value: Reflections on Money, Morality and an Uncertain World* (London: Penguin, 2011), 132.

Ethics needs to be built back into banking: through intentional education that teaches bankers what their professional duties to their customers are and how to fulfill them, through empathy that shows banks how to understand their customers' needs and rewards those who serve their customers effectively, through examples shown by the board of directors and others in their choice of who is promoted and respected, and all of this supported by effective enforcement by regulators and by banks' internal disciplinary measures.

Twitter: A Case-Study in the Character-Malformation Potential of Twenty-First-Century Digital Technology

Jonathan Cole

> I once said "shut up and sing" in response to a tweet by a celebrated entertainer of color who had said something I didn't like about the war between Israel and Gaza. His wife then accused me of being a racist—and suddenly I had thousands of people raging at me.
>
> The very fact that I tweeted those words offers a sense of what Twitter can do to compulsive users—it was a childish and obnoxious riposte, and, I am ashamed to say, it was something I wrote when I was 53 years old. And the thing is, it took me 10 seconds to tweet it and days to live it down.
>
> –John Podhoretz[1]

Introduction

Twitter has a reputation for being one of the most toxic platforms within the social media ecosystem.[2] The above confession from John Podhoretz, an American political commentator and editor of *Commentary* magazine, testifies to one side of the coin of Twitter toxicity: the ability of the platform to bring out the worst in its users.[3] The high-profile exit from Twitter by actress and rapper Awkwafina (Nora Lum) exemplifies the other side of the coin: the deleterious psychological impact toxic reactions can have on users. The Asian-American entertainer left the platform, which she described as an "ingrown toenail," on the

---

[1] John Podhoretz, "Why I Quit Twitter—And You Should, Too," *The New York Post*, Dec. 29, 2019, https://nypost.com/2019/12/26/why-i-quit-twitter-and-you-should-too/.

[2] Twitter is technically a microblogging site: "A combination of blogging and instant messaging that allows users to create short messages to be posted and shared with an audience online": Daniel Nations, "What Is Microblogging? A Definition with Examples," *Lifewire*, Dec. 19, 2019, https://www.lifewire.com/what-is-microblogging-3486200.

[3] Podhoretz maintains an account on Twitter, boasting 122,500 followers, but ceased posting in March 2019.

instructions of her therapist following incessant criticism and harassment for the sin of "cultural appropriation"–her alleged adoption of African American Vernacular English in her music and some of her movies.[4]

The anecdotal experiences of high profile users attesting to Twitter's toxicity is borne out by research conducted by the Pew Research Center (Pew), which has found that 24 percent of high-volume tweeters and 11 percent of less active tweeters have personally experienced harassing or abusive behavior on Twitter.[5] Pew has also found that 26 percent of U.S. adult users report that Twitter has increased their stress levels, and 21 percent report posting something that they later regretted sharing.[6] Indeed, Twitter, Inc., has conceded the problem of toxicity by repeatedly emphasizing its commitment to improving the "health" of public conversations on its platform, Twitter.[7]

This chapter hypothesizes that Twitter users are more likely to experience harassment and abuse, increased stress levels, and regret from using Twitter than is usual in social interactions in other contexts (social systems), particularly physical/analogue contexts.[8] This hypothesis raises the question: "What is it about Twitter that appears to generate social interactions with higher levels of negative experience?" Below, I identify and analyze five design features of Twitter that remove important norms which govern interactions in physical/ana-

---

[4] Corinne Heller, "Awkwafina Addresses 'Blaccent' Controversy and Quits Twitter," Feb. 5, 2022, https://www.nbcnewyork.com/entertainment/entertainment-news/awkwafina-addresses-blaccent-controversy-and-quits-twitter/3536892/.

[5] Colleen McClain et al., "The Behaviors and Attitudes of U.S. Adults on Twitter," *Pew Research Center*, Nov. 15, 2021, https://www.pewresearch.org/internet/2021/11/15/the-behaviors-and-attitudes-of-u-s-adults-on-twitter/, 2. The top 25 percent of U.S. adult users by tweet volume produce 97 percent of all tweets, which means that high users receive a disproportionate number of interactions on Twitter. Meltem Odabas, "10 facts about Americans and Twitter," *Pew Research Center*, May 5, 2022, https://www.pewresearch.org/fact-tank/2022/05/05/10-facts-about-americans-and-twitter/.

[6] Colleen McClain et al., "The Views and Experiences of U.S. Adult Twitter Users," *Pew Research Center*, Nov. 15, 2021, https://www.pewresearch.org/internet/2021/11/15/1-the-views-and-experiences-of-u-s-adult-twitter-users/, 4.

[7] Twitter, Inc.'s, 2020 annual report, for instance, undertakes to improve the health of conversations on Twitter by "devoting substantial internal resources" to reducing "abuse, harassment, spam, manipulation and malicious automation on the platform." Twitter, Inc., "Fiscal Year 2020 Annual Report," 17, https://s22.q4cdn.com/826641620/files/doc_financials/2020/ar/FiscalYR2020_Twitter_Annual_Report.pdf.

[8] "Physical/analogue" is used here and throughout to denote both physically embodied human interactions and those that occur on technologies that facilitate embodied interaction, such as television, radio, and landline telephones. (Mobile telephones, which I place in the digital category, can also be used for voice calls just like a landline telephone, but can also obviously be used to interact in digital media, such as social media).

logue social systems in ways that incentivize civility and disincentivize incivility. These features of Twitter are anonymity, brevity, interpolation, unmoderatability, and invisibility of mitigating circumstances.[9]

The paper will then proceed to argue that Twitter malforms the character of its users in ways that could, over the long term, potentially undermine important norms which have evolved to promote "healthy conversations" in physical/analogue social systems. Finally, the paper argues that Twitter's corporate rhetorical goal of promoting "healthy conversations" is in tension with its financial goals of increasing revenue and shareholder profit by selling advertising, and that this tension is a consequence of Twitter's (and Twitter, Inc.'s) genesis–an example of the way that twenty-first-century technology can pervert political economy in socially harmful ways.

Five Character-Malforming Design Features of Twitter Which Undermine Social Norms That Promote Healthy Conversation

Anonymity

Anonymity is the most significant design feature of Twitter which contributes to the toxicity experienced in its social system. Although personal identifying information is required to register an account on Twitter, users can set up their profiles in a way that allows them to interact on the platform with complete anonymity.[10] Users are free to give their account fictitious names and Twitter handles, for example: EarthWombat@EarthWombat and Sarcastic Whimsey | DoubleVaxxed and Boostered@StillNotThePope.[11] Users are also free to obscure their identities through the use of fictitious and/or nonidentifying images and bios.[12]

The use of real personal names and other identifying information in social interactions (including showing one's face) have long been an important and established component of physical/analogue social systems. It is customary, for example, to exchange real names when meeting a stranger for the first time or when beginning a new job, meeting new clients, or joining virtually any social

---

[9] This is not intended to be an exhaustive list of character-malforming design features. Other well-known and much-discussed problems with Twitter, such as bots, misinformation, and administrator censorship, fall outside the scope of this essay.
[10] Twitter also permits the creation of organizational accounts. I limit my focus here to the accounts of individual users interacting on Twitter as private citizens.
[11] The name is the part before the @ symbol and the handle is the part after the @ symbol.
[12] Nothing prohibits users from using real names, images, and biographical information on their accounts, and many do.

group, from a sporting club to a place of worship. Real names and other identifying information are also typically used, and often required, in interactions with governing authorities (for example, filing tax returns), businesses (opening a bank account) and educational institutions (enrolling at a college), and even in recreational and entertainment settings (for example, participating in team sport).[13]

Certain norms have developed in Western societies to obscure (protect) the identity of individuals in limited circumstances, such as whistle-blowers, journalistic sources, persons in witness-protection programs, minors, and intelligence officers. These cases, however, have traditionally been regarded as exceptions to the rule that individuals have a wide obligation (either legal or social) to live and interact according to their real identity. Indeed, it is illegal in many contexts for citizens to give or use false information about their identity. These norms reflect the reasonable anxiety and suspicion that arise in interactions with other humans unwilling to give their name or show their face, or worse, those who use a false name—actions associated with dishonesty, ill-intent, or criminality.

It is true that there are numerous routine social interactions in which humans do not offer or exchange names and other identifying information, particularly during simple, transactional exchanges, such as purchasing goods at a supermarket or buying the newspaper at a news agency, although such information is required for more complex purchases, such as buying a car or a house. The use of names and identifying information, including the amount of identifying information given or exchanged, is determined by a complex set of cultural norms that are context-specific and -determined. These norms are so deeply embedded in human cultural practices that most of us are oblivious to their existence and complexity.

A unique feature of Twitter is that it manages to combine many different physical/analogue social systems into one single networked speech forum, from sports and entertainment to news, political activism, and social commentary (and much more). Thus, tweets can range from the trivial to the politically consequential. Much of the toxicity occurs in the part of this broad canvass that involves speech dealing with substantive political, social, and moral questions, particularly those which are divisive.[14] It is in this arena that the ability to speak

---

[13] Indeed, one of the significant drawbacks from playing sport at the elite level or becoming a successful actor or actress is the ubiquitous and often stifling presence of journalists, paparazzi, and fans, who all know what the person of interest looks like, sometimes where they live, and other personal information about them.

[14] Pew estimates that 33 percent of tweets by U.S. adults are political in nature. Sam Bestvater et al., "Politics on Twitter: One-Third of Tweets from U.S. Adults Are Political,"

and interact anonymously is of most consequence, and a radical departure from physical/analogue norms. Commentators on television, for example, typically show their face on camera and are introduced by their real name, often with some accompanying information about their professional affiliation and/or qualifications. In print media, one routinely encounters the names of authors, again often with an affiliation and headshot, in close proximity to the article (above, below or beside).[15] Needless to say, it would be highly irregular for a person giving a public lecture, participating in a public debate or serving as a member of a panel discussion to be introduced as Westeros@OzGoofyPrincess and to appear with their face obscured.

The point is that the cultural norms governing the use of personal and identifying information in social interactions—norms that are present in virtually all social systems and, as such, taken for granted—have evolved in all human societies as a means of developing interpersonal trust by incentivizing civil behavior and disincentivizing uncivil behavior. This is achieved via the vital social function of reputation, with its connection to personal identity. Reputations stand or fall on records of social interaction. Civil, honest, kind, and generous social interactions generate reputations for integrity, which can make a person more desirable as a friend, romantic partner, business associate, or colleague, and in turn provide social and professional advantages and opportunities as a consequence. Conversely, dishonest, abrasive, abusive, and selfish behavior damages reputation in a way that can lead to ostracization and other social disadvantages and penalties.

By permitting users complete anonymity on its platform, Twitter, Inc., has removed a vital social norm that is essential for healthy human interactions, particularly in relation to substantive and divisive political, social, and moral questions. This negative impact of anonymity on human behavior in the online space has been dubbed the "online disinhibition effect" by psychologists.[16] "Dissociative anonymity"—which is to say, the ability of online users to dissociate their online self from the normal constraining context of a fully integrated online or offline identity—has been identified as one important contributing factor to the online disinhibition effect.[17]

Scholars have noted the way that the internet, and the media it facilitates, are eroding norms of privacy. Daniel Solove, for example, has highlighted the

---

Pew Research Center, Jun. 16, 2022, https://www.pewresearch.org/politics/2022/06/16/politics-on-twitter-one-third-of-tweets-from-u-s-adults-are-political/.

[15] It is becoming more common in online print media, particularly in highly partisan outlets, for authors to write under aliases.

[16] John Suler, "The Online Disinhibition Effect," *International Journal of Applied Psychoanalytic Studies* 2, no. 2 (2005): 184–88, at 185.

[17] Ibid.

very real danger of a kind of "enslavement" to human error, by virtue of the seeming immortality of information on the internet, which raises the prospect of mistakes, particularly those made early in life, having potentially life-long prejudicial impacts for people.[18] He validly fears that "the long-standing value of giving people a second chance, of allowing people to reinvent themselves, might soon become a relic of a bygone era."[19]

The protection of privacy is therefore one of the great challenges presented by the age of the internet, and in that context Twitter's anonymity is presented as a virtue by some privacy advocates, and by Twitter, Inc., itself.[20] It is important, however, not to conflate anonymity with privacy. There is a difference between, on one hand, widespread customs of identification in social interactions that serve to promote civil interpersonal relating and, on the other hand, the good of preserving a zone of privacy, particularly as it pertains to sensitive in-

---

[18] Daniel J. Solove, "Speech, Privacy, and Reputation on the Internet," in *The Offensive Internet: Speech, Privacy, and Reputation*, ed. Saul Levmore and Martha Craven Nussbaum (Cambridge, Mass.: Harvard University Press, 2011), 15.

[19] Ibid.

[20] A post on Twitter's blog, *Common Thread*, by "Twitter Safety," mounts a defense of anonymity on Twitter. The post is interesting both for the fact that it reveals sensitivity to the criticisms about the connection between anonymity and toxicity, which it claims "academic studies" have brought into doubt (see below), and the positive case it mounts for the virtues of anonymity, which revolve around freedom of expression, safety, and the very twenty-first-century ideal of "flexibility" in user presentation. Twitter Safety, "What's in a Name? The Case for Inclusivity through Anonymity," *Common Thread*, Sep. 21, 2021, https://blog.twitter.com/common-thread/en/topics/stories/2021/whats-in-a-name-the-case-for-inclusivity-through-anonymity. The "academic studies" referenced in this case are all nonpeer-reviewed articles, conference papers, and symposia proceedings. The methodologies and arguments employed in the papers are tendentious, often do not conclude what the Twitter blog suggests, and are specifically about social media platforms that are very different from Twitter, such as 4chan. One common argument, for example, runs that, because identified people harass online, it follows that anonymity is not the cause of harassment, without pausing to ask obvious questions, such as: "Are anonymous accounts more likely to harass than identified accounts? "Is there a qualitative difference in the nature of and duration/intensity of harassment from identified and anonymous accounts?" Suffice it to say that it is important to note that there are voices that question the link between toxicity and anonymity in online social systems that I make here. See, for example, J. Nathan Matias, "The Real Name Fallacy," *Coral by Voxmedia*, Jan. 3, 2017, https://coralproject.net/blog/the-real-name-fallacy/. Contrast these claims with the large and growing scholarship on the "disinhibition effect" online, referenced earlier.

formation that could be used in a prejudicial manner.²¹ The laudable, and increasingly necessary, fight to protect privacy in an era of privacy-eroding technology is not incompatible with my argument that complete and total anonymity in a social system in which political discourse occurs—that is, Twitter—is deleterious.

In this context, it is important to recognize that Twitter's anonymity does have one virtue, insofar as it provides a forum for marginalized groups and political/social reformers living under oppressive regimes to speak publicly in a way that could help to bring about positive social change in their contexts. I don't think it follows, however, that anonymity ought to be permitted to all users as a default setting, given the way anonymity is used and abused by users who have no valid fear of adverse repercussions, aside from the social opprobrium they are seeking to avoid for being rude, abusive, or harassing. Twitter, Inc., could operate Twitter in a way that makes the use and public display of real personal identities the default setting, with exceptions available by special application to allow vulnerable users to use the system anonymously, albeit in a way that flags to other users that a particular account is anonymous.

Brevity

A second design feature of Twitter that contributes to character malformation is brevity. Twitter imposes a 280-character limit per tweet. Users can like, reply to, and retweet tweets made by other users, but no tweet, including replies and retweets, can exceed the 280-character limit (characters include spaces and punctuation). It is possible to generate conversations, of a sort, by virtue of the fact that anyone, originator or reader, can reply to replies to tweets, which can then be read as a conversation by using the scroll function.²² Twitter also permits the attachment of images, GIFs, and videos (up to 140 seconds long and 512MB).

Former CEO and cofounder of Twitter, Inc., Jack Dorsey has highlighted Twitter's brevity as one of its virtues. When announcing the increase of permitted characters on individual tweets from 140 to 280 in 2016, he remarked: "That concept of brevity, speed and live conversation—being able to think of something

---

[21] Saul Levmore reminds us that there is a positive role for anonymity in the realm of feedback, a vital (and socially accepted) component of political polling, product feedback, staff surveys, and student evaluations of faculty. Saul Levmore, "The Internet's Anonymity Problem," in Levmore and Nussbaum, *The Offensive Internet*, 60.

[22] It is possible to create "threads" of tweets by attaching multiple tweets together (so that they appear in a linked sequence one below the other). This is one way around the character limit, although this is an exceptional, rather than typical, use of the platform.

and put it out to the world instantly—that's what's most important."[23] Suffice to say, however, conversations about substantive political, social, and moral questions in which each individual contribution to the exchange is restricted to 280 characters (approximately forty to forty-five words) is not particularly conducive to constructive conversation. The character limit incentivizes (forces) the sacrifice of nuance, subtlety, caveats, definitions, proper clarification, and, crucially, the citation of evidence in support of positions or arguments. These are important features of any physical/analogue social interaction, where a speaker can confirm that their interlocutor has understood their speech, can often detect lack of understanding through facial reaction, and can then proceed to clarify, and where the recipient of the speech can ask clarifying questions. It is easy to overlook the importance of the opportunity for both parties in a conversation to expand, elaborate, or seek clarification, as such speech habits are so deeply ingrained and widely used in all manner of social interactions, from a conversation between friends at a bar to a business meeting or university seminar. The brevity of speech required on Twitter, combined with anonymity, incentivizes provocative and inflammatory speech by removing penalties for abusive behavior and making it extremely difficult to speak with nuance and subtlety. As Dorsey noted, Twitter is optimized for instantaneity (not careful, considered speech).

Interpolation

Twitter is designed to bring strangers into contact with each other as a means of building networks of followers. It does so by exposing tweets to users who do not follow the author of the tweet, with the effect of exposing tweets to users who are not the intended audience of the tweet or who may be hostile to the content or author of the tweet.[24] This occurs in part via Twitter's "recommendation algorithms," which place select tweets from users not followed by an account into that account's Home timeline (feed) under the heading "you might like."[25] It is also accomplished by visibility (again in the Home timeline) of tweets liked or

---

[23] "Twitter Announces Changes to its 140-Character Limit," *Mediaweek*, May 25, 2016, https://www.mediaweek.com.au/twitter-140-character/.

[24] There is a sense in which even completely anonymous accounts cease to be strangers to users whom they follow, particularly if they interact regularly with that account. Although the identity of the follower is obscure, the account itself becomes "known" and familiar.

[25] Rumman Chowdhury and Luca Belli, "Examining Algorithmic Amplification of Political Content on Twitter," *Twitter Blog*, https://blog.twitter.com/en_us/topics/company/2021/rml-politicalcontent.

commented on by accounts followed by a user. It can also happen through troll-following and the use of hashtags. The latter make tweets visible to followers of the hashtag who do not follow the account using the hashtag. Hashtags are designed to allow users to follow interests and issues, such as #auspol (Australian politics), without having to follow thousands of individual accounts that might tweet on the topic of interest. Hashtags also allow users to tweet on a specific issue and reach a potentially larger audience beyond their own following. Troll-followers, as the name suggests, follow accounts with the sole intention of abusing and harassing them (and sometimes any other account that interacts with them).

The problem is that a user with strong opposition to a particular viewpoint, characteristic, or group identity, such as religion, might regularly abuse religious users by writing abusive responses to their tweets and by troll-following the accounts of high-profile religious people. The algorithm, noting that this particular account regularly engages tweets on religion, may mistake this interaction for positive interest and then recommend tweets by religious users not followed by the opponent of religion, thus exposing new religious users to potential abuse and harassment. Similarly, by regularly commenting (with hostility) on religious tweets, the opponent of religion exposes new potential victims to the opponent's own followers, some of whom are likely to share that user's hostility to religion, via the visibility of liked or commented-upon tweets by followed accounts.

The reason I dub this phenomenon "interpolation" is that the Twitter algorithms expose conversations to hostile voices in a way that is far less common in physical-analogue social systems, where opportunity costs, customs, and the reputational damage that accompanies rude, aggressive, or harassing behavior mitigate against the kind of negative interpolation that Twitter facilitates. This type of cyber interpolation would be akin, in the physical-analogue world, to an individual interrupting a dinner at a restaurant, or the meeting of an association, or a church service or public lecture with negative or hostile commentary on what is being discussed, or perhaps the personalities involved. That said, the increase in student protesters shouting down unpalatable speakers on university campuses is perhaps an indication of the ways in which norm-breaking habits in the cyber realm are bleeding into the physical-analogue realm and challenging norms there.

Unmoderatability

Unmoderatability describes the way Twitter makes it possible for users to amass extremely large followings (audiences), making moderation of the conversations generated by the tweets of such users impossible. Former U.S. President Barack

Obama has the largest following of any Twitter user, at 132.4 million.[26] Every tweet Obama makes elicits thousands of comments, retweets, and likes. A tweet from June 24, 2022, for example, generated 918,100 likes, 229,600 retweets, and 40,900 comments. The tweet commented on the controversial decision of the U.S. Supreme Court to overturn the precedent in the *Roe v. Wade* ruling in relation to abortion, one of the most vexed and polarizing social issues in the United States.[27]

With these kinds of engagement numbers, Obama can have only minimal visibility into the thousands of conversations and interactions (between followers) generated by his tweets. Twitter does include moderation tools that permit the owners of accounts to block, mute, or hide followers, conversations, and replies to tweets. It is therefore possible that Obama employs moderators to help manage his Twitter account and the high volume of interactions it generates. But even with the assistance of moderators, it is inconceivable that Obama could take any kind of realistic responsibility for the thousands, indeed millions, of conversations generated by his prolific tweeting, not to mention the abuses and harassment that must arise as a consequence.

The ability for Twitter users to garner followings larger than most countries is a novel development in interpersonal communication. There are ostensible analogues with television programs and books, both of which can reach audiences in the millions. The difference, however—and a significant one at that—is that consumers of popular television programs and books cannot instantly comment on the program or book to the author in a way that is immediately visible to the rest of the audience. Nor can individual audience members reply (instantly) to the comments of other viewers or readers, or, for that matter, harass and abuse other viewers and readers on the basis of their opinion on the program or book in question. Accordingly, there is no moderation dilemma for those who produce television programs or who write books, as they bear no responsibility for any abuse that might occur between audience members. By amplifying the visibility of attitudes, reactions, and opinions among audience members, Twitter greatly increases the scope and likelihood of conflict between them.

Accounts with large followings, which account for a disproportionate number of the interactions on Twitter, are undoubtedly responsible (in the sense of generating large conversations) for much of the abuse and harassment that oc-

---

[26] As of August 10, 2022. If Obama's following were a country, it would be the tenth largest in the world (after Russia and ahead of Mexico).

[27] The Tweet read as follows: "Today, the Supreme Court not only reversed nearly 50 years of precedent, it relegated the most intensely personal decision someone can make to the whims of politicians and ideologues—attacking the essential freedoms of millions of Americans." Barack Obama (@BarackObama), Twitter, 10:26 a.m., Jun. 24, 2022, https://twitter.com/BarackObama/status/1540340642848690176.

curs on the platform, yet the owners of those accounts have very limited capacity to moderate, and therefore mitigate, such negative interactions. Users with large followings and high interaction may genuinely be ignorant of the personal and social impacts their tweets have on those who engage with them.

Invisibility of Mitigating Circumstances

The final feature of Twitter that malforms character is not so much a design feature as a design consequence. Humans are adept at reading the subtle physical cues that accompany speech, right down to small changes in voice tone and pitch, eye movement, and other microfacial expressions. Most humans can tell rather quickly if their speech is upsetting an interlocutor, is confusing an interlocutor, or requires additional explanation or rearticulation. Humans can also tell if an interlocutor is tired, has Asperger's, or is uneducated, inebriated, distracted, or affected by a myriad of other factors that most speakers will then take into account in ways that make them adapt their communication strategy. For obvious reasons, these social cues are absent on Twitter. Moreover, given the brevity problem, escalatory misunderstanding and offense occur on the platform more regularly than in other social contexts on account of the invisibility of the physical elements that play an important function in human communication, along with the lack of visibility of other socially relevant information that can help moderate communication strategies, leading to greater tolerance.

Anonymity, brevity, interpolation, unmoderatability, and invisibility of mitigating circumstances are all design features or design consequences of Twitter that remove or attenuate important facets of communication which, in physical/analogue social systems, help to facilitate positive and constructive human interaction. Rather than promoting "healthy conversations," the stated social goal of Twitter, the platform is contributing to the malformation of human character by subverting norms that exist to promote constructive human engagement in physical/analogue social systems. Technological change, as Neil Postman has argued in *Technopoly*, is "ecological," in the sense that "one significant change generates total change," much in the same way that one single environmental change can affect an entire ecology.[28] There is reason for concern, then, that Twitter may have long-term negative impacts on human social ecology by undermining or eroding important, yet underappreciated, norms that have evolved over centuries to incentivize interpersonal civility and disincentivize interpersonal incivility.

---

[28] Neil Postman, *Technopoly: The Surrender of Culture to Technology* (New York: Vintage Books, 1993), 18.

The Technological Perversion of Twenty-First-Century Political Economy

As noted above, Twitter, Inc., trumpets its concern and desire to foster what it terms "healthy conversations": "We believe that public conversation is better when as many people as possible can participate. With that philosophy in mind, we work hard to promote healthy conversations on our service. We know that people are less likely to speak if they feel intimidated or fearful."[29] However, any desire Twitter, Inc., has to realize this goal of creating a space for healthy conversations is undermined by the reality that it is a business, and specifically a publicly traded corporation with responsibilities and explicit goals of maximizing shareholder profit.[30] This is abundantly clear from the corporation's reports to shareholders: "We made meaningful progress in 2021 against our 2023 goals: doubling development velocity by the end of 2023, delivering at least 315 million mDAU in Q4'23, and delivering $7.5 billion or more in revenue for the full year of 2023."[31] The reality is that Twitter is a product, not a public square for healthy conversations. Healthy conversations, to the extent that they do occur on Twitter, are a byproduct. Twitter, Inc., makes its revenue through the sale of user information, gleaned in large part from the conversations users engage in on Twitter, which yield insights into their interests, preferences, and atti-

---

[29] Twitter, Inc., *2020 Global Impact Report*, https://about.twitter.com/content/dam/about-twitter/en/company/global-impact-2020.pdf, 4.

[30] The initial conference paper that developed into the present chapter was conceived and completed before the announcement of Elon Musk's bid to purchase Twitter, Inc. At the time of the chapter's finalization, that bid looks to be in serious jeopardy, with Musk writing to Twitter, Inc.'s, board informing them of his intention to terminate the acquisition bid and the board responding with threats of litigation to ensure that the deal goes ahead. I have not considered the Musk acquisition angle here. That said, it is worth noting that the sticking point in the deal is the question of bot accounts, in particular transparency about the number of bot accounts on the platform. I note that Musk has not raised any of the character-malforming design features identified and discussed here as areas of Twitter in need of reform. *ABC News*, "Elon Musk Seeks to Terminate $64 Billion Twitter Buyout Deal," Jul. 9, 2022, https://www.abc.net.au/news/2022-07-09/elon-musk-seeks-to-terminate-64-billion-twitter-buyout-deal/101223448. Musk's other publicly stated concern in relation to Twitter, besides bot accounts, is the moderation policies of the company that Musk believes are too restrictive of free speech. See Kat Tenbarge, David Ingram, and Ben Goggin, "Under Musk, Some Fear Twitter's Moderation Progress Could Unravel," *NBC News*, Apr. 26, 2022, https://www.nbcnews.com/tech/internet/elon-musk-fear-twitters-moderation-progress-unravel-rcna25932.

[31] Twitter, Inc., *Q4 and Fiscal Year 2021 Letter to Shareholders*, Feb. 10, 2022, https://s22.q4cdn.com/826641620/files/doc_financials/2021/q4/Final-Q4'21-Shareholder-letter.pdf, 2. The term "mDAU" stands for "monetizable daily active users."

tudes. Twitter, Inc., is then able to monetize this information through the sale of targeted advertising:

> We enable our advertisers to target an audience based on a variety of factors, including who an account follows and actions taken on our platform, such as Tweets created and engagement with Tweets. We believe this data produces a clear and real-time signal of that person's interests, greatly enhancing the relevance of the ads we can display and enhancing our targeting capabilities for advertisers.[32]

Twitter, Inc., is in fact a digital advertising company. Twitter is the proprietary product through which it collects and packages the information required to sell targeted digital advertising. Twitter also functions as the medium through which Twitter, Inc., displays advertisements on behalf of its clients. What makes Twitter, Inc., unusual is that its business model is largely hidden to users by virtue of the fact that its product is free to use and is promoted as a public square or public service utility.[33] Many users have little cognizance that the actual contract of use for Twitter is free access to the product in exchange for the commodification and sale of their user history. This creates a glaring tension at the heart of Twitter, Inc.–its oft-repeated aspiration to provide a service that facilitates healthy conversations and its actual use of that service to sell advertising worth billions of dollars.

These two goals sometimes appear incongruously in the same sentences in corporate documents, as in the following example: "Twitter serves the public conversation. We have a massive opportunity in front of us to grow revenue and mDAU, to serve billions of people daily, and to lean into the $150 billion (and growing) digital ads market, where we have less than 3% market share today."[34] In fact, we could go further and say that Twitter, Inc.'s corporate aspiration of providing a service that facilitates healthy conversations is undermined by two separate factors: the design features discussed earlier, which remove important norms that incentivize healthy conversations and penalize unhealthy conversations, and its business model, which aims to increase revenue by capturing a greater share of the digital advertising market by selling user data.

---

[32] Twitter, Inc., "Fiscal Year 2020 Annual Report," 17.
[33] Twitter, Inc., also has a data-licensing business, although most of its revenue comes from advertising. Cofounder and inaugural CEO of Twitter, Inc., Jack Dorsey conceived of Twitter very early on in its life as a "utility," likening it to "electricity." Nick Bilton, *Hatching Twitter: How a Fledgling Start-up Became a Multi-Billion Dollar Business and Accidentally Changed the World* (London: Sceptre, 2014), iBooks, III. #Jack, "The Hundred-Million-Dollar Offer."
[34] Twitter, Inc., *Q4 and Fiscal Year 2021 Letter to Shareholders*, 2.

The fact of the matter is that healthy conversations are not necessary, or even essential, to achieving the corporation's business goals. With a market cap of $37.01B (at the time of writing), there is no commercial incentive to alter the design of Twitter to address any of the character-malforming design features identified and discussed here.[35] To increase profitability and improve the return for investors, Twitter, Inc., need only increase the number of users and engagements on the product in order to continually refine its ability to target ads and increase the reach it can offer advertisers. Indeed, it is plausible that unhealthy conversations might actually increase user engagement with the product and therefore be a more profitable strategy. Social media platforms are specifically designed to be addictive to users, irrespective of the positivity or negativity of the content of specific posts, according to some Silicon Valley insiders, such as Aza Raskin, inventor of the "infinite scroll," who has likened social media to "behavioural cocaine."[36] It is worth noting, as a final aside, that were Twitter, Inc., to accomplish its stated purpose of promoting healthy conversations through Twitter, then it would have succeeded in commodifying and monetizing healthy conversations.

The tension at the heart of Twitter, Inc., can be explained to some extent by the genesis of the company and its product Twitter.[37] Twitter was developed in 2006 as a side project by several individuals involved with a struggling podcasting company called Odeo and went live after just two weeks of development. It was originally conceived (and used in the very early days) as a "status update" service, but quickly evolved beyond this as more users joined the platform and began shaping its culture of usage. As a consequence of Twitter's lightning-fast development and public release *and* its rapid adoption by users, who effectively took control of shaping habits and practices of usage on the platform, the cofounders of Twitter, Inc., and the developers of Twitter found themselves in disagreement and confusion (and for some years thereafter) about precisely what the thing they had created was, and more importantly, what it was for. Despite disagreement and confusion about the nature and purpose of Twitter among its creators, venture capital quickly began pouring into the fledging company purely on the basis of consistent and impressive user growth (and a good deal of Silicon Valley hype). Remarkably, hundreds of millions of investment dollars flooded into Twitter, Inc., in just the first three years, even though "Twit-

---

[35] "Twitter Market Cap 2011–2021| TWTR," *Macrotrends*, Apr. 11, 2022, https://www.macrotrends.net/stocks/charts/TWTR/twitter/market-cap.

[36] Hillary Andersson, "Social Media Apps Are 'Deliberately' Addictive to Users," *BBC Panorama*, Jul. 4, 2018, https://www.bbc.com/news/technology-44640959. "Infinite scroll allows users to endlessly swipe down through content without clicking."

[37] The following account is taken from Bilton, *Hatching Twitter*.

ter still had no business model or even the faintest sign of one."[38] It wasn't until 2010 that Twitter, Inc., began "experimenting" with advertising.[39] By 2012, Twitter, Inc., was valued at ten billion dollars and was making one million dollars a day from advertising revenue, marking its transformation to a digital advertising company.[40]

Twitter was thus the product of experimentation by tech developers, who built and launched the platform with little care for, or understanding of, its nature, purpose, and effects. The developers quickly lost control of its culture through rapid user adoption, and managed to raise hundreds of millions of dollars without a business model, only to discover the kind of business Twitter could be—a digital advertising company—years after its launch. This is an inversion of the traditional genesis of new businesses, in which entrepreneurs and investors typically first identify a gap or need in the market for a particular good or service, followed by the design and production of the good or service, and only then launch to market.[41] In this regard, the creation of Twitter appears to illustrate Postman's concept of "technopoly," a term coined in 1992 to describe a state of affairs then already extant in America characterized by "the submission of all forms of cultural life to the sovereignty of technique and technology."[42] "New technologies," Postman observes, "may not always solve significant problems or any problem at all," but rather appear to exist sovereignly, which is to say that they exist for the sake of existing, and quickly for the sake of perpetuating technology itself.[43] This seems to be an apposite description of Twitter, a technology that solves no ostensible problem and appears to exist for the sake of the technology; Twitter exists because it was technically possible to create it, and what is technically possible to create must be created for the sake of a relentless and amorphous notion of technological "progress."

It is important to bear in mind that the investment dollars that poured into Twitter, Inc., in the early years were predicated on user adoption, and specifically on the monetization potential of such adoption, not on the social goal of promoting or facilitating healthy conversations. Indeed, Twitter was not conceived or created, in the first place, to foster healthy conversations. This corporate aspiration has arisen in the context of Twitter's growing negative reputation for producing exactly the opposite outcome, and thus is a tacit, or perhaps not so

---

[38] Bilton, *Hatching Twitter*, III. #Jack, "Rumours."
[39] Ibid., IV. #Ev, "Steve Jobs 2.0."
[40] Ibid., V. #Dick, "Make Better Mistakes Tomorrow."
[41] There are variations, of course, such as businesses based on producing existing goods or services at superior quality or price.
[42] Postman, *Technopoly*, 52.
[43] Neil Postman, "Technology as Dazzling Distraction," *The Education Digest* 59, no.8 (1994): 25–28, at 25.

tacit, admission that Twitter, Inc., must work toward making Twitter a forum for healthy conversations.

Postman also keenly understood the commodification potential of information. This potential, first realized with the creation of the telegraph, as he notes, stems from the insight that "the value of information need not be tied to any function it might serve in social and political decision-making and action," in which case information "can be bought and sold irrespective of its uses or meaning."[44] In Twitter's case, it is not the intrinsic value or utility of the content of tweets and the exchanges they generate which are commodified. Rather, it is the contextual byproducts of the contents of tweets and user engagements—user "interests"—which are commodified because of their value to advertisers in helping to efficiently target advertising. It is worth reiterating that Twitter, Inc., is not selling healthy conversation but rather user interest, and user interest can be revealed in both positive and negative interaction, through likes and dislikes.

Conclusion

It may be some time before the full scope of the adverse ecological effects of purposeless, sovereign, and monetizable technologies like Twitter becomes clear. But our early experience of the introduction of new technological species, like Twitter, into the human social ecology prompts concern about their far-reaching distorting effects on human culture, anthropological character, social systems, and even political economy.

The story of Twitter therefore serves as a cautionary tale about the potential of new digital technologies to pervert political economy in the twenty-first century. It illustrates, for example, the way that technological potential can drive the creation of products that neither serve any obvious social good nor solve any obvious social problem, but seem to exist for the sake of an undefined, mythological sense of progress, insofar as the technologically generated products in question are novel, if ultimately not useful. It further illustrates the way that a product can be designed and launched very rapidly, circumventing the usual processes of research, analysis, consultation, and care that have traditionally gone into product design and technological innovation. It also illustrates the way that contemporary investment culture, particularly in the tech sector, can finance the rapid growth of products designed too quickly, with too little care for their effects, and without a business model or even rationale for the product. Finally, it illustrates the way that a business model can be retroactively discovered and applied to a product long after the product has developed a reputation

---

[44] Postman, *Technopoly*, 68–69.

for being something very different, and in ways that create tensions between the corporation's public aspirations and its financial incentives and obligations.

Part Four: Navigating State Power

Resisting Political Authority to Protect Faith and Morality: Enduring Lessons from the Lutheran Reformation

John Witte Jr.[1]

Introduction

This chapter offers a historical perspective about the role of the state in the formation of moral character. And it offers a cautionary note that is as salient in late modern liberal societies as it was in the premodern Christian societies that will be my main focus. To be sure, like other authors in this volume, I recognize that the modern state forms and shapes our ethics, character, and habits through its laws and policies. This moral formation comes through the state's many "thou shalt" commands (pay your taxes; educate your children; register your properties) and "thou shalt not" commands (do not kill; do not steal; do not bear false witness).[2] It comes through its formal state-run systems of education from kindergarten to graduate school, and its less formal but pervasive instructions about private and public health, safety, and welfare.[3]

The state's moral character formation also comes through the myriad ways that its policies and procedures nudge, encourage, incentivize, and facilitate us

---

[1] This chapter draws in part from my *The Reformation of Rights: Law, Religion, and Human Rights in Early Modern Calvinism* (Cambridge: Cambridge University Press, 2007), hereafter RR; *and Law and Protestantism: The Legal Teachings of the Lutheran Reformation* (Cambridge: Cambridge University Press, 2002), hereafter LP. For Luther's writings referenced herein, see *D. Martin Luthers Werke: Kritische Gesamtausgabe*, repr. ed., 78 vols. (Weimar: Böhlau, 1883–1987), hereafter WA; and *Luther's Works*, trans. and ed. Jaroslav Pelikan and Helmut T. Lehmann (Philadelphia: Fortress Press, 1955–68), hereafter LW.

[2] Stephen Pickard, Michael Welker, and John Witte Jr., eds., *The Impact of Education on Character Formation, Ethical Education, and the Communication of Values in Late Modern Pluralistic Societies* (Leipzig: Evangelische Verlagsanstalt, 2022).

[3] John Witte Jr. and Michael Welker, eds., *The Impact of the Law on Character Formation, Ethical Education, and the Communication of Values in Late Modern Pluralistic Societies* (Leipzig: Evangelische Verlagsanstalt, 2021).

to adopt certain behaviors and avoid others. Tax deductions encourage marriage, charity, and home ownership. Heavy license fees and taxes discourage smoking. Zoning, land use, and nuisance laws guide the religious uses of our properties. Civil rights laws encourage more inclusive employment. Same-sex marriage rights invite changes to marital theology. Education licenses and accreditation define the baseline content of religious schools. Rather like trees and plants bending to the light, individuals and institutions, including religious ones, often naturally position and incline their moral choices and habits to enjoy the benefits of state policies, and sometimes contort themselves to avoid the political shadows.

But what happens when the state deeply betrays its responsibilities? What happens when the state's policies or actions malign a citizen's character, violate their morality, abridge their basic rights, compel them to act or forgo action contrary to their conscience or faith? Even worse, what happens when the state becomes an outright tyrant threatening the bodies, souls, and minds of citizens, the fundamentals of faith, freedom, and family? When, how, and on what grounds may citizens reject, resist, and even revolt against the state altogether, or against individual state officers who betray their office and the legal and political order they are called to protect? These are perennial questions in the Western tradition going back to biblical and classical times, and they have produced a sizeable library of reflections over the centuries. But these questions also remain the stuff of daily headlines, not only in late modern liberal societies, but indeed throughout the world today. Just ask people today in Ukraine, Hong Kong, Iran, Iraq, Afghanistan, North African countries, North Korea, the Philippines, Central America, and way too many other places around the world facing rogue and oppressive states.

When political intrusions on liberty, morality, and conscience are lower, as they often are in most late liberal societies today, oppressed citizens usually have "softer" force at their disposal to protect themselves. They can file a law suit, press for a conscientious exemption, lobby for legal change, invoke constitutional checks and balances, issue petitions and grievances, mobilize shame through media exposures, disobey laws or organize demonstrations against injustice as we have seen in campaigns against gross racism, police brutality, or controversial judicial decisions. But when the political intrusions on liberty, morality, and conscience are graver—as they were in earlier Western societies and still are in many parts of the world today—oppressed citizens use "harder force." When citizens have no other legal recourse, they can resist and rejoin, even with violence, those who violate their faith, freedom, family, and other fundamentals. When the rule of law breaks, when oppression and tyranny break out, a whole community can resort to revolt and rebellion, even organized revolution and regicide.

These modern distinctions—between resistance and revolution, soft force and hard force—are, in part, products of early modern Protestant political theology and constitutionalism. This short chapter introduces the resistance theories of one early branch of Protestantism, the Lutheran Reformation, which played such a central legal, political, and cultural role in Germany and Scandinavia from the sixteenth to the twentieth centuries, and which still shapes the personal ethics if not the political ethos of these northern European lands and their many former colonial and mission outposts. This chapter first rehearses Luther's original teaching on resisting the spiritual tyranny of the papacy and the church's canon law. It then works through the arguments of the Magdeburg Confession on resisting the spiritual tyranny of the emperor. The conclusion reflects on the contemporary implications and applications of these early Lutheran arguments against oppression and tyranny.

The Lutheran Reformation as a Resistance Movement

The Lutheran Reformation began as a powerful resistance movement, indeed a revolution,[4] not against a political tyrant, but against what Martin Luther and his early followers regarded as a "spiritual tyrant": the papacy and the Catholic Church's canon law and sacramental system. In his writings in the late 1510 s and early 1520 s, Luther railed against the pope as the "anti-Christ," "the whore of Babylon," a "werewolf" who stalked the vineyard of God to the peril of innocent Christians. Through false doctrines and abusive laws, Luther charged, the pope and his clerical retinue have destroyed the freedom of the Christian Gospel, tyrannized the Christian conscience, and stolen the German people blind. Luther then called on various lower magistrates—the princes, nobles, dukes, and cities of Germany—to stand up and throw off this spiritual tyrant for the sake of the freedom of the Gospel. "We must obey God, rather than men," Luther insisted, quoting Acts 5:29.[5]

It was one thing, however, for a conscientious Christian to resist and reject the tyranny of the pope and other clergy. It was quite another thing to resist and reject the tyranny of the emperor and other magistrates. After all, one of Jesus's most famous statements had been to "render to Caesar [the emperor] the things

---

[4] Steven Ozment, *Protestants: The Birth of a Revolution* (New York: Doubleday, 1993); and Harold J. Berman, *Law and Revolution II: The Impact of the Protestant Reformations on the Western Legal Tradition* (Cambridge, Mass.: Harvard University Press, 2006).

[5] See sources in LP, 53–65.

that are Caesar's, and to God the things that are God's."[6] Saint Paul had elaborated:

> Let every person be subject to the governing authorities. For there is no authority except from God, and those that exist have been instituted by God. Therefore, he who resists the authorities resists what God has appointed, and those who resist will come into judgment. For rulers are not a terror to good conduct, but bad. ... Therefore, one must be subject, not only to avoid God's wrath, but for the sake of conscience.[7]

Saint Peter was even more pointed:

> Be subject for the Lord's sake to every human institution, whether it be to the emperors as supreme, or to governors as sent by him to punish those who do wrong and to praise those who do right. ... Live as free men, yet without using your freedom as a pretext for evil; but live as servants of God. Honor all men. Love the brotherhood. Fear God. Honor the emperor.[8]

"Honor your father and mother" and by extension all other authorities, the Bible stated repeatedly, "so that your days may be long in the land which the Lord your God has given you."[9] All this seemed rather firm and clear biblical pronouncement that a conscientious Christian should respect and obey the political authorities, and suffer patiently and prayerfully if the authorities abused their office or, even worse, became tyrants.

Initially, these biblical passages gave Luther pause about resisting, let alone rebelling against, political magistrates. In his famous reply to the emperor at the Diet of Worms (1521), Luther defended his attack on the papacy by saying that "it is neither safe nor right to go against conscience," so long as one's "conscience is captive to the Word of God."[10] But two years later, when he addressed the question *Temporal Authority: To What Extent it Should be Obeyed* (1523) by conscientious Christians, he argued only vaguely that in this earthly life, all subjects must obey the political authorities in matters "of body and property" but not in spiritual matters, and should "thank God" if they are considered "worthy

---

[6] Matthew 22:21; Mark 12:17; Luke 20:25. I have used the Revised Standard Version throughout.
[7] Romans 13:1–5.
[8] 1 Peter 2:13–17.
[9] Exodus 20:12; Leviticus 19:5; Deuteronomy 5:16; Matthew 15:4; Mark 7:10; Ephesians 6:1–2. Luther set out these passages and others in LW 45:86–87, 110–12.
[10] WA 7:838.

to suffer for the sake of the divine word."[11] Luther became even more hesitant about political disobedience after the chaos and bloodshed born of the Knights' Revolt of 1522-23 and the Peasants' War of 1524-25. Both his Small and Large Catechisms of 1529 called the faithful to honor and obey parental, political, and spiritual authorities alike, making little provision for resistance in the event of abuse.

In the 1530 s and 1540 s, as Catholic political persecution of the new Protestant movement escalated, Luther and his followers gradually came to support more forms of political resistance—including organized rebellion by lower magistrates and estates; individual civil disobedience of ungodly laws; individual and group petitions and grievances against injustice; emigration from hostile territories; and the personal right to self-defense against "atrocious injury" and threat by any criminals, including political brigands.[12] Several Lutheran theologians and jurists refined and deepened this Lutheran resistance theory—including such leading lights as Philip Melanchthon, Martin Bucer, Johannes Bugenhagen, Gregory Brück, Andreas Osiander, Lazarus Spengler, Johann Oldendorp, Johannes Eisermann, and others.[13]

The strongest and most systematic Lutheran resistance theories along these lines were set out in scores of pamphlets issued by Lutheran cities and regions that had come under siege by imperial forces bent on reestablishing Catholicism in the empire and extirpating Protestantism root and branch. Of these pamphlets, the 1550 Magdeburg Confession offered the fullest and most radical Lutheran teachings on resistance to political tyranny, and it remained the strongest such statement for Lutheran lands for centuries. None of these Lutheran tracts, however, advocated violent revolution or regicide on the order of later sixteenth-century Calvinists, let alone the religious and secular democratic revolutionaries of the eighteenth and nineteenth centuries, the anticolonist, antifascist, and anticommunist forces of modern times, or the radical populist movements of our own day.

---

[11] LW 45:111-12. See also ibid. 86-87, 110-11.
[12] See, for example, LW 47:6 and WA 39/2:60. See further texts and analysis in Cynthia Grant Schoenberger, "Luther and the Justifiability of Resistance to Legitimate Authority," *Journal of the History of Ideas* 40 (1970): 3-20.
[13] Robert von Friedeberg, *Self-Defense and Religious Strife in Early Modern Europe: England and Germany, 1530-1680* (London: Routledge, 2017); Heinz Scheible, *Das Widerstandsrecht als Problem der deutsche Protestanten 1523-1546* (Gütersloh: Chr. Kaiser, 1969); Eike Wolgast, *Die Religionsfrage als Problem des Widerstandsrechts im 16. Jahrhundert* (Heidelberg: Carl Winter, 1980); and Quentin Skinner, *Foundations of Modern Political Thought* (Cambridge: Cambridge University Press, 1978), 2:195-206.

Martin Luther on Resisting the Pope and Canon Law

On December 10, 1520, before a group of his students and colleagues at the University of Wittenberg, Martin Luther burned the books of the canon law and of the sacramental theology that supported it. Consigned to the flames were Gratian's *Decretum* (ca. 1140) and four books of later papal laws. Also included were the popular confessional book *Summa angelica* (1486) and the papal bull that threatened Luther's excommunication. Luther's colleagues Johann Agricola and Philip Melanchthon, who had organized the event, had also hoped to burn the works of Thomas Aquinas and John Duns Scotus, two of the greatest theologians of the medieval church. But they could not find anyone in Wittenberg who would donate their copies for the fire. They selected instead some works by Luther's antagonists Johann Eck and Jerome Emser. Luther later wrote of his canonical bonfire: "I am more pleased with this than any other action in my life."[14]

If there was a single event that signaled Luther's permanent break with Rome, this was the event.[15] Three years before, on October 31, 1517, Luther had posted and published his *Ninety-Five Theses*, attacking the Catholic Church's crass commercialization of salvation through the selling of indulgences. In several publications in the next few months, Luther questioned with increasing stridency the biblical integrity of the church's theology of salvation and the sacraments.[16] On October 8-9, 1518, Luther answered a summons to appear in Augsburg before the pope's representative, Cardinal Cajetan, but refused to recant his views. On November 28, 1518, Luther appealed directly to the pope, insisting upon his rights, as a professor of theology, to an open hearing of his views at a general church council.[17] On July 4-14, 1519, with no such church council forthcoming, Luther engaged in a sensational public debate at the University of Leipzig with Johann Eck over fundamental questions of ecclesiastical authority—a debate that revealed the increasing radicality of Luther's theological doctrines of justification by faith, the primacy of the Bible, the nature of the church, and the priesthood of all believers.[18] On June 15, 1520, Pope Leo X issued *Exsurge, Domine*, the bull that condemned the teachings of that "wild boar" Martin Luther as heretical, scandalous, offensive, seductive, and "repugnant to

---

[14] LW 48:192; see also LW 48:186-87; and Heinrich Böhmer, "Luther und der 10. Dezember 1520," *Luther-Jahrbuch* 2, no. 3 (1920/1): 7-53.

[15] See generally Scott H. Hendrix, *Luther and the Papacy: Stages in a Reformation Conflict* (Philadelphia: Fortress Press, 1981).

[16] LW 31:35-70, 77-252; LW 35:3-113; LW 39:3-22; LW 42:95-115; LW 44:3-14, 15-114.

[17] LW 31:253-92.

[18] LW 31:307-26.

Catholic truth."[19] The bull gave Luther sixty days after receipt to repent, recant, and return to the Catholic fold. December 10, 1520 was the sixtieth day. On that day, Luther had his bonfire, burning his last bridge with Rome.

From Law to Gospel

Luther defended his iconoclasm in a torrent of writings in the early 1520 s. First, he argued that canon law fostered and featured papal tyranny. The canonists treated the pope not only as "lord of the world," but also as "the vicar of Christ," a veritable "demigod."[20] The pope thus enjoyed unbridled powers of legislation, adjudication, and administration that no one in Christendom—not even an ecumenical council—could effectively review, rejoin, or resist. Neither the pope nor his delegates were obliged to abide by scripture, tradition, or conciliar decree. Instead, they had power "to break up, change, or eliminate" rules of law as they saw fit. They passed laws and cast judgments for all of Christendom, yet they neither subjected themselves to law nor submitted to the judgments of others.[21]

Luther found particularly arbitrary the power of the pope and his delegates to grant equitable dispensations from vows, oaths, contracts, and other canonical strictures that worked injustice in particular cases. "These days," Luther grumbled, "canon law is not what is written in the books of law, but whatever the pope and his flatterers want. Your cause may be thoroughly established in canon law, but the pope always has his chamber of the heart in the matter, and all law, and with it the world, has to be guided by that." The very powers of dispensation that had made the medieval canon law the "mother of equity," Luther charged, had made the pope the father of tyranny.[22]

Second, Luther charged that the canon law was abusive and self-serving. The canonists over the centuries had spun a thick tangle of special benefits, privileges, exemptions, and immunities that elevated the clergy above the laity and inoculated them from legal accountability to local magistrates. Local clergy, Luther charged, used these prerogatives to amass huge holdings of tax-exempt property, supported by rich foundations and endowments, and controlled by parishes, cathedrals, monasteries, guilds, chantries, and other church institutions. These ecclesiastical units, in turn, used their properties to foster luxurious clerical livings and to engage in lucrative lending practices. To Luther's mind, these were flagrant violations of the canon laws of poverty and usury, and they

---

[19] Carl Mirbt, ed., *Quellen zur Geschichte des Papsttums und des römischen Katholizimus*, 2nd ed. (Tübingen: Paul Siebeck, 1901), 183–85.
[20] LW 31:341–42. See also LW 44:136.
[21] LW 31:383–95; LW 36:336–43; LW 44:86–89, 136–38, 141–44, 152–57, 164–68, 203.
[22] LW 44:202–03. See also LW 44:151–57; LW 36:79–80.

had served to "suck Germany dry."[23] When parties challenged these practices, local clergy used their privileges of forum to remove their cases to local church courts. Local church courts, in turn, used the false threats of the interdict and the ban to usurp the jurisdiction of the secular courts and to apply the canon law to subjects and persons far beyond their spiritual ken.[24]

Third, Luther charged that the church's canon law was an instrument of greed and exploitation. To support its luxury and bureaucracy, the church imposed heavy annates, tithes, and other religious taxes on the German people. The church invented all manner of relics, obits, ceremonies, altars, and pilgrimages to fleece the people of their charity. It reserved and sold German benefices and other lucrative church offices only to the highest bidder—often a foreigner with enough money to pay the "reservation fees" to receive his office, but without the pastoral or administrative skills needed to discharge it effectively. The church even sold salvation and purgation through its penitential works and indulgences.[25] "[T]oday nothing comes from Rome but a fair of spiritual wares which are bought and sold openly and shamelessly," Luther wrote:

> indulgences, parishes, monasteries, bishoprics, deaconries, benefices, and everything else that was originally founded for the service of God throughout the world. As a result, not only is all the money and wealth of the world drawn and driven to Rome, but the parishes, bishoprics, and prelacies are pulled to pieces and laid waste. Consequently, the people are neglected, and the word of God and God's name and honor perish and faith is destroyed.[26]

This is "bare-faced robbery, deceit, and tyranny of hell's portals."[27]

Fourth, and most fundamental, Luther argued that the canon law was devoid of authority. In his view, God vested legal authority in the prince, not the pope. The prince and other civil magistrates were, for Luther, God's vice-regents, called to appropriate and apply God's law in governing human society. The pope and all clerics, by contrast, were called to preach the Word, to administer the sacraments, to admonish the sinful, and to guide human consciences. This was the true meaning of "the power of the keys" described by Matthew 16:18-19.[28]

---

[23] LW 44:141. See also LW 44:95-96, 155-56, 163-64, 191-92, 213, 237-39; LW 45: 295-308.

[24] LW 44:130-33, 160-61, 181-82; LW 45:58-61.

[25] LW 44:141-44, 155-57, 169-72, 181; LW 31:175-77, 233; LW 45:109.

[26] LW 44:88-89.

[27] LW 44:156.

[28] LW 44:83-96, 127-30; LW 45:106-09, 118-26. See also his earlier exposition, *Luther: Lectures on Romans* [1516], trans. and ed. W. H. Pauck (Philadelphia: Fortress Press, 1961), 358-66, and Luther's later exposition in LW 40:321-77.

By promulgating and enforcing canon law, the pope and his bishops had usurped the prince's authority and "obscured the gospel, faith, grace, and true divine service." "Neither pope nor bishop nor any other [clerical] man has the right to impose a single syllable of law upon a Christian."[29]

Moreover, in Luther's view, the canon law opposed both the teaching and the authority of the Bible. The Bible, as Luther understood it, teaches that each person (1) stands in direct relation to God when confessing his or her sin and receiving God's grace; (2) is justified not by works but solely by faith in God's grace; and (3) is commanded to lead life in all its aspects in accordance with the Bible. By conferring on clerics the authority to dispense God's grace and to intercede for the souls of the laity, the canon law intruded upon the Christian's personal relation with God. It made clerics indispensable mediators between God and humanity, falsely according to them a greater sanctity and greater accessibility to God. By defining a hierarchy of meritorious works, the canon law sanctioned a salvation by works, not by faith, and elevated spiritual acts and vocations while deprecating those of the earthly life. By governing every step of the Christian walk with human rules and regulations, the canon law "tyrannized the Christian's conscience" "and "destroyed the spiritual love and freedom of the Gospel."[30]

From Church to State

On the strength of these criticisms, Luther in the early 1520 s urged that all legal authority be removed from the church to the state, from the clergy to the magistracy. The church is a community of faith and love, he insisted, not a corporation of law and politics. The consciences of its members are to be guided by scripture and the Spirit, not governed by legal traditions and clerical injunctions. All its members are priests and stand equal before God; they are not divided into a higher clergy and a lower laity. The church holds the power of the Word and is called to serve society, not to rule it. The state holds the power of the sword, and is called to rule society—by force, if necessary—to maintain public order, peace, and justice, and to facilitate the growth of the church and the moral improvement of civil society.

Having truncated the authority of the pope and the canon law, Luther exalted the power of the prince and the civil law. On one hand, Luther believed, the prince and other magistrates were God's vice-regents in the earthly kingdom, called to elaborate and enforce God's Word and will, to reflect God's justice and judgment on earthly citizens. The magistracy was, in this sense, a "divine of-

---

[29] LW 36:23–24, 55, 70–72, 96.
[30] LW 31:345–54.

fice," a "holy estate," a "Godly calling," within the earthly kingdom. Indeed, the magistrate was a god on earth, as Psalm 82:6 put it, to be obeyed as if God himself.[31] "Law and earthly government are a great gift of God to mankind," Luther wrote with flourish. "Earthly authority is an image, shadow, and figure of the dominion of Christ." Indeed, "a pious jurist" who served faithfully in the Christian magistrate's retinue is "a prophet, priest, angel, and savior ... in the earthly kingdom."[32]

The magistrate and his retinue not only represented God's authority and majesty. They also exercised God's judgment and wrath against human sin. "Princes and magistrates are the bows and arrows of God," Luther wrote, equipped to hunt down God's enemies in the earthly kingdom.[33] The hand of the Christian magistrate, judge, or soldier "that wields the sword and slays is not man's hand, but God's; and it is not man, but God, who hangs, tortures, beheads, slays, and fights. All these are God's works and judgments."[34]

On the other hand, Luther believed, the magistrate was the "father of the community" (*Landesvater, paterpoliticus*). He was to care for his political subjects as if they were his children, and his political subjects were to honor him as if he were their parent.[35] This was the essence of the *Obrigkeit*, the *ordo politicus*—the political authorities and their retinues that comprised the early modern state. Like a loving father, the magistrate was to keep the peace and to protect his subjects from threats or violations to their persons, properties, and reputations. He was to deter his subjects from abusing themselves through drunkenness, sumptuousness, prostitution, gambling, and other vices. He was to nurture and sustain his subjects through the community chest, the public almshouse, the state-run hospice. He was to educate them through the public school, the public library, the public lectern. He was to see to their spiritual needs by supporting the ministry of the locally established church, and encouraging their attendance and participation through the laws of Sabbath observance, tithing, and holy days. He was to see to their material needs by reforming inheritance and property laws to ensure more even distribution of parents' property among their children. He was to set an example of virtue, piety, love, and charity in his own home and private life for his faithful subjects to emulate and to respect. The Christian magistrate was to complement and support the God-given responsibilities of parents and family members for their children and dependents, without intruding on the paternal office. And he was to support the preaching and sacramental life of the local church without trespassing on the

---

[31] LW 2:139 ff.; LW 13:44 ff.; LW 44:92 ff.; LW 45:85 ff.; LW 46:237 ff.
[32] WA 30/2:554.
[33] LW 17:171.
[34] WA 19:626. See also WA 6:267; LW 45:113; LW 46:95 ff.
[35] WA 30/1:152 ff.; LW 13:58 ff.; LW 44:81–99.

ecclesiastical office, let alone that of the invisible church of the heavenly kingdom.[36]

These twin metaphors of the Christian magistrate—as the lofty vice-regent of God and as the loving father of the community—described the basics of Luther's and Lutheran political theory until modern times.[37] For Luther, political authority was divine in origin, but earthly in operation. It expressed God's harsh judgment against sin but also his tender mercy for sinners. It communicated the law of God but also the lore of the local community. It depended upon the church for prophetic direction but it took over from the church all jurisdiction—governance of marriage, education, poor relief, moral crimes, and other earthly subjects traditionally governed by the canon law. Either metaphor standing alone—vice-regent of God or loving father of the community—could be a recipe for abusive tyranny or officious paternalism. But both metaphors together provided Luther and his followers with the core ingredients of a robust Christian republicanism and budding Christian welfare state.[38]

Luther did not spell out his preferred form of state government, however. He had, at first, hoped that the emperor would endorse the Reformation, and accordingly included in his early writings some lofty panegyrics on the imperial authorities of the Holy Roman Empire of his day and of the Christian Roman Empire of a millennium before. When the emperor failed him, Luther turned at various times to the nobility, the peasantry, the city councils, and the princes, and in turn wrote favorably about each of them, and then sometimes unfavorably when they failed him.[39] Such writings must be read in their immediate political context, however, and not used to paint Luther as a theorist of political absolutism, or elitist oligarchy, or constitutional democracy. Luther did not sort out systematically the relative virtues and vices of monarchy, aristocracy, or democracy. He spent very little time on the thorny constitutional questions of the

---

[36] LW 45:83–84, 104–13 and sources in LP 105–14.

[37] See, for example, the recent reflections by Marie A. Failinger and Ronald W. Duty, eds., *Lutheran Theology and Secular Law: The Work of the Modern State* (London: Routledge, 2018); and Wolfgang Huber, *Kirche und Öffentlichkeit*, 2nd ed. (Munich: Chr. Kaiser, 1991).

[38] See, for example, Lisbet Christoffersen, Kjell Å. Modéer, and Svend Andersen, eds., *Law and Religion in the 21st Century: Nordic Perspectives* (Copenhagen: Djøf Publishers, 2010).

[39] For convenient excerpts of his political writings, see Hermann W. Beyer, *Luther und das Recht*, repr. ed. (Paderborn: Salzwasser-Verlag Gmbh, 2013); and J. M. Porter, ed., *Luther—Selected Political Writings* (Philadelphia: Fortress Press, 1974). See further LP; Virpi Mäkinen, ed., *Lutheran Reformation and the Law* (Leiden: Brill, 2006); and Mathias Schmoeckel, *Das Recht der Reformation* (Tübingen: Mohr Siebeck, 2014).

nature and purpose of executive, legislative, and judicial powers, let alone finer questions of checks and balances, judicial review, and other such questions.

In the same vein, Luther did not work out a systematic theory of resistance, rebellion, revolt, and all-out revolution against political authorities that had become tyrannical. He remained restrained in part by the numerous biblical texts that counseled political obedience. He was also restrained by his own exalted view of the political office of magistrate. The reality was that, after his narrow escape from the Diet of Worms in 1521 and protection in the Wartburg Castle for several months that followed, he was largely protected by his political patrons, and did not face personally the dire consequences of his theory of political obedience.

The Magdeburg Confession on Resisting the Emperor and Imperial Law

Shortly after Luther's death, in 1546, his followers in the German city of Magdeburg did face these dire consequences. It drove them to distill the biblical basics of Lutheran theories of political obedience, and to strengthen the case for political disobedience against imperial laws that intruded on religious freedom.[40] The leaders of the small Saxon city of Magdeburg had drafted this confession in response to the order of the Holy Roman Emperor Charles V to impose by civil law the uniform Catholic doctrines and liturgies being crafted by the Council of Trent, and to stamp out the "raging Lutheran heresy" that had "infected" the empire for three decades.[41] Those Lutheran polities that did not peaceably accept this new imperial law, called the Augsburg Interim, would face military conquest and destruction. Several Lutheran polities and leaders had already capitulated. Magdeburg would not. Imperial forces put the city under siege. The Magdeburg leadership stood firm, and began to write boldly in defense of their actions.

---

[40] *Confessio et apologia pastorum & reliquorum ministrorum Ecclesiae Magdeburgensis* (Magdeburg, 1550), hereafter MC. David M. Whitford kindly furnished me with a working translation of this document, which I have adapted herein based on review of the original text. See further David M. Whitford, *Tyranny and Resistance: The Magdeburg Confession and the Lutheran Tradition* (St. Louis, Mo.: Concordia Press, 2001). For another translation, which I have not seen, see *The Magdeburg Confession 13th of April 1550 A.D.*, trans. Matthew Colvin (North Charleston, S.C.: CreateSpace, 2012).

[41] "The Interim, or Declaration of Religion of His Imperial Majesty Charles V," in *Tracts and Treaties in Defense of the Reformed Faith*, trans. Henry Beveridge, ed. T. F. Torrance, 3 vols. (Grand Rapids: Eerdmans, 1958), 3:190.

The 1550 Magdeburg Confession was the most important of a hundred plus pamphlets in defense of their stand. The Confession recited the essential Lutheran doctrines that the ministers held contrary to the new Catholic establishment laws. The Confession then rehearsed the arguments to justify the ministers' refusal to obey the new laws, and to resist their implementation—with force of arms, if necessary. Its main conclusion was set out in the preamble:

> If the high authority does not refrain from unjustly and forcibly persecuting not only the lives of their subjects but even more their rights under divine and natural law, and if the high authority does not desist from eradicating true doctrine and true worship of God, then the lower magistracy is required by God's divine command to attempt, together with their subjects, to stand up to such superiors as far as possible. The current persecution which we are suffering at the hands of our superiors is primarily persecution by which they attempt to suppress the true Christian religion and the true worship of God and to reestablish the pope's lies and abominable idolatry. Thus the Council [of Magdeburg] and each and every Christian authority is obliged to protect themselves and their people against this.[42]

The Magdeburg Confession first countered the many biblical texts that called faithful Christians to honor, respect, and obey the emperor and other political authorities for the sake of conscience and the Gospel. Yes, the Confession argued, we must honor the authorities "so that our days may be long." But if our days are being cut short, then we should not honor those authorities who shorten them. Yes, political authorities were "appointed by God to do good." But if they are not doing good, then they could not have been appointed by God. Yes, the magistrate is not "a terror to good conduct but to bad." But if he himself becomes a terror to good conduct, then he must be a bad magistrate. Yes, we must "render to Caesar the things that are Caesar's, and to God the things that are God's." But if Caesar wants or takes what is God's, then we must withhold or retrieve it for God's sake. Yes, "he who resists the authorities resists God." But if the authorities resist God, then surely we must avenge God's honor. Yes, "vengeance is mine," says the Lord. But "we are his instruments" for good, and "God punishes in such a way that those who execute the punishment are not doing wrong but are carrying out God's will and command."[43]

Citing sundry biblical texts, the Confession argued that God has ordained the three main estates of church, state, and family to keep order and peace in this sinful world, so that the Gospel can flourish and each person can pursue his or her God-given calling. None of the authorities of these three estates may get "mixed up with one another," or intrude on each other's created mandate. None

---

[42] MC, A1v.
[43] MC, G3r–H1r; K1r–K3r; L2r–M1r.

may abandon, betray, or exceed their God-given office. And most important, none may violate the sovereignty of God. All authorities thus rule conditionally. If any authorities

> seek the extermination of religion and decent morals, and persecute true religion and decent living, then they dispose of their own honor, and they can no longer be considered to be authorities or parents either before God or within the conscience of their subjects. They become an ordinance of the devil instead of God, an ordinance which everyone can and ought to resist with a good conscience, each in accordance with his calling.[44]

The calling to resist abusive political authorities lies first and foremost with lower magistrates. The Bible makes clear that God instituted multiple authorities, not just one. The Bible speaks of "the powers that be," not just one power, of the multiple "authorities that rule," not just a single authority. All political authorities are equipped with the power of the sword to do good and to punish evil. That power must be exercised internally within the government as well as externally within the community. When an inferior magistrate does evil, a fellow or superior magistrate must correct or remove him. When a superior magistrate does evil, his fellow or inferior magistrates must, in turn, correct and control him, albeit always within the limits of the honor and respect that the higher magistrate deserves. If the higher magistrate commits only a minor or personal offense, lower magistrates should admonish him privately and gently. But if he unjustly endangers the "life and limb," "wife and child," and "local liberties of the people," the lower magistrates "may make use of their rights to defend themselves" and their subjects. Even worse, if the higher magistrate commits a premeditated attack on "the highest and most essential rights of the people"—indeed, if he attacks "our Lord himself, the author of these rights"—then even the most "insignificant and weakest regents" must rise up against him. If necessary, those lower magistrates must call upon "every pious and reasonable Christian" to join them in the resistance, armed not only with the sword but also with the Word's assurance that "God is on our side."[45]

The Magdeburg Confession did not spell out systematically the "local liberties of the people," or "the highest and most essential rights of the people" that could trigger these steps of escalating resistance and revolt. It did make clear that the "procedural rights" of the people had been abridged: "Divine, natural, and secular laws" alike recognize that criminals have a right to a public hearing and their day in court. But we have been "accused only on hearsay evidence," and have not had a chance to "face our accusers." Just because other Lutheran

---

[44] MC, G3r, G4v, L1r.
[45] MC, J4r–K1r, K2R–L1r, M1r–M2r, P2r–P3r.

towns have capitulated, does not mean that we good citizens of Magdeburg should lose "our rights by default." "Our case must be judged in accordance with proper justice."[46]

But the Confession's main concern was that the emperor was violating the people's "essential rights" of religion. Those violations merited a more forceful response. We "seek nothing else but the freedom to remain and be left in the true recognized religion of the holy and only redeeming Gospel." We act peaceably. We educate our children to be good and useful citizens. We pray daily for our rulers. We pay our taxes and tributes. We register our properties. We "desire no one's land and people and covet no one's worth and goods." "Your Imperial Majesty allows both Jews and heathens to follow their religion, and do not force them from their religions to the Papacy." But "we are not even allowed to have the same freedom of religion that is granted to non-Christians." Instead, the emperor seeks "to reintroduce the pope's idolatry, to suppress or exterminate the pure doctrine of the Holy Gospel ... in violation not only of divine law but also of written civil law."[47]

In these circumstances, the Bible requires "a lesser God-fearing magistracy and all those over whom it has been set to give protection against such unjust force and maintain true doctrine and worship, and preserve body and life, soul and honor." Those lower magistrates who fail to discharge their duty are ignoring the admonition of Proverbs 24:10–12: "Rescue those who are being taken away to death; hold back those who are stumbling to the slaughter." Others must come to help, too, lest they ignore the lesson of Judges 5:23, where God is said to have cursed a people "because they did not come to the help of the Lord, to the help of the Lord against the mighty." It was God who "ordained force," and he expects it to be used to "advance and defend His word, true divine worship, and appropriate reverence for God."[48]

Not only the Bible but history makes it abundantly clear that resisting tyrants who tread on the religious rights of their people is not only a right but a duty of the faithful. Biblical history is full of examples: Jonathan and David resisted King Saul, as did Saul's own servants when he became tyrannical. The leaders of Zebulun and Naphtali defied Jabin, the Canaanite king. Elias, Jehu, and Naboth refused to obey King Ahab. Asa deposed his own tyrannical mother, Queen Maacah. Daniel disobeyed King Darius. The Maccabees attacked the Romans. The Confession returned to these examples again and again as illustrations of a person's duties in the face of tyranny. Roman history, too, is full of examples. Think of Ambrosius refusing Justine, Moritz resisting Maximinus, Ambrose admonishing Theodosius, Laurentius refusing the orders of Decius,

---

[46] MC, H2r, K4r.
[47] MC, H4r–J2r, K1r.
[48] MC, K1r, L3r, P2v.

and more.[49] Even the pagan Roman ruler Trajan handed his deputy a sword with the words: "In so far as I command what is right wield this sword against my foes; but if I do the opposite, then wield it against me."[50]

These and other examples from religious and secular history, the Confession continued, underscored the universal and natural validity of the "law of legitimate self-defense."[51] Defense of oneself and of third parties against attack—using force and violence when necessary—was a familiar legal doctrine of the European *ius commune*. When a person is unjustly attacked by another, the victim has the right to defend himself, to resist—passively, by running away, or actively, by staying to fight with proportionate force. Other parties, particularly relatives, guardians, or caretakers of the victim, also have the right to intervene to help the victim—again, passively by assisting escape, or actively by repelling the assailant with force.

When a magistrate exceeds his authority, the Confession argued by analogy, he forfeits his office and becomes simply like any private person. If he uses force to implement his excessive authority, his victims and third parties may resist him passively or actively, just as if he were any other criminal brigand. Furthermore, if the higher magistrate giving the orders has exceeded his authority, then all lower magistrates, ministers, and military folks implementing his orders have also exceeded their authority. They are accomplices in the crime of the former higher magistrate, now private citizen. And the accomplices are all themselves now merely private citizens engaged in criminal actions. Both the victim and third parties also have the right of passive or active resistance against these assailants.

The Confession drew from this law of self-defense several lessons for how to respond to the emperor and his political allies, who now sought to coerce the Lutherans to return to Catholicism. First, all those who aided and acted for this tyrant were themselves accomplices to his crime of tyranny, and they were all guilty before God. This included all lower magistrates who implemented his orders. It also included soldiers and allies who marched for the tyrant, citizens and subjects who paid taxes in support of the tyrant, even subjects who knowingly prayed for the success of the tyrant.[52]

Second, all those called to care for others must assist their dependents to resist tyrannical attacks. Lower magistrates, judges, and police must protect the local citizens. Pastors, elders, and sextons must protect their local congregants. Fathers, mothers, and masters must protect their children, servants, and wards. Teachers and tutors must protect the students in their schools. If any of these

---

[49] MC, J3r, L1r–L4r, M4r–N1r, O3r–O4r.
[50] MC, M4r.
[51] MC, K1r, N.
[52] MC, N4r–O1r, P3r–P4r.

dependents were attacked on the street by a simple criminal, their caretakers would have to intervene. Failure to do so would render them an accomplice to the criminal attack. Tyrants are simple criminals, the Confession argued, and innocent victims must thus be defended against them. Those who fail in their defense become criminals themselves. "God will judge guilty not only those who themselves commit unjust killing, but also those who have not helped to protect and save, according to their ability."[53]

Third, invoking the Lutheran doctrine of the priesthood of all believers, the Confession argued with escalating rhetoric that "all pious Christians should concern themselves with this common emergency and take it as much to heart and treat it as seriously as if it concerned each person individually." All Christians are called to be priests to their peers, Good Samaritans to strangers in peril. All Christians are thus responsible to intervene when a victim is assailed by a common criminal, or when a community is ravaged by a criminal tyrant. This becomes doubly imperative when the victim of this criminal attack is ultimately Christ himself, whose people and preaching are being unjustly assailed. "As much as you do it to them, you do it to me," Christ had said.[54]

The Confession stopped short of arguing that every Christian member of the community could and should seek the violent overthrow of tyrants. That was a recipe for anarchy, and the Magdeburg ministers worked hard to counter such an insurrectionary conclusion. A more structured response was called for—with the higher magistrates passing instructions down the hierarchy of lower magistrates and ultimately down to the local caretakers about the best means and measures of response. A private individual's first reflex should be prayer and patience, then passive disobedience of false authorities and advice to others on how to disobey, then petitions for help from the lower authorities and insistence on the vindication of essential rights that have been violated. Only after exhausting peaceable remedies and receiving orders from a legitimate lower authority to join a just war or rebellion was a private person entitled to violent disobedience. But once so entitled, he or she could and should fight with all due alacrity. None of this was a violation of the individual Christian's duties to God and conscience: "The laws and liberties of our German Empire are such that Christians may use them in [good] conscience, just like they make use of other secular rules that are not against God. Indeed, if Christians do not make use of them, they will lose out to their own eternal shame before the world and to the harm of their successors."[55]

The Magdeburg Confession was a forceful distillation and extension of earlier Lutheran teachings on resistance to political tyranny, as well an impressive

---

[53] MC, P1r, P2r–P4r.
[54] MC, N3r–N4r, P1r, P4r.
[55] MC, G1r, H2r–J3r, O4r.

reconstruction of biblical, patristic, and medieval prototypes.[56] The Confession was also an impressive political achievement, for it eventually turned popular opinion against the emperor and the military enforcement of the Augsburg Interim. After a year of laying siege to the city of Magdeburg, the emperor's military ally, Duke Maurice of Saxony, ultimately switched back to the Lutheran side, and the threatened conquest of Magdeburg turned into a stalemate. This, in turn, led to the gradual collapse of other imperial military campaigns against other Lutheran towns and abandonment of the emperor's program to enforce the Augsburg Interim law throughout the empire. Ultimately, the emperor accepted the Peace of Augsburg (1555) that allowed each polity in Germany to have its own religious confession, whether Catholic or Lutheran, under the principle of *cuius regio, eius religio.*[57]

The 1550 Magdeburg Confession's three main lines of arguments for resistance against political tyranny—from the Bible, from history, and from the law of self-defense—provided a sturdy template on which later Protestants built their arguments about rights, resistance, rebellion, revolution, and regicide. In the 1550s and 1560s, John Ponet, John Knox, Christopher Goodman, and other English and Scottish Calvinist exiles, who had fled to the Continent to escape the persecution of Mary Tudor and Mary of Guise, added further arguments from popular sovereignty, private regicide, and inalienable rights. In the 1560s and 1570s, French and Swiss jurists like Pierre Viret, Theodore Beza, Hugo Donnellus, Lambert Daneau, and François Hotman added further arguments from covenant theology, classical republicanism, and constitutional history.[58] All these arguments and more came to ever more radical political expression and application in the hands of later Dutch, English, American, and French revolutionaries.[59]

Early modern Lutherans in Germany and Scandinavia, however, rarely pressed their resistance theories to such radical revolutionary conclusions.[60] For

---

[56] See summary in J. H. Burns, ed., *The Cambridge History of Political Thought, 1450-1700* (Cambridge: Cambridge University Press, 1991), 159-245.

[57] In Sidney Z. Ehler and John B. Morrall, eds., *Church and State through the Centuries: A Collection of Historic Documents with Commentaries* (Westminster, Md.: Newman Press, 1954), 164-73.

[58] See detailed sources and discussion in RR. But cf. caveats in Cornel Zwierlein, "The Importance of 'Confessio' in Magdebourg (1550) for Calvinism: A Historiographical Myth," *Bibliothèque d'Humanisme et Renaissance* 68 (2005): 27-46.

[59] See, for example, David M. Whitford, "John Adams, John Ponet, and a Lutheran Influence on the American Revolution," *Lutheran Quarterly* 15 (2001): 143-57.

[60] See, for example, Kjell Å Modéer and Helle Vogt, eds., *Law and the Christian Tradition in Scandinavia: The Writings of the Great Nordic Jurists* (London: Routledge, 2021); and Ma-

all the clever biblical casuistry illustrated by the Magdeburg Confession, it was hard for *sola scriptura* Christians to ignore the repeated biblical commands to honor, respect, and obey the political authorities and to bear persecution with patience, prayer, and perseverance. And outside of the Magdeburg Confession, it was hard for faithful Lutherans to find much traction for resistance theories in the foundational creeds, confessions, and catechisms of the Lutheran Reformation. It was not until modern times, when faced with the dire and destructive waves of monarchism, fascism, nationalism, and Nazism, that the Lutheran tradition reconsidered and reconstructed these original Lutheran teachings. Brave Lutheran reformers like Dietrich Bonhoeffer, Martin Niemöller, Eugen Bolz, Eivind Berggrav, and others returned to earlier Lutheran endorsements of resistance, most importantly the Magdeburg Confession, to work out a sturdy new Christian logic of organized political resistance, self-defense, and just warfare against tyranny.

These Christian theories of resistance, revolt, and revolution remain tragically salient in many parts of the world today, where Christians and other people of faith face fascism, nationalism, tribalism, jihadism, and plain political and popular brutality.[61] Empirical studies over the past decade by the Pew Research Center, various nongovernmental organizations, and the United States Department of State report that Christians are more widely harassed than the members of any other religious tradition, experiencing social and political hostility in at least 110 countries.[62] These hostilities have been carried out by a variety of private groups and governmental entities and include arrests and detentions; desecration of holy sites; denial of visas, corporate charters, and entity status; discrimination in employment, education, and housing; and closures of worship centers, schools, charities, cemeteries, and religious services—let alone outright rape, torture, kidnapping, and slaughter of believers in alarming numbers in war-torn areas of the Middle East, Eurasia, and Africa.[63] Here, the prophetic words of Luther and the Magdeburg Lutherans, and their echoes during the Nazi

---

thias Schmoeckel and John Witte Jr., eds., *Great Christian Jurists in German History* (Tübingen: Mohr Siebeck, 2020).

[61] See Timothy Samuel Shah and Allen Hertzke, eds., *Christianity and Freedom: Historical and Contemporary Perspectives* (Cambridge: Cambridge University Press, 2016); and Daniel Philpott and Timothy Samuel Shah, *Under Caesar's Sword: How Christians Respond to Persecution* (Cambridge: Cambridge University Press, 2018).

[62] See Pew Research Center, Jan. 2014, "Religious Hostilities Reach Six-Year High," at 21. By comparison, Muslims were harassed in 109 countries, Jews in 71, "others" (for example Sikhs, Zoroastrians, Baha'i, etc.) in 40, "folk religionists" in 26, Hindus in 16, and Buddhists in 13.

[63] Ibid.

reign of terror, ring with as much power, profundity, and purpose today as they did in the 1520 s to 1550 s and the 1930 s and 1940 s.

It seems less propitious in liberal lands today to adduce these magisterial writings to complain about political movements, COVID restrictions, vaccination requirements, travel limits, new liberal school curricula, changes in family policies, overreaching regulations, and controversial constitutional cases. Yes, Christians in late modern liberal lands have every right to use soft force to protest those intrusions that impede or threaten their ability to "worship God rather than men." They can file law suits, seek injunctions, file petitions, blanket the media to expose abuses and press for reforms. Those soft force exercises are essential popular checks and balances to keep the modern state at bay when it strays beyond its appropriate sphere. But, in my view, we dishonor the Lutheran heritage by equating these small shadows on our liberty in the liberal West today with the dark night that our parents and grandparents faced under the Nazis, or what our spiritual ancestors faced in the brutal religious genocide of the sixteenth century. And we insult the courage and genius of the authors of magisterial tracts like the Magdeburg Confession when we reduce their anguished arguments against their imperial oppressors to applause lines in sermons or speeches against the latest governmental insult.

Constitutional Rules and the Political Economy of Character Formation: Conditions on Government Aid to Religious Schools as a Case Study

Nathan S. Chapman

Introduction

For at least the past one hundred years, mainstream American society and traditional religious groups have been locked in a culture war over sexual mores, gender roles, and, more recently, questions of sexual and gender identity.[1] Because schools are powerful institutions for forming the habits, beliefs, and values of children–what this volume refers to as "character formation"–they have often constituted the front lines.[2] Both sides have sought to influence the subjects and content of instruction at public schools (those that are fully funded and operated by the government). For instance, the state of Florida recently enacted a law restricting some public-school teachers from providing instruction in sexual and gender identity.[3] In part, such disputes are about which beliefs, desires, and practices about sexuality and gender are true and desirable. In part, though, they are about the state's proper role in the formation of students' character regarding their own and others' sexuality and gender.

At the same time, religious Americans have long turned to private schools to inculcate their respective faiths. For many, this includes instruction and character formation in their faith's teachings about gender and sexuality. The proper use of public funds to support private religious education has been one of the most enduring and hotly contested political and social issues of American history, beginning with the refusal of Protestant proponents of the common school movement in the 1830 s to publicly fund Catholic schools on the ground that

---

[1] Matthew Avery Sutton, *American Apocalypse: A History of Modern Evangelicalism* (Cambridge, Mass.: Belknap Press of Harvard University Press, 2014), 114–47.

[2] James Davison Hunter, *Culture Wars: The Struggle to Define America* (New York: Basic Books, 1991), 197–225.

[3] 2022 Fla. H.B. 1557 (adopted Mar. 28, 2022); see Matt Lavietes, "Here's What Florida's 'Don't Say Gay' Bill Would Do and What It Wouldn't Do," *NBC News*, Mar. 16, 2022.

they were sectarian.[4] These disputes have not been exclusively religious; they have been about the state's support for a kind of formation of character seen to be inimical to the state's interests, especially the fostering of a contested notion of civic virtue.

The political economy of religious character formation through schools has always been framed by constitutional rules. Since the early twentieth century, state policies have been subject to federal rules as defined and implemented by the United States Supreme Court. Constitutional law has thus been a central feature of the culture wars over education in two different senses. Constitutional rules have themselves set the boundaries around which the competing sides must navigate at the federal, state, and local levels. At the same time, control over the Supreme Court has increasingly become a political objective, for controlling the Court is the way to control the rules of the political and economic game.

This chapter considers an especially hard constitutional question about state funding of religious schools as a case study of the effects of constitutional rules on the political economy of character formation. The question is this: when the government provides funds to private religious schools, may it condition those funds on the school's acceptance of a policy of nondiscrimination against employees or students because of their sexual or gender status or identity? The Court has never considered the question, but its recent school-funding decisions, coupled with political sentiment in some states, ensures that it will have to do so in the coming years.[5]

The legal battle on the horizon is a microcosm of the impact of political economy on character formation. Policy disputes about the government's proper role in education and character formation often arise from deeper theological and philosophical disputes among groups with incommensurable views of the good.[6] In a liberal constitutional state, such as the United States, such disputes are channeled into legal battles over constitutional doctrine, with courts sitting as the final arbiters of how society may proceed. Small differences to the constitutional framework can dramatically change the incentives that moral communi-

---

[4] John C. Jeffries Jr. and James E. Ryan, "A Political History of the Establishment Clause," *Michigan Law Review* 100, no. 2 (2001): 279–370.

[5] Associated Press, "Religious Schools Shun State Funding Despite Maine Victory," Aug. 30, 2022.

[6] See, for example, William Galston, "Parents, Governments and Children: Authority over Education in the Liberal Democratic State," in *Child, Family and the State*, Nomos XLIV, ed. Stephen Macedo and Iris Marion Young (New York: New York University Press, 2003), 211–33.

ties must navigate as they decide whether, and how, to maintain, compromise, or abandon their distinctive views.[7]

This chapter begins by laying out the constitutional framework of the political economy of private education. The current framework essentially holds that public schools must be as religiously neutral as possible, families have a right to private education, and the government may provide funds to private schools, but it may not discriminate against religious schools when it does so. Although the framework provides relatively clear answers for many cases, it is unclear about the conditions that the government may impose on private schools that receive funding for education, including whether the government may condition funds on the adoption of an LGBT nondiscrimination policy. The chapter considers three possible rules the Supreme Court might articulate to answer that question, and their respective implications for the political economy of private religious education. The point is not to identity the "right" rule, but to use the legal conundrum as an illustration of the practical influence of constitutional rules in shaping the market for dissenting approaches to character formation.

The Constitutional Framework of the Political Economy of Private Education

Four constitutional principles articulated by the Supreme Court establish the framework for the political economy's influence on religious education. Any constitutional rule about conditions on support for religious schools—and whatever effects such a rule would have on the political economy of education—would operate within this framework.

The first principle is that primary authority over education belongs to the states, which have traditionally given authority to local school districts. The U.S. Constitution delegates limited power to the federal government, and that power does not include authority over education; the power over essentially local concerns remains with the states. The states' power over education is subject, however, to two important caveats. The first is that the states are bound by constitutional rights provisions. The Fourteenth Amendment prohibits the states from violating the privileges or immunities of U.S. citizenship, the due process of law, or equal protection of the laws. The Supreme Court has held that these provisions incorporate fundamental rights articulated in the Bill of Rights—such

---

[7] See, for example, Richard A. Posner and Michael W. McConnell, "An Economic Approach to Issues of Religious Freedom," *University of Chicago Law Review* 56 (1989): 1–60.

as the rights of speech, the free exercise of religion, and nonestablishment of religion–against the states.[8]

The second caveat to state (and therefore local) control of education is that the federal government can *influence* state educational policy with conditions on grants of money to the states. The federal government has the power to spend for the general welfare, and the Court has interpreted this to include the power to place significant conditions on grants to the states, conditions that incentivize the states to adopt federal policies. It must be kept in mind, therefore, that conditions on educational spending that may affect religious character formation not only occur at the level of state grants to religious schools but also could arise from conditions on federal grants to the states. The federal government may not use a grant to induce a state to violate the Bill of Rights, so the constitutionality of such a grant would largely turn on a similar analysis to the one below.[9]

As a result of state authority over education, the long history of the political economy of religious education in the United States has played out at the state level. States have taken various approaches to religion in government-run schools and to support for religious schools. Cities, and then states, began developing publicly funded and controlled school systems in the middle of the nineteenth century. The common school movement, as it was known, sought to homogenize education in republican values that would be palatable to as many members of the community as possible. Because most Americans adhered to a Protestant denomination, common (public) schools incorporated instruction and devotional exercises that would have been accepted to all but the most conservative Protestants. Growing Catholic communities understandably objected to sending their children to the common schools. They sought funding and support for their own schools. A watershed movement in the American political economy of religious formation culminated in many state constitutional prohibitions against government funding of sectarian schools. In practice, this meant that state governments funded and operated public schools that integrated generic Protestant instruction and practice into their curriculum, but they refused to fund (or operate) Catholic, Jewish, or more evangelical Protestant schools.[10] At the same time, states began to require children to attend schools that satisfied

---

[8] See, for example, Cantwell v. Connecticut, 310 U.S. 296 (1940); West Virginia State Bd. of Ed. v. Barnette, 319 U.S. 624 (1943); Everson v. Bd. of Ed., 330 U.S. 1 (1947).

[9] See South Dakota v. Dole, 483 U.S. 203 (1987).

[10] See, for example, Kyle Duncan, "Secularism's Laws: State Blaine Amendments and Religious Persecution," *Fordham Law Review* 72, no. 3 (2003): 493–593; and Steven K. Green, "'Blaming Blaine:' Understanding the Blaine Amendment and the 'No-Funding' Principle," *First Amendment Law Review* 2, no. 1 (2003): 107–52; and Joseph Viteritti, "Blaine's Wake: School Choice, the First Amendment, and State Constitutional Law," *Harvard Journal of Law and Public Policy* 21 (1998): 657–718.

state curricular criteria. Requiring attendance and providing free, government-run schools were strategies to enculturate as many students as possible in what were seen as fundamental American norms, which included not only basic civic education but also instruction in the Ten Commandments, the Lord's Prayer, and, in some cases, Protestant hymns.[11]

The second principle essential to the constitutional framework of the political economy of education is that despite state control over public schools, parents, children, and teachers have the fundamental right to private education. In *Pierce v. Society of Sisters* (1925), at the request of two schools—one a military academy for boys and the other a Catholic school—the Supreme Court invalidated a state law prohibiting all private education. In an oft-quoted passage, the Court said:

> The fundamental theory of liberty upon which all governments in this Union repose excludes any general power of the State to standardize its children by forcing them to accept instruction from public teachers only. The child is not the mere creature of the State; those who nurture him and direct his destiny have the right, coupled with the high duty, to recognize and prepare him for additional obligations.

The decision secured the right of private religious education, but it did not change the political economy of education. At the time, there was little appetite for government funding of private religious education, and many places remained hostile to Catholic insularity, which was perceived to be threatening to the Protestant norms of democratic individualism that underlay the republic.

The third principle of the constitutional framework is that public schools may not engage in religious instruction or practice. In a series of cases beginning in the 1950s, the Supreme Court dismantled the soft Protestant establishment of the public schools. Up to that time, it was common for public schools to begin the school day with teacher- or student-led prayer and Bible reading and to endorse the basic norms of Christianity. The Court held that those practices were inconsistent with the Establishment Clause of the First Amendment, which prohibits the government from making a law "respecting an establishment of religion." The Court's concern was twofold: the official prayers and Bible reading amounted to a government-controlled and
-sponsored form of religious worship; and children are especially sensitive to social pressure, so those acts of worship were more likely to infringe on their

---

[11] Jeffries and Ryan, "A Political History of the Establishment Clause"; and Charles Leslie Glenn, *The Myth of the Common School* (Amherst: University of Massachusetts Press, 1987).

religious freedom than, say, an official prayer that begins a legislative session.[12] At the same time, the Supreme Court has made it plain that public schools need not be religion-free zones. Teachers and students are free to engage in religious speech and religious exercise so long as they are not attributable to the government.[13]

The result of the mid-twentieth-century settlement was that public schools were officially secular, but parents with the financial means could send their children to private schools. Feeling the economic pressure of the post-World War II baby boom, and realizing that religious schools could provide quality educations for a fraction of the cost of public schools, the political economy of government funding of religious schools began to change. Many states began to experiment with subsidizing some aspects of private education, mostly as a cost-saving measure that met with increased public support, especially from Catholic communities, which wielded considerable political power in some states.

At first, the Supreme Court adopted a doctrine that invalidated most forms of state subsidy of religious schools. States could act with neither the purpose nor the effect of advancing religion, nor could they become "excessively entangled" with religious institutions. The result was that even modest attempts to subsidize the many nonreligious public benefits provided by religious schools were invalidated, either because they had the incidental effect of advancing religion (by freeing up other private funds for religious indoctrination) or because the government had to become entangled with the schools to be sure the funds were not used to advance religion.[14]

The Court finally settled on what has become the fourth principle of the constitutional framework of religious education: the government may provide some indirect funding to religious schools, so long as it is religiously neutral and the product of the free, independent choice of parents and students. The leading case, *Zelman v. Simmons-Harris* (2004), involved government-funded vouchers that parents could use to offset the cost of private-school tuition.[15] The vouchers were good for any private school, religious or nonreligious, and there were multiple schools to choose from (though there were many more religious schools, and the nonreligious schools tended to cost more). The vouchers went from the government to parents, who could then pay them to the school of their choice. The Court evaluated the voucher program in light of all of the available educa-

---

[12] Engel v. Vitale, 370 U.S. 421 (1962); Abingdon Sch. Dist. v. Schempp, 374 U.S. 203 (1963).

[13] Kennedy v. Bremerton Sch. Dist., 597 U.S. ___ (2022); Widmar v. Vincent, 454 U.S. 263 (1981).

[14] Lemon v. Kurtzman, 403 U.S. 602 (1971); see John Garvey, "Another Way of Looking at School Aid," *The Supreme Court Review* (1985): 61–92.

[15] 536 U.S. 639 (2002).

tional options, including several varieties of public schools that were, of course, entirely government-funded. The sum total of the regime, the Court concluded, was religiously neutral and allowed parents genuine choice among educational options. The government funds flowed to the religious schools as the result of the individual exercise of religion, not because of governmental religious preferences.

Constitutional Vagueness, Democracy, and Rights

The constitutional framework provides the basic rules for the political and economic competition between secularist and religious educational interests. The rules have been established by the Supreme Court through its power to interpret and enforce constitutional restrictions on state power over church-state relations and individual and corporate freedom. They set the outer bounds of the government's relationship to religious character formation through schools: the government may not directly undertake such formation through schools that it controls; it may not shut down such formation by private schools; and it may facilitate such formation only through a program that is religiously neutral.

Each of these principles, and the judicial decisions that articulate them, is somewhat vague. The rules they create, like most rules, have some applications that are clear and others that are doubtful. Clear cases, those within what H. L. A. Hart describes as the "core" of the rule's meaning, are easy; those that fall within the rule's doubtful "penumbra" are hard.[16] Moreover, vagueness in rules delegates decision-making authority to those responsible for applying them.[17] The vagueness of the constitutional principles of religious freedom have effectively delegated authority to state governments to adopt a wide variety of policies, so long as they comply with the rules' clear application.[18] Such de facto delegation has some merits: it facilitates democratic governance, allows for policy experimentation, and permits geographic heterogeneity that reflects the preferences of local majorities.

At the same time, however, vagueness that promotes self-governance leaves the rights of political minorities unsettled and vulnerable to the "tyranny of the

---

[16] H. L. A. Hart, "Positivism and the Separation of Law and Morals," *Harvard Law Review* 71 (1958): 593–629, at 606–08; Lon L. Fuller, "Positivism and Fidelity to Law–A Reply to Professor Hart," *Harvard Law Review* 71 (1958): 630–72, at 662–65; and Ronald Dworkin, "Hard Cases," *Harvard Law Review* 88 (1975): 1057–109.

[17] See Frederick Schauer, *Playing by the Rules: A Philosophical Examination of Rule-Based Decision-Making in Law and in Life* (Oxford: Clarendon Press, 1991), 150–51, 158–62.

[18] Kathleen M. Sullivan, "Foreword: The Justices of Rules and Standards," *Harvard Law Review* 106 (1992): 22–123.

majority."[19] Such rules give the government a long leash to promote secularism or, alternatively, to facilitate religious education without regard for conflicting rights. That discretion always remains subject to oversight by the U.S. Supreme Court, which may always revise or clarify the applicable constitutional rule, turning what was once a hard case into an easy one.

Consider the following implications of the vague aspects of the constitutional framework for the political economy of religious education.

1. When the government seeks to subsidize private education, what factors are relevant to determining whether a parent's decision to use the money on religious education was sufficiently "free"? The economic baseline is that secular public education is free. In most cases, parents pay taxes to support transportation to public schools, instruction, and extracurricular activities. The cost of special education services for students with disabilities is especially high. No state government has attempted to provide anything like a comparable amount of money per pupil for education at a religious school. At the same time, religious schools, including those that cost far less per pupil than public schools, may offer a far better overall education than the local public schools offer. The question is whether the government's partial subsidy of those schools—even if it covers only a fraction of the parent's actual payment—induces the religious formation of children that the parents would not have otherwise freely chosen.

2. What counts as a subsidy? Governments have many tools to affect economic decision-making, and the Supreme Court has not always drawn conceptually defensible distinctions among them. For instance, most economists would say that a tax exemption has the same economic effect as a direct payment, yet the Court has treated them differently with respect to religious institutions, permitting tax exemptions for religious institutions, including churches, that would almost certainly be unconstitutional in the form of a direct payment.[20] Likewise, the Court has drawn a line between direct payments to religious schools, even on a per capita basis, and vouchers or tax credits to parents of religious school students for the same amount. The theory is that a direct payment symbolizes a closer relationship between church and state than a payment that goes first to the parents and then to the religious school.[21]

3. The Supreme Court has recently begun to articulate a new principle that will narrow the freedom of states to experiment with educational policy and will raise significant questions about the scope of religious liberty and competing individual rights. Recall that many states have adopted constitutional provisions, many of them more than a century old, that prohibit the expenditure of state funds on religious schools. As political interest in school choice has grown,

---

[19] See Alexis de Tocqueville, *Democracy in America*, part 2, chap. 8.
[20] See Walz v. Tax Commission of the City of New York, 397 U.S. 664 (1970).
[21] Mitchell v. Helms, 530 U.S. 793 (2000).

however, states have often avoided these provisions through mechanisms such as tax credits or deductions for parents who spend money on religious schools, on the ground that this does not involve a formal transfer of money from the state to religious schools.[22] Other states have avoided funding or reimbursing religious schools, even when they subsidize nonreligious private schools. In *Trinity Lutheran Church v. Comer* (2017), the Court held that the Free Exercise Clause of the First Amendment prohibits states from discriminating against religious schools when it subsidizes nonreligious public services provided by private schools.[23] The case involved a state program that reimbursed private schools for resurfacing their playgrounds with recycled rubber. Citing its own constitution, the state declined to include a religious school. The Court held that such discrimination violates the free exercise of schools, parents, and teachers. More recently, in *Carson v. Makin* (2022), the Supreme Court made it clear that the nondiscrimination rule extends well beyond playground surfaces to include subsidies for education more generally.[24] Under this new principle, states are free to decline to subsidize private schools altogether, but they may not subsidize nonreligious schools without extending the same subsidy to religious schools.

The Coming Battle over Conditions on Government Funding

On the horizon looms a legal battle over the extent to which the government may place conditions on funding for religious schools. The new principle prohibits states from excluding religious schools from private school funding simply because they are religious, but it says nothing about whether the state may place conditions on those funds. In general, states have the authority to set basic curricular requirements on all schools, whether public, private, or home-based schools, to ensure that the education they provide comports with minimum requirements and that the students who attend them comply with the state's mandatory attendance rules.[25] Although there is no case precisely on point, it seems clear from the totality of the relevant doctrine that the First Amendment prohibits the states from using curricular requirements to interfere with religious instruction and devotion in private schools. The doctrine is far less clear, however,

---

[22] See, for example, Arizona Christian Sch. Tuition Org. v. Winn, 563 U.S. 125 (2011); Gaddy v. Ga. Dept. of Rev., 301 Ga. 552 (2017).
[23] 137 S. Ct. 2012 (2017).
[24] 596 U.S. ___ (2022), docket number 20-1088, decided Jun. 21, 2022.
[25] See Pierce v. Society of Sisters, 268 U.S. 510 (1925).

about the extent to which states may use conditions on funding to influence the religious practice or the character development of religious schools.

The leading case on point is *Bob Jones University v. United States* (1983).[26] Bob Jones University is a Christian college in South Carolina. Based on its religious beliefs about race, the college forbade interracial dating or marriage among faculty and students. Most universities, including religious colleges, are exempt from federal taxes as charitable institutions. The Internal Revenue Service determined that a school discriminating on the basis of race could no longer be considered charitable, and it revoked Bob Jones's tax-exempt status. The Supreme Court rejected without detailed discussion the university's argument that revoking its tax-exempt status—a form of subsidy—violated its right to free exercise of religion.

More recently, in *Christian Legal Society v. Martinez* (2010), the Court held that a state-run law school could impose a nondiscrimination policy on student groups as a condition of receiving certain extracurricular benefits.[27] A Christian student organization forbade leaders from engaging in sexual relationships outside of marriage, which at that time would have excluded anyone in a same-sex relationship. The group argued that the school's nondiscrimination condition interfered with their constitutionally protected freedoms of expressive association and religious exercise. The group argued that requiring it to accept leaders who do not share its religious and moral views would change its ability to express its views and carry out its mission. In a close decision that turned on contested facts, the Supreme Court held that the university's antidiscrimination condition was "viewpoint neutral" because it applied equally to all student groups.[28] One could conclude from *Bob Jones* and *Christian Legal Society* that the government may freely condition funds to religious organizations on their adoption and enforcement of a nondiscrimination policy, at least so long as the government applies the same condition on all other recipients.[29]

At the same time, in a series of decisions, the Court has articulated an extraordinarily robust right of religious organizations to make employment decisions about clergy and other ministers. Known as the ministerial exception, the rule says that churches, religious schools, and other organizations' hiring, firing,

---

[26] 461 U.S. 574 (1983).
[27] 561 U.S. 661 (2010).
[28] 561 U.S. 661, 669 (2017).
[29] Consider also *Rust v. Sullivan*, 500 U.S. 173 (1991), in which the Court upheld a federal program that funded family planning on the condition that recipients not use the funds to encourage or facilitate abortions. The recipients argued that this condition violated their rights under the Speech Clause of the First Amendment, but the Court held that it did not because the recipients could still use private funds to engage in their desired speech.

and disciplinary decisions about employees who function as ministers are entirely exempt from employment antidiscrimination law. The Court unanimously agreed that:

> By imposing an unwanted minister, the state infringes the Free Exercise Clause, which protects a religious group's right to shape its own faith and mission through its appointments. According the state the power to determine which individuals will minister to the faithful also violates the Establishment Clause, which prohibits government involvement in such ecclesiastical decisions.[30]

This doctrine extends to teachers who are responsible for religious instruction and worship at religious schools, but it probably does not extend to teachers, administrators, and staff who do not perform those functions.[31] It says nothing about student admissions or discipline.

By now, the coming constitutional conflict should be obvious. Many states have refused to subsidize religious schools on the ground that the religious schools engage in discrimination in hiring or admissions, especially discrimination on the basis of LGBT status or conduct that the schools believe to be inconsistent with their religious beliefs and their mission of forming religious character. After *Trinity Lutheran* and *Carson v. Makin*, however, those states may no longer fund nonreligious schools without extending the same funds to religious schools. The question is whether they will condition those funds on schools adopting and enforcing a policy against discrimination in employment and student admissions on the basis of LGBT status—even when that discrimination is based on the institution's interest in religious integrity and religious moral formation. Maine, for one, has already done so.[32]

Evaluating the Dispute

How should courts evaluate conditions on funding of religious schools that would require the schools to change their religious conduct? In particular, what about the condition that the school decline to discriminate in hiring and admissions on the basis of LGBT status? I will first analyze the contours of the current legal regime and the difficult conceptual and value questions they raise. I will then consider the consequences of different doctrinal results for the political economy of character formation in religious schools.

---

[30] Hosanna-Tabor Evangelical Lutheran Church & Sch. v. EEOC, 565 U.S. 171, 188 (2012).
[31] See Our Lady of Guadalupe v. Morreissey-Berru, 140 S. Ct. 2049 (2020).
[32] See David Sharp, "Religious Schools Shun State Funding Despite Maine Victory," *AP News*, Aug. 30, 2022.

The Doctrinal Question

At the outset, although this chapter focuses on the implications of constitutional rules for the political economy of character formation, it is worth noting that the Supreme Court's articulation of such rules is, of course, itself a product of a political economy that shaped the terms of the Constitution and the contours of the prior doctrine, determined the personnel on the Court, and influenced their jurisprudential approaches and political values. No court is an island; the constitutional doctrines the Supreme Court announces are creatures of political economy as much as they affect it.

The first step is to clarify the legal question. The doctrine is clear that the government may not directly subject religious schools to nondiscrimination rules. Doing so would violate their rights of expressive association and, to the extent the discrimination is based on religious beliefs, would potentially also violate their rights of religious freedom.[33] It is also clear that the government may not require religious schools to change their religious beliefs or the religious content of their speech. The government may not use the threat of punishment to shut down religious or political beliefs or speech.

The conceptual puzzle arises from the nature of the government's influence with a condition on funding. It does not directly interfere with the recipient's right. It does not forbid or tax the recipient's exercise of a right. Instead, it provides a benefit or privilege on the condition that the recipient forgo the exercise of a right. The conditional nature of the benefit implicates, or at least appears to implicate, the recipient's free choice. The government is under no obligation to provide the benefit (although if it provides the benefit to nonreligious private schools, it must extend it on the same terms to religious schools). The question is whether it may incentivize certain behavior by offering a subsidy that is contingent upon enforcing a policy of nondiscrimination on the basis of LGBT status.

The constitutional status of conditions (or "strings") on government privileges and benefits that induce someone to forgo a constitutional right is one of the most conceptually fraught issues in U.S. constitutional law.[34] The Supreme Court has been inconsistent with what are known as unconstitutional conditions cases. Sometimes the Court has concluded that conditioning a benefit on forgoing a right is a violation of the right,[35] while other times it has come to the op-

---

[33] Boy Scouts of America v. Dale, 530 U.S. 640 (2000).
[34] See, for example, Cass R. Sunstein, "Is There an Unconstitutional Conditions Doctrine?," *San Diego Law Review* 26 (1989): 337–45; and Kathleen M. Sullivan, "Unconstitutional Conditions and the Distribution of Liberty," *San Diego Law Review* 26 (1989): 327–36.
[35] See Sherbert v. Verner, 374 U.S. 398 (1963).

posite conclusion.³⁶ In some cases, it is silent about the conditional feature of the government's imposition on rights altogether, simply analyzing the effect of the condition as a burden on the exercise of a right.³⁷ It has rarely expressly discussed the underlying conceptual problems, and it has never provided a coherent theory of when, why, and by what sort of conditions constitutional rights are infringed.³⁸

Perhaps the most straightforward articulation of a doctrine on unconstitutional conditions was in an early religious liberty case. In *Sherbert v. Verner*, the Supreme Court held that conditioning unemployment benefits on a Seventh-Day Adventist's being available to work on Saturday—her sabbath day—imposed a burden on her religious exercise that the government could not justify. The claimant had no fundamental or constitutional right to unemployment benefits. The state was not obligated to set up a system of such benefits. Once it did, however, it could not deny a benefit on the basis of an applicant's religious conduct when she otherwise would have been statutorily entitled to it. As Justice William Brennan wrote for the Court, "It is too late in the day to doubt that the liberties of religion and expression may be infringed by the denial of or placing of conditions upon a benefit or privilege."³⁹

On the other hand, in the *Christian Legal Society* case, discussed above, a majority of the Court held that denying extracurricular benefits to a university student group did not materially affect its religious exercise. After all, the group could still meet, pray, study, and exclude students who did not share their beliefs; they just could not do so with the same benefits and on the same terms as the groups who declined to discriminate. The same is true in the Court's decision in *Bob Jones:* the school could continue to discriminate on the basis of race, but not without forgoing its tax exemption. In both cases, there is no question that the Constitution forbids the government from punishing religious groups from discriminating on the basis of religious belief and practice; the cases suggest, however, that the government may decline to fund such groups.

Bob Jones and *Christian Legal Society* seem to apply to nondiscrimination conditions on funding of religious schools, but the question is unsettled. Some scholars have argued that laws prohibiting discrimination by race and sexuality are different because, at least in the 1960 s and 1970 s, there would have been so many religious objectors seeking accommodations from racial nondiscrimination laws that they would have undermined the civil rights regime. There would

---

36 *Christian Legal Society v. Martinez*; *Bob Jones University v. United States.*
37 Fulton v. City of Philadelphia, 141 S. Ct. 1868 (2021).
38 For a highly critical appraisal of government conditions, see Philip Hamburger, *Purchasing Submission: Conditions, Power, and Freedom* (Cambridge, Mass.: Harvard University Press, 2021).
39 Sherbert v. Verner, 374 U.S. 398, 404 (1963).

not be nearly as many objectors from LGBT antidiscrimination laws, the argument goes, so the government does not have as strong an interest in a rule without exceptions.[40] In addition, the judgment in *Christian Legal Society* depended heavily on a contested and narrow factual record that may not apply to other cases, and the benefits at issue in the case were minor compared to the thousands of dollars per student at a religious school.

Given the doctrinal background and the apparent binarity of the legal question, it seems likely that the courts will adopt some version of one of two rules to govern nondiscrimination conditions on funds to religious schools. This chapter means to take no normative stance on which would be the most persuasive application of prior doctrine or constitutional principles; rather, it seeks to tease out the potential implications for political economy of one or the other.

The first rule would hold that the government may not secure as a condition for receiving public funds a promise to forgo any constitutional right; that is, a promise to forgo a belief or practice that the government could not prohibit outright. Call this the no-conditions rule. It is almost certain that the government may not directly prohibit religious schools from imposing religious requirements, including requirements of both belief and conduct, on employees and students. Under the no-conditions rule, the government may not condition funds to a religious school on its agreement to adopt and enforce a nondiscrimination policy. The rule finds support in the Court's previous unconstitutional conditions cases and in the principles of religious freedom and religious equality embodied in the First Amendment. It is, however, somewhat at odds with the principles of separation of church and state and the liberty of conscience of taxpayers, insofar as the government's support for discriminatory institutions implies that the government and taxpayers are complicit in a school's discriminatory policy. But proponents of the rule would argue that the government may avoid such complicity by declining to fund any private schools, and that, even if the government were to fund discriminatory schools, doing so does not implicate the *religious* conscience of taxpayers, for their objection is not to the religious beliefs of the recipients, but to their conduct, whether it is inspired by religion or not.

The other rule would provide that the government may place a nondiscrimination condition on the receipt of funds—the nondiscrimination rule—either because the condition, accepted voluntarily, imposes no burden on the recipient's religious exercise, or because the government has a sufficiently strong interest in declining to support such discrimination. This rule finds support in the *Bob Jones* and *Christian Legal Society* cases, protects LGBT persons from discrimination by institutions receiving government funds, and avoids governmental com-

---

[40] See Andrew Koppelman, "Gay Rights, Religious Liberty, and the Misleading Racism Analogy," *Brigham Young University Law Review* (2020): 1–32.

plicity in such discrimination and the symbolic abrogation of rights such complicity may convey.

So far, the chapter has proceeded as though the proposed rule would be all or nothing—either the government or the religious schools get a clear victory, and the other a clear loss. This assumption, however, proceeds from framing the dispute according to the conceptual views of one of the parties, in this case the government. The greatest challenge for fairly resolving the dispute is that the parties understand the issues in light of fundamentally different paradigms, and there is no religiously neutral way to choose between them. Most of the objecting schools understand the discrimination to be on the basis of religious beliefs and/or conduct—not on the basis of LGBT identity or status. The views of Christian schools, in particular, are informed by a moral tradition based on religious forms of reasoning about God, anthropology, sin, redemption, and spiritual life. The government's paradigm, and the view of LGBT advocates, is entirely different. For them, LGBT identity or status is a biological and social fact. LGBT persons have been, and continue to be, subject to an immense amount of regulation, coercion, and harm by governments and private parties. In the West, this treatment has been influenced by traditional Christian sexual mores. Nondiscrimination rules are meant to thwart the continuing unfair treatment of LGBT persons and ensure them equal status as citizens and members of society. The two sides have incommensurable moral paradigms—one based on an ongoing religious tradition, the other in a conscious response to that tradition. Despite the aspirations of American constitutionalism to religious neutrality, there is no entirely neutral viewpoint from which to adjudicate the dispute.

Perhaps there is room for a third rule, one that attempts to narrow the gap between these competing paradigms, to preserve as much of both of them as possible. Under the no-conditions rule, the government may not require schools to forgo any rights in exchange for funds—including the right to discriminate on the basis of belief and conduct. Suppose, however, that the Court took a middle path for conditions cases, perhaps on the ground that the recipient's consent ameliorates, even if it does not eliminate, the dangers to religious liberty. Suppose the Court were to conclude that the government could condition funds on a recipient forswearing discrimination on the basis of LGBT *conduct* but not on the basis of the recipient's religious belief. In other words, in exchange for the same funding available to other private schools, the religious school agrees to not discriminate against staff or students on the basis of their status and conduct, but may continue to discriminate against them on the basis of their religious beliefs. This would apply what has long been understood to be the core of the Free Exercise Clause—the freedom of religious belief—to religious institutions.

Under this no-status-discrimination rule, schools could continue to make employment and admissions decisions on the basis of shared religious beliefs about morality. Perhaps neither side would get everything it wants, but such a ruling would approximate the liberal ideal of governmental neutrality, because the government would not have to adopt the religious framework, and though the religious schools would be obliged to adopt the government's status-based framework, their enduring freedom to discriminate on the basis of religious beliefs would enable them to maintain their moral integrity. Religious schools could screen employees and students for their beliefs about moral theology rather than their conduct or status. More specifically, schools could require employees and students to affirm traditional Christian (or Jewish or Muslim) views on sexual and family ethics for religious reasons. The school could hire and admit persons who identify as LGBT, but only when they share the school's beliefs about gender and sexuality. Such a solution would allow schools that wish to maintain the integrity of their moral theology to do so on their own terms—for religious reasons—without permitting them to violate the antidiscrimination norm as conceptualized by the state and LGBT rights communities—discrimination on the basis of sexual status or conduct.

There would still be hard cases—for instance, when a school wishes to discipline an employee or student who purports to adhere to the school's moral theology but whose conduct is in tension with those beliefs. Under the no-status-discrimination rule, religious schools who have accepted conduct- and status-discrimination conditions on funding would be unable to remove the employee or student on those grounds. A school could, however, inquire into the employee's or student's continued religious beliefs, and if the employee or student maintained the school's beliefs despite contrary conduct, the school would have the opportunity for pastoral care rather than removal.

The Political Economy Implications of Different Doctrinal Rules

So far, we have considered the doctrinal and conceptual components of the legal question. Now we shall turn to possible influences of various rules on the micro-political economy of religious-sexual character formation in religious schools. What difference will a decision make, one way or the other? Consider three possible scenarios.

1. The No-Conditions Rule. Religious schools win—the government may not condition funds on private schools adopting any nondiscrimination policy, whether for staff or students, and whether based on belief or status and conduct. Since this would thwart the government's interest (in some states), the question is how the government would respond. The response would differ by state, depending on its unique legal and political economy of education. Many states provide some amount of funding to private schools as a matter of course to cover costs of safety and other public services. Presumably this would continue. The question is whether the government would increase funding of all private

schools, even those that discriminate, or would instead reduce or eliminate additional funding for all private schools.

If the government increases funding apace, religious schools that want to engage in traditional religious moral formation will be able to do so unimpeded and on equal terms with other private schools. Their ability to do so will still extend only to parents who can afford the school—the vast majority of students will continue to attend public schools out of financial need or civic persuasion. States in this situation may reinforce their understanding of family and sexual ethics by increasing instruction in that understanding in public schools, with the hope of culturally overwhelming minority religious communities over time.[41] In truth, this is likely to happen, at least in progressive-dominated states, regardless of the constitutional rule, simply because of strong government nondiscrimination policies, the media, and the popular zeitgeist. In those states, a no-conditions rule would allow minority religious communities to continue to attempt to inculcate their own values with minimal government influence. Indeed, the decision to fund private schools would likely be long-lasting; it is often politically difficult to withdraw government entitlements, especially from a highly motivated and politically engaged group.

Some states may respond to a difference-reinforcing doctrine by declining to provide additional funding to any private school. There would likely be overlapping political economy reasons for this. Public schoolteachers' unions are a powerful constituency in many states, and they typically oppose any state funding for private schools out of self-interest. Other groups oppose school choice on the ground that it will benefit only families who can afford private schools and will reduce political support for providing an adequate education in public schools. Others oppose private education on the ground that civic republicanism demands common schools. Separately, there is some evidence that when the most engaged families vacate the public schools, the remaining students are worse off. Other groups will oppose any funding of any religious institution on religious liberty grounds—they don't want their tax dollars funding religious beliefs with which they disagree. And still others will oppose such spending out of concern about discrimination on the basis of LGBT status. There is, of course, significant overlap in the constituencies of these political factions, but those who do not overlap are likely to make common cause. All of these groups oppose government funding for religious schools for various self- and others-regarding rea-

---

[41] See, for example, Linda C. McClain, "Bigotry, Civility, and Reinvigorating Civic Education: Government's Formative Task Amid Polarization," in *The Impact of the Law on Character Formation, Ethical Education, and the Communication of Values in Late Modern Pluralistic Societies*, ed. John Witte Jr. and Michael Welker (Leipzig: Evangelische Verlagsanstalt, 2021), 109–26.

sons based on a combination of incommensurable values and untested empirical hypotheses about consumer responses.

The result of abandoning funding for private schools would be plain. Religious schools would continue to be able to engage in moral formation as they wish, but their reach would be limited to what parents can and want to pay (unless they are privately subsidized by churches, denominations, or individual donors). In most cases, only the well-off would be able to afford the education, and in virtually no cases would the neediest be able to participate. Even a program that fully funded tuition for private schools would probably leave some modest educational costs that some families would struggle to pay. The economics of survival would lead some schools to soften their hiring and admissions policies, especially in parts of the country with smaller religious communities.

There is another aspect of the no-conditions rule that might have an effect on the political economy of religious schooling that is difficult to predict. Supreme Court decisions in "culture war" cases often have far greater symbolic than practical effect. A win for religious schools might galvanize the LGBT rights movement in a way that increases its local and statewide influence, at least in the short term. On the other hand, such decisions also make law, and law has a moral-forming effect of its own. To reduce the symbolic effect of such a decision, the Court might signal both that religious schools should not be understood to reflect the moral norms of society and, at the same time, that religious schools' distinctiveness plays a vital role in the lives of religious individuals and communities that a healthy liberal society may not only tolerate but support.

2. The No-Discrimination Rule. Now consider what might happen if the government wins, in the sense that it may condition school funding on the recipient's enforcement of a nondiscrimination policy. This would be a major symbolic victory for the government's view of LGBT status and rights. The political response of the dissenting religious communities would be unpredictable, but it is likely that they would see themselves as not only political minority dissidents, but those with views that society increasingly wants to purge as morally repulsive. As a practical matter, however, it is unclear the difference such a rule would make for religious formation in schools. Here we must distinguish between two plausible responses by religious schools: accept the conditions alongside the money, or refuse both.

Consider first the schools that would refuse the money and conditions. They would be at an obvious economic disadvantage to the schools that accepted them. This would create a powerful economic incentive to accept the conditions. The more the state has an appetite for supporting private schools and imposing secularizing conditions, the harder it would be for nonconforming religious schools to compete with government subsidies at other private schools, and therefore to resist the incentive. Nonconforming schools would be accessible only to wealthier students unless the schools received significant private subsidies.

We should keep in mind the larger political economy of education, though: the government completely subsidizes secular public schools—they will always have a powerful edge in the education market.

3. Schools Accept the No-Discrimination Rule. Now consider what might happen if the schools accept the government's nondiscrimination condition alongside the funds. Those schools would undoubtedly be subject to the secularizing influence of the nondiscrimination rule; the interesting question is how much. Under current doctrine, the government could not require the schools to change their religious beliefs, doctrine, or speech. That means they could maintain and profess the tenets of their traditional beliefs about family and sex. Would that be enough to enable them to form the character of their staff and students according to their religious beliefs?

In the literature on constitutional rights, this issue has usually been framed as a question of expressive association rather than one of character formation. The reason is that the Supreme Court has adopted a relatively robust "expressive association" doctrine under the Free Speech Clause of the First Amendment that protects groups' ability to exclude from their membership those whose inclusion would dilute or change the group's message. According to this doctrine, a white supremacist organization does not have to admit Black members, and the Boy Scouts of America does not have to admit openly gay members.[42] The assumption of this doctrine is that sometimes the medium is the message; in the case of groups, the identity of members is part of the message the group means to convey to its own members and to outsiders.

Framing the issue as one of expression, however, neglects moral formation. For communities defined in part by a commitment to reasoning within and embodying a particular moral tradition, excluding those who reject that tradition is not merely a question of internal or external expression or social symbolism; it is about integrity and the ability to maintain and pass along the tradition.

Consider a Christian school that accepts funds in exchange for a nondiscrimination policy on the basis of LGBT status and conduct. The school wants to maintain its traditional morality and form students accordingly: sexual desire and conduct are understood in light of a Christian account of creation, sin, and redemption. Under current doctrine, the school could continue to profess and teach those beliefs, but they would be at odds with the nondiscrimination policy, which requires it to act according to the professed identity and conduct preferences of teachers and students. The problem is not one of group expression—or not principally one of group expression—but one of rational coherence; not of social but of intellectual integrity. Because the reasoning pertains to morality, the incoherence threatens not only intellectual integrity but also the integrity of resulting habits, dispositions, and practices.

---

[42] Boy Scouts of America v. Dale, 530 U.S. 640 (2000).

To make this as concrete as possible, consider what the school's website must say under two different versions of a no-discrimination rule. First consider the no-status discrimination rule—that is, by accepting the funds, the school may discriminate on the basis of religious belief, but not on the basis of LGBT status or conduct. As a condition for receiving the government funds, and as a matter of truth-in-advertising, the website *must* declare that the school does not discriminate on the basis of LGBT status with respect to hiring or admission. The website may, however, also say that although it does not discriminate on the basis of status, it does require employees and students to affirm a statement of religiously informed beliefs about sexuality. Such an approach would allow potential employees and students to self-select and would allow the school a chance to maintain its beliefs and moral formation.

Now suppose a strict no-discrimination rule: accepting the funds precludes the school from discrimination on the basis of status or conduct *or* agreement with the school's religiously informed moral doctrine. The school may still *hold* and *attempt to teach* those beliefs. But it may not discipline employees and students for disagreeing in thought, word, or deed. It could try to avoid internal conflict with dissenting employees and students by publicizing its views and its intention to transmit them. The website would state the school's adherence to certain religious doctrines about human sexuality as one component of its theologically informed anthropology. To make its position as plain and coherent as possible, the school will have to expressly say that it does not accept the moral framing of its own antidiscrimination policy.

The likelihood of a school attempting this balancing act is approximately zero. Not only would it render its moral reasoning incoherent, it would invite questions into its sincerity. After all, the state did not *obligate* the school to adopt a nondiscrimination policy. The government funding was an incentive to do so, but, at least in principle, the school could have declined the funding and nondiscrimination condition (although this may not have been economically feasible). Despite the school's ongoing right to maintain its own religious beliefs and to instruct students accordingly, adopting a nondiscrimination policy premised on contrary anthropological, epistemological, and theological beliefs would almost certainly have the effect of diluting and eventually altering those beliefs. Experience with dissenting employees and students would also influence the school's moral views and formation. Nondiscrimination conditions on funding that do not allow religious schools to exclude staff and faculty on the basis of their religious beliefs would ultimately have a dramatic effect on the ability of religious schools to maintain and transmit traditional norms and practices.

The centrality of schools for character formation should not be overstated. Schools play an important but not necessarily a dominant role in this process. Family, friends, neighbors, churches, synagogues, sports clubs, and the media—now, especially, social media—all have a tremendous amount of influence over character formation. Religious schools rarely perfectly live up to their own lofty ideals, and students often come to reject the views and practices of their parents and teachers. At the same time, students of public or nonreligious private schools often maintain or adopt traditional religious morality through the influence of family, church, synagogue, or friends. Schools are a battleground for political economy because they implicate a liberal republic's interest in forming citizens, but they are only one site of moral formation.

Conclusion

This chapter has explored the role of constitutional rules in the political economy of character formation by examining an emerging constitutional dispute, the possible rules that the Supreme Court might announce to resolve that dispute, and their potential effects on the political economy of private religious education. The dispute itself arises from the current constitutional doctrine that creates a framework for public policy and private decision-making about education. That framework raises a question that is likely to eventually come before the Supreme Court: when states choose to fund private schools, may they condition those funds on the school's adoption of an LGBT nondiscrimination policy, even when the recipient school has a religious objection to the policy? Current doctrine does not resolve the question, and may reasonably be understood to point in both directions.

The relative implications of the possible rules for the political economy of character formation are fairly clear. Where the state may not impose such a condition, the state may not use subsidies to induce religious schools to abandon their commitment to traditional sexual mores and beliefs about gender identity, but the same rule may lead governments to decline to fund religious schools altogether, further reducing their ability to compete economically with government-funded schools. Where the states may impose a no-discrimination condition, schools will be faced with a difficult choice to either reduce their competitiveness with private schools that do accept the funds, or to accept the funds at the risk of eroding their ability to engage in traditional moral formation. A no-status-discrimination rule that permits the government to condition funds on schools adopting a policy against discriminating on the basis of LGBT status or conduct, but that allows them to continue to discriminate on the basis of religious *belief* about sexual morality and gender identity, would be unlikely to entirely satisfy either constituency. It may, however, achieve at least some of the government's interests without allowing the government to induce religious schools to abandon their religious beliefs about sexual moral formation altogether.

Contributors

Roshan Allpress is National Principal of Laidlaw College, in Auckland, New Zealand.

Nicholas Aroney is Professor of Constitutional Law in the T. C. Beirne School of Law at the University of Queensland, in Brisbane, Australia, and Affiliated Faculty at the Center for the Study of Law and Religion at Emory University, in Atlanta, Georgia.

Sergio Belardinelli is Full Professor of Sociology of Culture in the Department of Political and Social Science at the University of Bologna, Italy.

Rüdiger Bittner is Professor of Philosophy, Emeritus, at Universität Bielefeld, Germany.

Nathan S. Chapman is the Pope F. Brock Associate Professor of Professional Responsibility at the University of Georgia School of Law, in Athens, Georgia.

Jonathan Cole is Assistant Director of the Centre for Religion, Ethics, and Society at Charles Sturt University, in Canberra, Australia.

Andreas Glaeser is Professor and Chair of the Department of Sociology at the University of Chicago, in Illinois.

Amanda Gouws is Distinguished Professor of Political Science and South African Research Chair in Gender Politics, Stellenbosch University, South Africa.

David McIlroy is Visiting Professor of Banking Law at the University of Notre Dame (USA) in London.

Piet J. Naudé is Professor of Ethics, Emeritus, at the University of Stellenbosch Business School, in Stellenbosch, South Africa.

Paul Oslington is Professor of Economics and Theology at Alphacrucis University College, in Sydney, Australia, and Honorary Research Professor at the Australian Centre for Christianity and Culture, Charles Sturt University, in Canberra, Australia.

John Witte Jr. is the Robert W. Woodruff Professor of Law, McDonald Distinguished Professor of Religion, and Faculty Director of the Center for the Study of Law and Religion at Emory University, in Atlanta, Georgia.

www.ingramcontent.com/pod-product-compliance
Lightning Source LLC
Chambersburg PA
CBHW062023220426
43662CB00010B/1443